Working and Living
PORTUGAL

Contents

About the author

Harvey Holtom has lived in Madrid for 20 years, where has worked as a teacher, translator, photographer and writer. He is currently the correspondent for the *Time Out* website. He is married to Spain but confesses to a long-standing affair with Portugal and has visited the country on many occasions.

Author's acknowledgements

The author would like to give thanks to all of the people who agreed to be case studies in this book. Special thanks go in particular to Kevin Rose, Rupert Eden and Martin O'Donnell for giving me much more time and information than I initially asked for. Special thanks also go to Alison Roberts, of Lisbon, and Len Port, of the Algarve, for patiently putting up with my pestering questions and providing valuable insights and contacts. In addition I would like to thank Maria Lindo, of the Automobile Clube de Portugal, and all those anonymous people working for institutions and private companies who kindly provided me with information by telephone or e-mail. Thanks too to Rupert Wheeler, for being so patient. Finally I would like to thank my wife, Maggi, and my children, Sebastian and Ella, for putting up with me.

Conceived and produced for Cadogan Guides by
Navigator Guides Ltd, The Old Post Office, Swanton
Novers, Melton Constable, Norfolk, NR24 2AJ
info@navigatorguides.com
www.navigatorguides.com

Cadogan Guides
Network House
1 Ariel Way
London W12 7SL
info@cadoganguides.co.uk
www.cadoganguides.com

The Globe Pequot Press
246 Goose Lane, PO Box 480, Guilford,
Connecticut 06437–0480

Copyright © Cadogan Guides 2004
"THE SUNDAY TIMES" is a registered trade mark
of Times Newspapers Limited.

Maps © Cadogan Guides, drawn by
Map Creation Ltd.

Cover design: Sarah Gardner
Colour essay design: Smith, Cowan and Wilkinson
Cover and photo essay photographs: © John Miller
   and © Alamy
Editor: Susannah Wight
Proofreader: Mary Sheridan
Indexing: Isobel McLean

Printed in Italy by Legoprint

A catalogue record for this book is available from
the British Library
ISBN 1-86011-127-0

The author and publishers have made every effort
to ensure the accuracy of the information in this
book at the time of going to press. However, they
cannot accept any responsibility for any loss,
injury or inconvenience resulting from the use
of information contained in this guide.

Please help us to keep this guide up to date. We
have done our best to ensure that the information
in it is correct at the time of going to press. But
places are constantly changing, and rules and
regulations fluctuate. We would be delighted to
receive any comments concerning existing entries
or omissions. Authors of the best letters will receive
a copy of the Cadogan Guide of their choice.

Introduction

01

Portugal has become increasingly familiar to northern Europeans over recent decades as a result of the availability of cheap air travel. Yet much of this charming little country remains unknown to the visitors who flock in droves to spend a week or a fortnight in the sun-drenched southern coastal region of the Algarve, or take a city break in Lisbon, and ignore the rest.

This book is aimed at those who plan to go to Portugal to live and work and who will inevitably venture further afield, north and inland. They will discover a land delightfully full of variety – of landscapes and weather – and contradictions – not all of which are good. State-of-the-art modernity exists side-by-side with idiosyncratic old-fashioned ways. Gleaming public projects and advanced infrastructures often hide pockets of extreme backwardness, urban blight and rural poverty. Those who end up settling in Portugal find such contrasts to be on the one hand part of the country's unfailing charm and, on the other, annoying and infuriating. But most who stay find that the good aspects outweigh the bad, and accept it all as part and parcel of life in Portugal. The country's recent modernisation and transformation has not divested it of its more enchanting qualities – a slower, laid-back lifestyle; a quaint, old-fashioned approach to work and business; and exquisite manners, which put some northern Europeans to shame.

Getting to Know Portugal

02

This chapter introduces Portugal to those thinking of moving there and describes its geographical and climatic diversity. It also gives an overview of Portugal's long, complex and passionate history – the country has gone from being a far-flung outpost of the Roman and Moorish empires to become one of Europe's oldest nation states; it had a vast overseas empire, which then declined into a backwater, a state from which it has only recently emerged on becoming an EU member state. Finally there is a look at the history and development of the Portuguese language, from a vulgar form of Latin to a modern language, one of the most widely spoken in the world.

Climate and Geography

A glance at any map of the Iberian peninsula shows just how small Portugal is. It occupies approximately a sixth of the land mass and is only marginally bigger than the neighbouring Spanish 'Autonomous Communities' of Castilla y León and Andalucía. Or, put another way, Portugal is only slightly larger than Scotland. Roughly rectangular, Portugal extends slightly less than 600km in length, from north to south, and 220km at its widest point, from the Atlantic coast to the Spanish border. Belonging to Portugal, too, are the offshore islands: Madeira, about 1,000km southwest of Lisbon, close to the west African coast and north of the Canary Islands; and the Azores, almost 1,500km west of Lisbon, about a third of the way to the US eastern seaboard.

Despite its diminutive proportions, Portugal offers an astonishing variety of landscapes and climatic conditions. The principal contrasts are between the north, the centre and the south. However, the combined influence of the Atlantic and the Gulf Stream brings summer temperatures in the Algarve and the northerly coastal areas of Costa de Prata and Costa Verde that are not greatly different. Faro's average summer midday temperature, for example, is 28°C and Oporto stays around 25°C, a small disparity. Within these three bands, in fact, the more significant differences are between the littoral and the interior. The offshore islands also differ greatly in terms of landscape and climate from continental Portugal. Wherever you are you will find attractive, often stunning countryside and a far milder climate than in northern Europe.

The Douro

The Minho river is Portugal's northern border. Its south bank is in Portugal; on the other side is the 'Autonomous Community' of Galicia, Spain's most north-westerly region. Further inland, the border meanders southwards and then eastwards, encompassing the mountain ranges (*serras*) of da Peneda, do Soajo, do Gerês, do Larouco, da Coroa and de Montezinho. Here the border swings southwards again, hugging the eastern side of the Serra de Mogadouro and following the Douro river (one of the peninsula's major waterways, which crosses northern Spain before penetrating into Portugal) for many kilometres in a roughly southwesterly direction. The Douro International Natural Park straddles the river and is managed by the Portuguese and Spanish authorities.

The mountains in Portugal's northeastern corner form a natural frontier with Spain. They are green and lush, and traversed by several fast-flowing rivers, which flow roughly east–west, for instance the Lima, the Cavado and the Támega, which joins the Douro (by now firmly in Portugal) at Castelo de Paiva. The Douro itself eventually comes out at Porto (Oporto to English-speakers), Portugal's second city, a major port and commercial centre. Further south, another important river, the Mondego, flows through the historic university city of Coimbra, and comes out at Figueira da Foz, showing the boundary of what is considered northern and central Portugal.

Central Portugal

Central Portugal has much in common with the north, as the mountainous terrain does not stop at the Mondego. There are a good many more *serras* between this river and the Tejo (Tagus), which, entering from Spain in an east–west direction a little to the south of Castelo Branco before turning south towards Lisbon, really marks the great divide between the country's northern and southern halves. Such mountainous features are reflected in the Portuguese tourist authorities' divisions of the country, which transcend provincial boundaries and create more logical areas, based on geographical features. The northeastern quarter of the country is thus known as 'Montanhas' and includes all of the above-mentioned *serras* as well as the Trás-os-Montes ('behind the hills') region and the Serra da Estrela. The climate here is varied in temperature and precipitation. Summers can be fierce, with 40°C midday temperatures not unknown, but there are frequent spring and summer showers in the higher areas. Winters can be very cold; the thermometer often plummets to 0°C. The city of Bragança, in the far northeastern corner, averages only 8°C in winter, and rainfall is abundant in Montanhas, multiplying that of the Algarve by about five; Bragança averages over 140mm of monthly rainfall throughout December and January. Snow is also common here – the Serra da Estrela has Portugal's only winter sports facilities.

The Costa Verde

The northern coastal areas comprise two tourist regions. The most northerly is the Costa Verde (Green Coast), which runs south from the Spanish border and includes the provinces of Minho and Douro Litoral as well as the cities of Viana do Castelo, Braga and Oporto. No linguistic genius is needed to work out why this coastline is thus named. The abundance of rivers and the precipitation coming in off the Atlantic make for a colourful, beautiful landscape, crisscrossed by deep, verdant, highly fertile valleys. Oporto is rainy, with a monthly average of over 100mm from October to March, peaking at 168mm in December. Temperatures, though, are quite mild, and the thermometer rarely reaches freezing point in winter, while summers are more than bearable. Oporto's average minimum temperatures go from 11°C in October, down to 5°C in December, January and February and in July and August the maximum temperatures sit around the 25°C mark.

The Costa de Prata

The Costa de Prata (Silver Coast) extends southwards from just below Oporto to the fishing town of Ericeira, northwest of Lisbon. This coast comprises most of the provinces of Estremadura and Ribatejo as well as that of Beira Litoral. From the fishing port of Peniche to Figueira da Foz, at the mouth of the Mondego, it is practically one long, unbroken sandy beach. Inland are forest-clad hills and yet more mountains. Climatically it is similar to the Costa Verde, though it gets slightly milder the further south you go. Inland, Coimbra, which is roughly halfway between Oporto and Lisbon, has average summer maximums and minimums of 29°C and 15°C, respectively, ranging from 14°C to 5°C in winter. These temperatures are similar to those enjoyed in the Lisbon area. Perhaps surprisingly, year-round average temperatures in the Costas Verde, Prata and Lisbon hold up well when compared with those in the Algarve, as a result of the effect of the Gulf Stream.

Lisbon

Lisbon itself, a little to the south of central Portugal, has a pleasant climate because of its situation and proximity to the sea. Summer lasts from June to October, with average temperatures of 27°C, although they can hit 40°C. In winter the thermometer stays around 14°C, rarely dropping below 10°C, though the wind chill factor can make it seem colder. Lisbon is wet most of the year, except in summer; showers are frequent in spring and autumn and lashing rain is common in winter, with December and January registering average precipitation of over 100mm.

South of Lisbon

South of the Tejo and Lisbon, things start to change geographically and climatically. Temperatures in coastal regions differ less from north to south than one might expect, thanks to the Gulf Stream, but winter weather becomes progressively drier and warmer the further south you go. The coastline from the salt flats in the estuary of the Rio Sado, just south of Setúbal, practically all the way to the Algarve, for the moment remains barely exploited and has few noteworthy resorts. The unattractive sea port of Sines is the only town of any size.

The Alentejo

Inland is the area known as the Alentejo, a corruption of 'além do tejo' ('beyond the Tagus'), an immense plain covering almost a third of Portugal's surface area but which only accounts for two per cent of the country's population of more than 10 million. The Alentejo is divided administratively into two districts, the 'Alto' (Upper) and the 'Baixo' (Lower) Alentejo, but the tourist board joins both together under the name of 'Planícies' (Plains). The Alto is bounded by the Spanish border, with the Serras de Marvão and Mamede, dotted with fortified hill villages, forming a natural frontier region. The Tejo bounds the area to the north and west, and a fairly straight line, running east–west just to the south of the city of Évora, marks the southern limits. From then on, and all the way to the Algarve, the imposing and hauntingly beautiful Baixo Alentejo plains take over. To the east, the frontier with Spain is marked mainly by the course of the Rio Guadiana and to the south the province borders on the Algarve.

The most striking feature of the Alentejo is its flatness and emptiness. Where smallholdings, subdivided over the generations, characterise the north and make it look from the air like a patchwork quilt, the form of landholding in the south has since Roman times been the 'latifúndio': enormous estates, originally established to make maximum advantage of poor soil and scarce water. As a result there is a largely unbroken undulating landscape, dotted with ancient olive trees and cork oaks, lone bulls enjoying ample pastures, gently rolling hills and a 'big sky'.

Weather-wise, the Alentejo offers oven-hot, incredibly dry summers, with temperatures averaging over 30°C but frequently climbing above 40°C and, conversely, extremely chilly winters. There are showers in spring and autumn; wildflowers bring a riot of colour in spring and the autumn is pleasantly mild. The lack of rain is not only a principal climatic feature but a major problem, leading to agricultural setbacks, restricted water supplies and serious forest fires in summer. In an attempt to palliate the problem, the government undertook the massive and controversial Alqueva dam scheme, close to the Spanish border, which has been in use since 2002. Environmentalists opposed the dam vigorously throughout its construction, claiming it is a white elephant. It may well be, but this man-made lake, Europe's largest, is now a permanent feature of the Alentejo landscape, occupying about 160 square miles when full.

The Algarve

South of the Alentejo is the Algarve, Europe's warmest region in winter, if the term 'winter' is appropriate for a place where January temperatures average around 15°C. It can get a lot colder but snow and ice are extremely rare. Summers here can be very hot, with daytime temperatures averaging 28°C and often climbing way above 30°C, though Atlantic breezes keep things bearable. The Algarve also suffers from many of the Alentejo's endemic problems – droughts and water shortages – especially during the main tourist season.

The southern coastline has stretches of dramatic, abrupt cliffs that seem to crash into the sea, spectacular sandy beaches and intimate coves. The eastern Algarve has flat, marshy land and a series of sand spits that accompany the coastline almost to the Spanish border. Just inland are hills that offer an astonishing variety of flora and fauna and which are carpeted in wildflowers in February and March, followed by orange blossom in April. Here, slick, sophisticated resorts and fashionable golf and villa developments are in marked contrast to quaint little inland villages, just a short drive away.

Offshore Portugal

Madeira has a subtropical climate and so does not suffer too much from thermal extremes. The range is from about 16°C in winter to more than 22°C in summer. The island boasts 2,000hrs of sunshine annually, though there is a rainy season from October to March, and August is famous for the misty season, known as the *capacete*. Otherwise the island gets warm winds known as the *leste* coming off the Sahara; they sometimes bring deposits of sand. There are sometimes tropical storms as well.

The Azores, further out into the Atlantic, enjoy a mild climate, perhaps surprisingly given the location. Winter temperatures rarely drop below 14°C and in summer average around 21°C. Rainfall is frequent but it comes in the form of showers rather than in downpours.

Portuguese History

Portugal is one of Europe's oldest countries, with over nine centuries of history as a nation within, give or take some minor tweaking, the borders that it still has today. Until medieval times, though, there was little to distinguish historical developments on this western edge of the Iberian peninsula from the interior, so it is more accurate to talk of there being a common Iberian history until that time. Portugal's long, complex and passionate history merits several volumes. The few pages that follow are a greatly boiled-down overview.

Prehistoric Portugal

There is plenty of evidence of early human settlements within the confines of present-day Portugal. Remnants of pottery and cave burials, found along the Tagus valley and in parts of modern Alentejo and Estremadura, are thought to date from around 8,000 to 7,000 BC. In the Beira Alta region, in Vila Nova de Foz Côa, the largest-known **Palaeolithic** 'art collection' was discovered in the 1980s. The late **Neolithic** period had some of the first cultural focal points that might be defined as having 'Lusitanian' characteristics, distinct from others in the peninsula: the construction of dolmens and cromlechs.

During the **Bronze and Iron Ages** the whole peninsula was colonised by **Celts** and **Iberians**, thought to have originated in northern Africa, who introduced a pastoral and agrarian culture, including the use of a primitive form of plough and wheeled carts, to the whole area. The Iberians also had a form of writing and made offerings to the dead. Around this time, also, the Phoenicians, the Greeks and the Carthaginians, at different moments, established trading posts on the coast, exploited mines and colonised much of the south.

The first real permanent settlements in Portugal were the *'castros'*, fortified hilltop villages whose construction and development were refined by Celtic peoples between 700 and 600 BC. Vestiges of these constructions still remain in parts of northern Portugal.

Romans, Visigoths and Moors

Until the Middle Ages, Iberian history would be defined by periods of invasion and colonisation, first by the Romans, then by the Visigoths and later by the Moors. After their victory over Carthage in the 3rd century BC, the **Romans** made the former Carthaginian territory a new province of their expanding empire. They met resistance from the **Lusitani**. This tribe was led by the warrior chieftain Viriato, who held up the Roman invasion for several decades until he was betrayed and murdered in his bed by three of his own people – who had been bribed by the Romans. Viriato's death brought the end of the Lusitanian resistance but provided Portugal with its first national hero and the name for the province – Lusitania. The term 'Luso' still refers to all things Portuguese.

From then on the Roman conquest of the rest of the peninsula was rapid. Julius Caesar made Olispo (Lisbon) the administrative centre in 60 BC, a role it played until the founding of Emerita (nowadays Mérida, in the neighbouring Spanish region of Extremadura) in AD 25. A senate was established in Ebora (Évora) and other important towns such as Scallabis (Santarém) and Pax Julia (Beja) were founded. As well as this, industries such as brick-making, tile-making and iron-smelting were established; many roads and bridges were built to connect the different administrative centres; and the temple of Diana was erected in Évora.

The process of Romanisation served to accentuate the differences between the two main regions. In the rugged northern mountains its impact was less, but on the southern plains the Romans created the large estates known today as 'latifúndios' and introduced olives, wheat, oats and vines. The Romans also imposed towns, 'citânias', into which they gradually forced the Lusitanian peoples. In the citânias the Lusitanians acquired Roman civilisation and learned Latin, the language from which modern Portuguese developed. When the Romans converted to Christianity in the 3rd century AD, so did the Lusitanians.

Roman cultural, economic and administrative influence would last for a long time throughout the entire peninsula; even the road network was used until well into the Middle Ages. Roman remains in Portugal are scarcer and less impressive than those found at Tarragona and Mérida in Spain, but important sites may still be seen in Évora and Conímbriga, southwest of Coimbra.

With Roman rule in decline, the first wave of barbarians invaded the Iberian peninsula in AD 409. First the **Vandals**, followed by the **Alans**, then the **Suevi** (or Swabians) and finally the **Visigoths**, all came and conquered. The Visigothic empire ruled most of the peninsula from 585 until the early 8th century but it was always a rickety alliance of factions and when the first Moorish armies crossed from North Africa in 711, initially to help one Visigoth faction in a dispute with another, the whole system collapsed. Within a decade the **Moors** had occupied practically the whole of the peninsula apart from the mountainous northern Spanish regions of Asturias and the Basque country.

The Muslims, like the Romans, made a huge impact on the peninsula and their imprint remained long after their departure. Though they were less influential in the north, a great civilisation flourished in the south, centred on Córdoba in modern-day Spain, under the rule of wise, tolerant governors who founded schools and libraries and fostered the arts and sciences, especially mathematics. This civilisation was known as 'Al-Andalus', from which the modern name of Andalucía is derived, and at the time no other civilisation in Europe could match its splendour. In Portugal, the Arabs settled principally in what is nowadays the Algarve (the name derives from the Arabic 'Al-Gharb', meaning 'the land beyond'), though they controlled the Alentejo and other areas as far up as Lisbon and the Tagus. In the mid-9th century a caliphate grew up around Shelb (nowadays Silves), which was independent of the main centre at Córdoba.

Throughout the period of Arab domination, the economy flourished. Mines were exploited, Roman irrigation techniques were improved upon and crop rotation was introduced. Hitherto uncultivated crops such as cotton, citrus fruits and rice, important products even today, were also introduced. More important still, trading links with the north of Africa were established and urban centres such as Lisbon, Évora, Santarém and Beja grew, prospered and became sophisticated. Many Visigothic peasants quickly converted to Islam, since their conversion to Christianity had been superficial; others continued to practise Christianity, which was tolerated. At this time there was also an important Jewish community, mainly in the urban centres, who played a significant role in the fields of commerce and scholarship.

The decline of Moorish Portugal started in the 11th century, when certain rich, powerful local nobles began to carve up the caliphate into independent regional city-states (*taifas*). This meant they became weaker and more vulnerable to attack from small groups of Visigothic Christians, who were able to take the initiative from their mountain refuges in the northwest and begin the Christian reconquest of Iberia.

The Reconquest

The reconquest had, in fact, begun as early as the 8th century. Individual Visigothic nobles, taking refuge in the northern stronghold of Asturias (Spain), resisted the Muslim onslaught. One of the first was **Pelayo**, who defeated the Muslims at Covadonga in 737 and earned himself the throne of Asturias (later to become Asturias-León) in the process. Over the next couple of centuries, subsequent kings of Asturias-León reconquered parts of northern Spain, in what is nowadays known as Castilla-León, and the northern Portuguese cities of Braga, Oporto, Viseu and Guimarães. Here they established strongholds and settled Christians around them. The region became a buffer zone and the borders between Muslim- and Christian-dominated territory shifted back and forth endlessly as the two sides attacked, retreated and counter-attacked.

Portugal's status as an independent monarchy originates from the organisation of the military frontier against the Muslims in this area. The buffer zone was constantly being reorganised under counts appointed by the **kings of León**. The territory, known as Portucalense, was made a province of León, and the appointed counts enjoyed considerable autonomy owing to the province's physical separation from León by rugged mountains. In 1096 King Alfonso VI of León gave hereditary title to the province of Portucalense and Coimbra as dowry to the crusader-knight **Henrique** on his marriage to the king's favourite (if illegitimate) daughter, Teresa. Henrique and Teresa's son, **Afonso Henriques**, led the next stage of the reconquest. Wresting control from his mother in 1128, he also challenged the power and sovereignty of Alfonso VII, king of León, to whom he was still a vassal. On two occasions, in 1137 and 1140, he attacked Galicia, finally forcing Alfonso VII to recognise his claim to the throne of an independent kingdom in 1143, though papal approval would still not come until 1179.

In the meantime, Afonso Henriques had made some daring incursions into Muslim territory, including the impressive victory at Ourique, in the Alentejo, in 1139. A brilliant military commander, Afonso Henriques reconquered more Muslim territory than any other Christian king in the peninsula. Establishing his capital at Coimbra, he continued to harass the Moors and, in 1147, exploiting their internal divisions, and aided by a passing fleet of English, Flemish and German crusaders bound for Palestine, took Lisbon after a three-month siege.

Further internal wrangling among the Muslims, Lisbon's strategic location and continued help from passing crusaders finally allowed Afonso Henriques to cross the Tejo and capture and hold large sections of the Alentejo. These victories earned Afonso Henriques papal recognition as king of Portugal in 1179 and he was granted all conquered lands over which neighbouring kings could not prove rights. When he died in 1185, Afonso Henriques had established an officially recognised Christian kingdom that extended well into Muslim Iberia. This was the embryo of current-day Portugal.

Afonso Henriques' descendants, first his son and heir, Sancho I, then his grandson Afonso II, and later his great grandson Sancho II, all further enlarged the realm. By the early 1200s the reconquest had penetrated into the Algarve and was completed by Afonso III in 1249 when he attacked and defeated an isolated enclave of Muslims ensconced at Faro in the Algarve. This last battle, which extended Portuguese territory to the sea, established the approximate territorial limits Portugal has had ever since.

The Moors, even after that defeat, held on to much of Al-Andalus (southern Spain) until as late as 149,2 when the Catholic kings finished the task by taking Granada. Throughout the southern Iberian peninsula the Moorish influence is present, and in the Algarve especially, it can be seen in place names such as Albufeira, Aljezur and Almancil, in ruined castles, in building styles still used today, and in some of the crops that continue to be cultivated, like citrus fruits. The modern Portuguese language, also, has some 600 words of Arabic origin.

Consolidation and Growth

Successive kings, especially **Dom Dinis**, a poet and brilliant administrator who ruled from 1297 to 1325, set about consolidating the country as a unified monarchy. Dinis established the frontiers of Portugal (and made them secure by building castles) via the Treaty of Alcañices, signed by King Fernando IV of Castile in 1297. He founded the University of Lisbon and created the Order of Christ to substitute the Knights Templar, who had been instrumental in the reconquest. He also fomented maritime trade as far north as the Baltic and into the Mediterranean, encouraged agricultural development and even planted pine forests along the coast to avoid erosion.

Dinis was succeeded by his son, **Afonso IV**, who continued his father's development policies and helped neighbouring Castile in its fight against the Muslims. When his grandson and heir, **Fernando I**, came to the throne, plagues had debilitated the economy and he had to take far-reaching measures to stimulate food production, forcing landowners to rent or sell unused land and obliging all who had no useful occupation to work the land. The measures brought about the desired effect and the economy recovered. Fernando was also able to stimulate the development of the country's maritime fleet, which would have a crucial role to play in future centuries.

On Dom Fernando's death, in 1383, he left no male heir and his wife Leonor tried to enthrone the couple's only daughter, **Beatriz**, married to Juan I of Castile, which would effectively have ended Portugal's independence. The Portuguese bourgeoisie opposed this and, after Spanish forces were defeated, João of Avis, Fernando's illegitimate stepbrother, occupied the throne, becoming **João I**, the first of the House of Avis dynasty. Help from the English in defeating the Spaniards led the way for the 1386 Treaty of Windsor, an Anglo–Luso alliance that would last until the 20th century.

The Age of Discoveries

With Castile no longer a threat, for the moment at least, Portugal started looking outwards. Portugal's maritime expansion began in the early 1400s and the occupation of Ceuta, nowadays a Spanish enclave in northern Morocco, assured Portuguese domination of the straits of Gibraltar. A participant in that campaign was the Infante Dom Henrique (**Henry the Navigator**), who afterwards settled in Sagres, on the extreme end of Cape St Vincent, where in 1418 he founded a naval school. Henrique used the wealth of the Order of Christ, of which he was a master, to finance maritime research. He was motivated by scientific curiosity and religious fervour – seeing further maritime voyages as a continuation of the crusades against the Muslims and the conversion of new peoples to Christianity – as well as by the desire to open a sea route to India.

By the time Henrique died in 1460, the Portuguese had explored down the west coast of Africa as far as modern-day Sierra Leone and discovered the archipelagos of Madeira, the Azores and Cabo Verde. During the successive reigns of João II, Manuel I and João III, overseas expansion continued. **Vasco da Gama** reached India in 1499, by sailing around the African continent, and opened up important commercial routes. **Pedro Alvarez Cabral** set foot in Brazil for the first time in 1500.

In 1494, the **Treaty of Tordesillas** established the share-out of the newly discovered territories between Portugal and Spain. – It should not be forgotten that Columbus first reached America in 1492. An imaginary line to the west of the Cabo Verde islands left in Portuguese hands anything that should be 'discovered' thereafter, meaning **Brazil** would become a colony shortly afterwards. Portugal was by now the world's chief maritime power, with strategic posts in Goa, the Moluccas and Macao.

Imperial Decline and Spanish Intervention

Decline was not long in coming. Throughout the Middle Ages, the country's finances had been in the hands of Jews, who had never been persecuted in Portugal as they were in the rest of Christendom. But during the reign of Manuel I, in 1497, under pressure from Spain and Rome, they were expelled or forced to convert to Catholicism. As the Protestant Reformation erupted in the early decades of the 16th century, so the Roman Catholic Church's response, the Counter-Reformation, a determined campaign to strengthen the Catholic Church's role in Europe and to restore religious unity, gathered pace. One of its principal arms was the **Inquisition**. In 1536 João III was granted permission to establish the Court of the Inquisition in Portugal and this body began to root out heresy from 1539 onwards. The first Inquisitor General was replaced by a religious zealot, the archbishop of Évora, who stood for public confession and immediate execution.

Although the Inquisition in Portugal dealt with all forms of heresy, corruption and disbelief, its main victims were the so-called New Christians, the same Jews who had converted to Christianity 40 years earlier, many of whom were suspected of secretly practising Judaism at home. The Inquisition was the instrument used to stop such an 'abomination'. Courts of the Inquisition functioned all over Portugal. The first *auto-da-fé*, or public burning of a heretic, took place in 1540 in Lisbon and over the next 150 years an estimated 1,400 people perished this way.

Persecution of the Jews was one factor that helped to bring about the beginning of the end of Portugal's imperial splendour. Since the Jews possessed vital technical skills, their elimination robbed the country of an important force for modernity and reinforced feudal elements. Other factors that contributed to the empire's decline were the use of profits from Asian monopolies to import manufactured goods, rather than laying the basis for economic and industrial development. The Asian empire was a state-run affair and so produced no independent middle class or commercial sector as in other European countries with overseas possessions. In addition, the vast sums spent on sumptuous palaces and churches meant a further severe drain on the economy.

João III's successor, **Dom Sebastião**, was aged three when his father died and assumed the throne at 14. He was not fit for this position, being sickly, poorly educated and mentally unstable. In 1578, at the age of 24, fanatically obsessed with launching a great anti-Muslim campaign, Sebastião embarked on a costly crusade to the north of Africa, which would result not only in the young king's death but also in that of most of the Portuguese nobility. As Sebastião had no heirs, a crisis of succession ensued, and to make matters worse the state's coffers were stretched to the limit to pay the ransoms demanded by the Moors to return captured nobles.

Sebastião's successor was his uncle, Henrique, the last surviving son of Manuel I, an aged and infirm cardinal who was refused papal dispensation to marry, thus denying any possibility of a new heir being engendered. Henrique, in any case, died in 1580. One of the pretenders to the throne was Felipe II of Spain, João III's nephew, who sent an army, led by the Duke of Alba, to attack Portugal and step into the power vacuum caused by Sebastião's débâcle in north Africa. The Spanish intervention in Portuguese affairs led to Felipe II's being crowned **Felipe I** of Portugal in 1581, aided and supported by the remnants of the Portuguese nobles. **Spanish domination** was to last little more than half a century, but was sufficient to create a resentment against their eastern neighbours that many Portuguese still feel to this day, especially since much of Portugal's overseas trading power was lost as a result.

Spanish rule ended in 1640, thanks to an uprising led by the **Duke of Bragança** who proclaimed himself **João IV**, thus beginning the rule of the House of Bragança, which would last until the proclamation of the Republic in 1910. João IV died in 1656, having consolidated and restored the monarchy by making peace with former enemies, recouped some lost colonial possessions and defeated Spanish attempts to reincorporate Portugal into the Iberian Union. Only in 1666, three years after Spain's final military defeat at the hands of the Portuguese, did the neighbouring kingdom recognise Portugal's independence. Asia, however, had been lost so the Portuguese monarchy, in the figure of **Pedro II**, who had assumed the throne after the voluntary abdication of his inept brother Afonso in 1667 (as well as marrying Afonso's former wife, Marie-Françoise Isabelle of Savoy – their marriage had been annulled) attempted to put order into domestic affairs. He implemented mercantilist policies in Portugal similar to those of France, seeking to protect Portuguese industries against foreign competition. He also published laws to enforce sobriety and criticised luxury, and his personal appointee to the treasury, Luís de Menenses, the Count of Ericeira, organised the textile industry and imported looms from England. He stimulated national production of wool and silk by decreeing that only Portuguese woollens and silks could be worn.

As well as the attention given to the domestic situation, much energy at this time was directed towards the development of Brazil. The cultivation of cotton, sugar and spices was nurtured, requiring large mounts of labour; slaves were imported from Angola and Guinea. The discovery of gold and precious stones in Brazil led to a gold rush from all over the world. While these discoveries would mean a fantastic source of revenue for Portugal, this came at the expense of Brazil's emerging agricultural sector, which was devastated. In addition, much of the wealth was squandered on megalomaniac projects such as the convent at Mafra, ordered by the absolutist **João V**, Pedro II's successor.

Despite these excesses, João V was an energetic king who copied the style of Louis XIV of France and introduced absolutist rule into Portugal. Brazilian gold allowed João V to spend lavishly on major architectural works, the greatest being the royal palace at Mafra, begun in 1717, which sought to rival the Escorial in Spain. He also endowed Coimbra University with an elegantly decorated library and built the aqueduct that supplied Lisbon with water. He encouraged the development of decorative arts and pursued mercantilist policies to protect indigenous industries as well as subsidising the publication of notable literary works. The period of João V's rule has often been referred to as Portugal's second renaissance.

On João V's death in 1750 he was succeeded by his indolent son **José I**, who placed the reins of government into the hands of **Sebastião José de Carvalho e Melo**, later the **Marquês de Pombal**. This petty noble was able to climb through Portugal's rigid class system by a combination of energy, intelligence, good looks and a shrewd marriage. He eventually wielded power in Portugal. Having been Portugal's ambassador to Britain and Austria, Pombal had been exposed to Enlightenment ideas and, aware of Portugal's backwardness, sought to reform it and create a middle class by means of ruthless despotism.

Natural Disasters and Napoleonic Invasion

The great earthquake that destroyed Lisbon in 1775 did further damage to the country's shaky finances, although José I, predictably, entrusted rebuilding to Pombal, who applied his principles of enlightened despotism (dictatorship) to get the country back on its feet. Dom José died in 1777, leaving the throne to his daughter, Dona Maria, who went mad in 1791 and delegated power to the Prince Regent, later to be called **Dom João VI**. The three **Napoleonic invasions** between 1807 and 1811 also knocked the country back again. The Portuguese royal family went into exile in Brazil while the fighting continued, leaving military affairs in the hands of British generals, and the Portuguese army effectively in charge of the country. The French were finally pushed out of Portugal and Spain in 1814. Meanwhile, in Brazil, the prince regent had declared the colony an independent kingdom leaving Portugal, technically speaking, half a colony of Brazil and half a British protectorate. In the absence of royal power, and inspired by the liberal airs blowing throughout Europe, the military drew up a new constitution that the king was forced to sign – much against his will – when he returned from Brazil in 1821. This brought the end of absolutist monarchy.

The Crisis of the Monarchy

The backlash came after Dom João died in 1826. **Prince Pedro**, his son and successor, drew up a new, less liberal constitution and then abdicated in favour of his own 7-year-old daughter, Maria, naming his brother, **Miguel**, prince regent on the condition that Miguel would marry Maria when she came of age. Miguel did so but later backtracked on the constitution and returned to his absolutist convictions, nullifying Pedro's constitutional charter and repressing all protests. What became known as the '**War of the Two Brothers**', essentially between absolutist ideas, strong in the country, and enlightenment, strong in the cities – was to divide Portuguese society for much of the 19th century, even provoking a civil war in 1846. A two-party system of alternation held things together for the rest of the century but the monarchy was practically bankrupt and republican ideas grew ever stronger, above all in the army and the urban working-class. In

1908 **King Carlos I** and his son were assassinated and in 1910 a **military uprising** abolished the monarchy.

The Republic

Parliamentary elections held in 1911 brought a republican triumph, the royal family went into exile and the provisional government of the First Republic took office. But there was no political stability. The ruling **Partido Democrático** was led by **Afonso Costa**, a man of a dictatorial bent who manipulated successive elections to keep power. The bureaucracy, a legacy of the monarchy, was corrupt and inefficient and the military took an ever-greater role in governmental matters. Neither president nor prime minister had the authority ever to dissolve parliament, and military intervention – of which there were 45 between 1920 and 1926 – became the 'normal' way of changing governments.

Salazar, the 'Novo Estado' and the Revolution of the Carnations

Finally, in 1926, a coup led by **General Carmona**, a Catholic monarchist, took power definitively and suppressed the republican constitution. Unsure how a restoration of the monarchy would be received, Carmona called elections in 1928, standing as sole candidate. That same year he promoted an economics professor from Coimbra, **Dr Salazar**, to the post of tax minister. As a result of his strict control of the public purse he became prime minister in 1932, a post he held until 1968. While, in terms of pure ideology, it is difficult to portray Salazar and his '**Novo Estado**' (New State) as fascist in the sense that Hitler's Germany and Mussolini's Italy were fascist, his methods certainly were fascistic. Parliamentarians were elected from a sole party, the **União Nacional**, trade unions were vertical and run by industry bosses, strictly controlled education fomented the Catholic religion, censorship was absolute and the political police, the PIDE, watched over everyone. The 'three Fs' – Fátima, *Futebol* and *Fado* – were the regime's watchwords and its way of controlling the people, in a modern variant of 'bread and circus'.

Although Salazar's regime created the infrastructure of a modern economy, the benefits did not filter down to the ordinary people, who continued in poverty, especially those in the countryside, which was largely abandoned. Discontent was rife, but what made the regime fall had more to do with external factors than internal ones. Salazar's colonial wars cost the country dear and earned Portugal enemies in many places. Military officers, based in Africa, also began to realise how unjust their country's system was, and, when Salazar was incapacitated by a stroke in 1968, his successor Marcelo Caetano tried to make certain concessions towards democratisation of the country. Too little, too late: by 1974 military discontent had grown and the revolutionary **Movimento das Forças Armadas (MFA)**, led by Otelo Saraiva de Carvalho, organised the overthrow of the government on 25 April that year. This moment of great change has since become known as the '**Revolution of the Carnations**'.

Into Europe

Since 1974 Portugal's history has been, if not uneventful, one of progress towards liberties and democracy. The last quarter of a century can be seen as two separate periods with a watershed in the middle. After the revolution, Portugal divested itself of its colonies, provoking an inrush of Portuguese citizens who had formerly been mainly resident in Angola and Mozambique. These '*retornados*' came at a moment of great economic chaos, a situation that continued until the mid-1980s. However, in 1986 Portugal gained access to the European Economic Community, as the European Union was known then. This has brought massive investments in infrastructure and great changes in society, mainly for the better.

Today, Portugal, though still poor by the standards of most of its EU partners, is a prosperous, stable democracy that has finally begun to look forward instead of to the past. The country still has many problems, though. A series of scandals, involving cronyism in government and an extended paedophile ring including several public figures, coupled with tax hikes, cuts in public spending and job losses, have all rocked Portugal's collective confidence. While relationships with neighbouring Spain, always strained, have become more fluid in recent years, sections of the Portuguese business and finance communities are worried about the increasing presence of Spanish enterprises in Portugal and fear being swallowed up into a Spanish-dominated Iberian market.

Apart from this, nobody knows what the future holds, as the EU subsidies from which Portugal has benefited for the last 15 or 20 years, begin to head east to the former communist countries incorporated into the union in May 2004. There is certainly a great deal of concern about this issue at present, and fears that Portugal will simply not attract the investors any more, given the cheap, but highly qualified labour force available in the new member states. One of the residents interviewed for this book stated it quite clearly: 'If you want business opportunities, go to Hungary!' But despite the pessimism currently reigning, the foundations have, at least, been set for a tomorrow that will almost certainly be rosier than yesterday and the day before.

The Portuguese Language

Every day, somewhere in the region of 200 million people in the world greet each other with '*Bom dia*'. Portuguese is the eighth most-spoken language in the world, and third among Western languages, after English and Castilian. It is the official language of seven countries – Portugal, Angola, Brazil, Cabo Verde, Guinea Bissau, Mozambique and the São Tomé and Príncipe Island group. Since 1986 it has also been an official EU language.

It originated from Latin, introduced by the Romans and adopted by the inhabitants of Lusitania thereafter. From that time until the 9th century, everybody spoke Romance, an intermediate stage between vulgar Latin and the modern Latin-root languages, which include Portuguese itself, Castilian, French and Galician, modern Portuguese's closest cousin, spoken in northwestern Spain.

Between the decline of the Roman Empire and the arrival of the Moors in 711, the Germanic invasions influenced Romance and had the effect of breaking the peninsula's linguistic uniformity, leading to the eventual emergence of the different tongues now spoken in modern Spain and Portugal. During the period of Moorish domination, the population continued to speak Romance although Arabic influences are also evident in modern words such as *arroz* (rice), *alface* (lettuce), *alicate* (pliers) and *refém* (hostage). The 9th–11th centuries were a period of transition; genuinely Portuguese words began to appear in written Latin texts, and Galician–Portuguese began to emerge as the spoken language of Lusitania. During the reconquest this language also became the area's written language, and the interaction between the northern Galician–Portuguese and the southern Mozarabic dialects also brought about a linguistic metamorphosis. By the time of Portugal's independence, in 1185, an early and distinguishable form of Portuguese had emerged. This process continued with the consolidation of Portugal as a nation, the expulsion of the Moors and the 1385 defeat of the Castilian armies in their attempts to conquer Portugal.

Portugal's overseas expansion spread the language to Asia, Africa and America, but the language absorbed some words from these places: *chá* (tea), of Chinese origin, is an example of this. The Renaissance also made an impression on Portuguese, which imported some Italian expressions and erudite words of Greek origin. Modern Portuguese, as such, emerged in the 16th century when the first grammars defining morphology and syntax were published. By 1572, when Luis de Camões wrote *Os Lusíadas,* the language was already close to its current structure. Since then, linguistic changes have been minor and more or less limited to lexical input from Castilian, French and English, the latter particularly in terms of technical vocabulary in the 19th and 20th centuries.

Anyone who aims to live and work in Portugal should take learning Portuguese seriously. This is not only as a matter of common courtesy to your hosts, but also a necessary step if you are to make the best of your time there. In tourist areas and larger cities there are many English-speaking property agents, lawyers, doctors and other professionals, but you cannot always bank on this. Further off the beaten track, you are less likely to find people who can help you in your own language. Even if your life and dealings are mainly within the expat community, there will be times when understanding and making yourself understood in Portuguese will be necessary. Dealing with officialdom, bank clerks, plumbers, waiters, shopkeepers and policemen will usually mean having to communicate in Portuguese, and in emergencies this could be a matter of life or death. That said, you may be pleasantly surprised at the number of English-speakers you do come across, especially if you have spent time in neighbouring Spain. With a history of overseas trading and emigration to other countries, the Portuguese have many centuries of interaction with other peoples and their languages and have, consequently, become a nation of talented linguists who approach other languages with few complexes and a certain gusto.

A word of warning. Portuguese, as seen above, belongs to the same family of languages as Spanish, French and Italian, all derived from Latin. You might be familiar with these languages if you have spent some time in those countries. On paper, Portuguese looks remarkably like its neighbour, Castilian. But it has certain characteristics that can make it difficult to learn, at least initially. The pronunciation is considerably complex and the abundance of closed vowels and shushing consonants make it sound to the unfamiliar ear like an eastern European language. This makes understanding spoken Portuguese difficult at first. While you can often make an inspired guess about the meaning of written Portuguese – you do not have to be a genius to work out what '*modere a sua velocidade*' means on the highway – it might not be so obvious if someone says this to you at machine-gun speed. You might well ask this person to moderate their speaking velocity! But learning Portuguese need not be traumatic. Quite the contrary, language learning can be fun if you approach it positively, with an open mind and a sense of humour for those times when you put your foot in it. Attempts at speaking Portuguese, however clumsy, will be appreciated and people will listen patiently, speak back to you slowly and try to help you.

For tips on learning the language, both at home before you leave and once in Portugal, *see* **Living in Portugal**, 'Learning Portuguese', pp.100–104. For pronunciation and useful words and prases, *see* **References**, pp.230–39.

Profiles of the Regions

03

Talking about Portugal by region immediately raises the thorny question of definition. Portugal is, administratively speaking, made up of 11 mainland provinces plus the two offshore island groups. They are: Minho, the most northerly; Douro Litoral, the 'river of gold' and including the city of Oporto (Porto); Trás-os-Montes, 'beyond the hills'; Beira Alta (Upper Beira); Beira Baixa (Lower Beira); Beira Litoral (Coastal Beira); Ribatejo, alongside the Tejo (Tagus); Estremadura (which includes Lisbon); Alto Alentejo (Upper Alentejo); Baixo Alentejo (Lower Alentejo); the Algarve. The two offshore provinces of Madeira and the Azores are known as the *'Adjucentes'*, meaning the 'Adjacent Islands', a strange term for territories which are about 1,000 and 1,500km from the mainland respectively.

These divisions are a little capricious, though, and many neighbouring provinces have much in common in terms of landscape, climate, customs and economic development. It therefore makes more sense to talk of Portugal in the larger groups of provinces defined by the Portuguese National Tourist Office when describing areas that, broadly speaking, share climatic and geographical characteristics:

- **The Algarve**: very much a province and a region of its own.
- **Planícies**: the Plains, comprising most of the two Alentejos.
- **Costa de Lisboa**: the Lisbon Coast, including the capital itself, slices of Ribatejo and Estremadura provinces and the northern, coastal part of the Alentejo.
- **Costa de Prata**: the Silver Coast, comprising most of the provinces of Estremadura, Ribatejo and Beira Litoral.
- **Costa Verde**: the Green Coast, encompassing Minho and Douro Litoral.
- **Montanhas**: the Mountains, made up of Trás-os-Montes, the inland part of Douro and the upper and lower Beiras.
- **Offshore Portugal**: Madeira and the Azores.

The Algarve

For many regular holidaymakers and would-be residents the Algarve *is* Portugal or, maybe, Portugal *is* the Algarve, such is the southern region's popularity among northern Europeans, British and Irish people among them. It is easier to get to the Algarve than it is to travel to Lisbon in these days of cheap charters and regular budget airlines. Faro airport, in the centre of the region, operates pretty much around the clock during the main holiday season. It can also get quite busy off-season, as the principal allure of the Algarve is its fantastic climate, a place where the word 'winter' is almost a misnomer, making it an ideal place for a low-season break.

A considerable number of northern Europeans and foreigners from further afield have made their home in the Algarve over the last 30 years. The expatriate community now makes up a sizeable minority of the region's population and there is a whole array of services provided by and for foreigners. These include sports and leisure facilities, golf courses particularly, where English is spoken, schools offering education in English and following the National Curriculum, social clubs for English-speakers and a small army of tradespeople and service providers who also come from the British Isles. Most local waiters can deal with English-speaking customers. After Lisbon and Oporto, the Algarve is one of Portugal's best-equipped regions in terms of infrastructure, services and leisure facilities. And, however much people might complain about the poor functioning of the administration, it is probably no worse here than anywhere else. Many residents either run businesses directly connected to the tourist industry, or get involved in the property market. Others find employment in the businesses run by their compatriots. Still others provide services for the expat community, which has become a sub-industry of itself. Many English-speaking people with skills – ranging from plumbers, electricians, hairdressers and gardeners to more highly qualified professionals such as doctors, dentists and vets – find there is enough demand to keep them in work.

The Algarve's climate, natural beauty, coastline and relaxed, laid-back way of life go a long way to explaining its popularity. But anyone who wants to find the 'real' Portugal and integrate may be advised to look at another part of the country to settle. One Algarve-based journalist interviewed for this book puts it quite clearly: 'In the Algarve there are two separate, parallel societies. The locals and the foreigners live apart even though they are mutually dependent, respect each other greatly and co-exist peacefully.' This is fine if learning Portuguese and integrating is not top on your list of priorities, but if you are working to a different agenda, living surrounded by expats may not be so appealing.

Faro

The administrative capital and transport hub of the Algarve is Faro, an attractive city of some 40,000 people. Tourists generally arrive at the airport and then go immediately to their holiday destination, which is their loss but possibly the city's gain. Residents of the central Algarve will need to become familiar with Faro, as most administrative departments are located there. Destroyed twice by earthquakes, in 1532 and 1755, the city still has its original Roman walls, some Moorish ruins, a 13th-century cathedral, an 18th-century episcopal palace and a 16th-century convent. The city's archaeological museum is within the convent, with a section dedicated to the Moorish period. In addition, the 'golden' church of Nossa Senhora do Carmo is thought to be the best example of gold-leaf woodwork in southern Portugal; it has a somewhat macabre chapel lined with the bones from over 1,200 monks.

Faro has a good modern marina and a naval museum full of scale-model boats and galleons which illustrate the Algarve's maritime history. The city also has a fairly active cultural scene and reasonable shopping facilities. Nearby is the Ria Formosa lagoon, a large nature reserve where hundreds of species of birds stop over during the spring and autumn migratory periods. The beach is almost 7km away from the city, a long sandy spit reached by crossing a bridge.

East of Faro

The region either side of Faro is divided into the central, west and east Algarve. East of Faro there is much less tourist development and, so far, fewer foreign residents. It is generally quieter, lower-key and cheaper, for property, than the area to the west of Faro. Going a little eastwards, close to Faro is **Olhão**, a fishing port of about 30,000 inhabitants. From the late 19th century until quite recently this town was the centre of the tuna- and sardine-canning industry, then the most important industry in the Algarve. The flat, terraced roofs and straight, box-shaped chimneys characteristic of the town lend it a Moorish feel and the fish market is a riot of noise and colour every morning. Further east is the prettiest town in the eastern Algarve, **Tavira**. This picturesque town straddles the river Gilhão and its history started some time before 400 BC. Like many other coastal towns and villages it was practically flattened by the 1755 earthquake, and as a result of this most of the interesting architecture dates from the 18th century. The local economy combines increased tourism with a still-functioning tuna fishing industry, though this is no longer the main source of income. There are many excellent fish restaurants, the most attractive on the river banks – fat tuna steaks are the standard fare. In the more basic, down-to-earth fishermen's bars and cafés, eating and drinking is still very reasonably priced.

West of Faro

The majority of foreign residents live west of Faro, where there is a booming expat 'scene' and property market. Located in the absolute centre of the Algarve is the town of **Albufeira**. Its 'strip' is possibly the most tourist-intensive spot on the whole of the Algarve and it offers, Costa del Sol style, many English pubs offering a full range of ales, karaoke sessions, wet T-shirt contests, quiz nights and Premiership football on large TV screens. Discos are in abundance and there are holiday apartment blocks galore. The town's long beach is pleasant enough but can get very crowded in the high season; nearby are many other nice beaches and coves. Albufeira is easily reached as it sits at the junction of the main Algarve–Lisbon motorway and the trans-Algarve Via do Infante; it is also easy to escape from for those who prefer to avoid crowds of lager louts.

Going west, there are several towns and villages that are very pleasant indeed. Many have not become overly developed owing to the building restrictions that have curbed excesses over the last decade. Inland, the other side of the Via do Infante, is **Silves**, the Moorish capital of the Algarve. Nowadays a quiet market town, Silves was considered the major cultural centre of the Iberian peninsula around the turn of the 11th century and was the scene of many epic battles between the Moors and the Christians during the later reconquest. Its principal attraction is the vast Arab fortress with orange groves inside its walls, which endured many sieges before finally falling to the Christians. There is also a 13th-century church (formerly a cathedral), a survivor of the 1755 earthquake.

Inland from Silves are pleasant forests of pine, eucalyptus, cork and oak, the spa village of **Caldas**, the market town of **Monchique** and **Fóia,** the highest point in the Algarve, which affords splendid, sweeping views of the whole western end of the province. The nearest beaches to Silves are down at **Portimão**, the second largest city in the region. Not especially attractive, Portimão does have good shopping and entertainment facilities and nearby are several sites of historical interest such as the caves of Estombar, the mosaic floor of the Roman villa at Figueira, and the recently restored burial tombs from the Dolman period (around 3,500 BC) at Alcalar. The long Praia da Rocha is Portimão's main beach and there are plenty of other beaches within striking distance. Many expats have fixed their residence in the nearby charming picture-postcard beach village of **Carvoeiro**. Close by, and probably a factor in many people's decision to move here, is a reputable international school.

Further west still is **Lagos**, a town that, while taking tourism on board, is also acutely aware of its historical importance. Nowadays laid-back and picturesque in the extreme, Lagos was the place where Prince Henry the Navigator had his ships built and prepared for the voyages that were to discover the Atlantic islands and explore the west African coast. There is a modern marina, for latter day seafarers, and lovely beaches, both within a stone's throw of the town itself and either side of the Ponta da Piedade headland, just to the south. The town has good eating and drinking and a fairly active cultural scene. Lagos is becoming more popular with expats now as improved communications, in the form of the Via do Infante, which finally reached here in spring 2003, mean it is now far more accessible from Faro airport.

The western tip of the Algarve is the **Cabo de São Vicente**, which before the age of discoveries was thought to be the end of the earth. It now has an impressive lighthouse. Nearby, at **Sagres**, Henry the Navigator is said to have founded a navigation school, possibly within the confines of the thoroughly renovated Fortaleza de Sagres. Little remains to show that the school was really here.

Planícies (The Plains)

The Planícies region comprises most of the Upper ('Alto') and Lower ('Baixo') Alentejo districts. The Alto Alentejo is bounded by the Spanish border, to the east, the Tagus river to the north and west; a fairly straight line running east–west just to the south of the city of Évora marks the southern limits. From then on, and all the way to the Algarve, the imposing Baixo Alentejo plains take over. The Baixo part of the region is bounded to the west by the Lisbon coast tourist region but has its own, unspoilt coastline starting just south of the industrial port of Sines. To the east, the frontier with Spain marks the edge of the region, and to the south the province borders on the Algarve. Inland, the plains are vast, flat, unrelenting and murderously hot in summer but quite cold in winter. Spring, when the countryside is a riot of colourful wildflowers, and autumn, pleasantly mild, are the most agreeable seasons.

One of Portugal's poorest and most backward regions, the two Alentejos together account for almost a third of continental Portugal (while the Planícies tourist region occupies about a quarter), and are sparsely populated. These two facts are clearly related. Since Roman times the landholding structure in the Alentejo has been one of huge estates (*latifúndios*). As a result, agricultural workers there have long been a landless peasant class in what was essentially a feudal system. The region, along with the Algarve, remained under the control of the Moors for at least a century longer than most of the rest of Portugal. After it was incorporated into the kingdom, Dom Dinis directed some of his attention there, building fortress towns along the Spanish border to contain Castilian expansionism. Once Portugal embarked on its overseas adventures the region fell into a state of abandonment, which continues to this day. After the 1974 Revolution, many of these estates were expropriated and given to peasant collectives, but lack of capital and know-how impeded their successful development and the estates are now, largely, back in the hands of their original owners. The lack of job opportunities – agriculture has become increasingly mechanised – have forced many *Alentejanos* to seek their fortune elsewhere.

Despite this, the two Alentejos are collectively known as Portugal's 'bread basket' as most of the country's wheat is grown there. In addition, olives and cork represent a considerable part of the region's production and Alentejo wines are very highly regarded, as is the distinctive and delicious cuisine (*see box, p.152*). The region is also famous for the Arab horses and bulls bred here.

There are many contrasts between the northern and southern halves of the region. Dotted throughout the north are historic towns, villages and prehistoric sites. The capital, **Évora**, a major political centre in Roman times, is now a UNESCO World Heritage site, with more listed buildings than anywhere else in Portugal except Lisbon. A Roman temple, Moorish alleys, a medieval city wall, itself built over the original Roman fortifications, a Romanesque cathedral, an aqueduct from the 16th century and Renaissance palaces and churches from every period are the chief attractions of this city of 55,000 inhabitants. Elsewhere, away to the northeast is the marvellous, fortified hill-village of **Marvão**, built to keep watch for marauding Spaniards. This village, along with its slightly plainer neighbour **Castelo de Vide**, the larger **Portalegre** and several other villages make up what is known as the Rota dos Castelos (Castle Route), located within the **Serra de São Mamede** natural park, bordering on Spain. To the south of these are more fortress towns, many built of marble, such as **Elvas**, and **Monsaraz**, which rivals Marvão for picturesque beauty. Inland from the border is **Estremoz**, the largest of the so-called 'marble towns'.

The southern half contains much less to see and is, if anything, even more sparsely populated. The only city of any size in the area is **Beja**, important in Roman and Moorish times, architecturally rich and close to several important archaeological sites. South of Beja is the charming little town of **Mértola**, close to the Guadiana river, which has a Moorish watchtower still standing and where an Islamic festival of music, dance and theatre is held every May. Nature lovers are well served in the southern Plains region. In the southeast corner is the practically uninhabited **Parque Natural do Vale do Guadiana**, traversed by the Guadiana river. To the west, the coastal strip between the port of Sines and the Cabo de São Vicente (part of the Algarve) is a nature reserve called the **Paisagem Protegido do Sudoeste Alentejano**.

Studies show that only about 5 per cent of foreign property-buyers in Portugal prefer the Alentejo to other areas. The reasons are obvious: it does not have the job or business opportunities of other areas, nor the attraction of the sea. But for those seeking peace and quiet in an unspoilt area, Planícies could be the answer, especially as the government is giving incentives for businesses in the field of ecotourism. The Alqueva Dam, a recently completed project just inside the border, is the largest artificial lake in Europe. Though it was fiercely opposed by environmentalists, politicians claim it will help to regenerate the region. Thousands of planning applications for golf courses, luxury hotels, health spas and island resorts have been filed since the dam was completed, and locals hope this will help the area to become an inland Algarve.

Costa de Lisboa (The Lisbon Coast)

The Lisbon Coast tourist region extends far beyond the capital itself over areas that are, administratively speaking, neighbouring provinces. Its most northerly point is the small fishing village of Ericeira, in the southern half of the coastal province of Estremadura (which Lisbon is itself a part of). Inland it takes some of the Ribatejo ('beside the Tagus') province. To the south, between Setúbal, Portugal's third largest and most industrialised city, and the unattractive port town of Sines, it includes a strip of coastline that is technically part of the Baixo Alentejo. The area has a wealth of beautiful resort towns, charming villages and towns on the coast and inland, a good number of iced-cake palaces, fairytale castles, historic monuments and other sights.

As the capital is here. the infrastructure is considerably better developed than in other, more isolated parts of Portugal. This is especially true of communications, which have improved immensely in recent years. Lisbon itself is a favoured destination for many foreign residents. It has more job opportunities than other areas and it is an absolutely enchanting, quirky and increasingly cosmopolitan city that has much to offer everyone, be they night-hawks, museum-goers, gastronomes, ethnic music lovers, beach bums, the trendy, the traditional, gay or straight. It is also possible to live within striking distance of the city, by the sea or inland, in great surroundings never far from the action.

Lisbon

Lisbon, capital of the Republic, formerly the metropolis at the heart of a huge ocean-going empire, is a city that most enjoy and leaves few disappointed. Like several others of the world's greatest cities, part of its physical attraction lies in the fact that it straddles seven hills, affording a variety of stunning views. Nowadays it stretches several kilometres along the northern bank of the Tagus estuary, though the original city was the hilltop fortress built by the Moors on top of a previous Roman construction. This is called the Castelo de São Jorge and is visible from most vantage points in the city. Surrounding the castle are the medieval neighbourhoods of **Alfama**, a corruption of the Arabic *Al Hama*, meaning 'hot springs', which spreads down the eastern side of the hill, and, on the other side, **Mouraria**, so called because that is where the Moorish population was concentrated after the Christian reconquest in 1147. There is a jumbled maze of narrow streets, steps and alleyways, an absolute nightmare for map-makers. No map ever gives you a true idea of the city's impossibly steep slopes.

By the end of the 13th century the city's commercial centre had moved down the hill to the **Baixa**, literally the 'low district', where most of the Jewish population was concentrated in medieval times. After the 1755 earthquake destroyed much of this district, the Marquês de Pombal ordered it to be rebuilt on a grid pattern. This area, while no longer the financial centre it was, is still regarded as Lisbon's centre, and the massive Praça Dom Pedro IV, known more commonly as Rossio, for centuries the city's main crossroads, is here.

The city would grow and engulf more hills over the following centuries, particularly to the west of the Baixa. From the early 16th century, after Dom Manuel I moved his residence from the castle to the waterfront, port activity increased in the area now known as Cais do Sodré. Jesuits and the merchant class soon colonised the hill behind the port area and it became known as the **Bairro Alto** (the 'high neighbourhood'). Between this area and the Baixa is the **Chiado** neighbourhood, less splendid than it was in its 19th-century heyday but still packed with theatres, fashion shops, bookshops and grand old cafés.

The city's continuing westward growth reached areas such as **São Bento**, where the Parliament is situated, **Alcântara** and, eventually, **Belém**, from where Vasco da Gama set out on his voyage to India in 1497. In this area are the Manueline style Torre de Belém, originally built to guard the river entrance to Lisbon's harbour and declared a UNESCO World Heritage site, the Jerónimos monastery, the fascistic Padrão dos Descobrimentos, a monument to the discoveries (both of which frequently adorn the covers of tourist brochures) and arguably the best custard tart shop in the world. Crossing the river at this point is the impressive Ponte 25 de Abril, an important, if congested bridge that links the capital with its southern-bank suburbs.

During the 20th century expansion was inland and to the north. Neighbourhoods such as **Saldanha** and **Avenidas Novas**, dominated by huge office blocks, are where much of the city's day-to-day business life takes place. Close by is the university and the Praça de Espanha, location of the Fundação Calouste Gulbenkian, one of Portugal's most important cultural institutions. A little beyond this are the neighbourhoods of **Sete Ríos** and **Benfica**, including the fabulous new Estádio da Luz, home of the famous football club, the Centro Colombo, one of the biggest shopping malls in Europe. There is little of central Lisbon's charm in these neighbourhoods, dominated as they are by grim apartment blocks. Not far away are the shanty towns (*barracas*), which are a source of much shame, though the authorities have made genuine attempts in recent years to rehouse many of the poor who live in them.

The most important development in recent times has probably been the redevelopment of the eastern side of town for Expo '98. The project, much in the manner of London's Docklands, has seen a post-industrial wasteland transformed into a booming area now known as **Parque das Nações** (Park of the Nations). It has riverside promenades, restaurants and cafés, some futuristic architecture such as Álvaro Siza's Pavilhão de Portugal, which houses the Council of Ministers, Regino Cruz's Pavilhão Atlântico next door, used for tennis competitions and rock concerts and, the centrepiece Oceanário, one of the largest aquariums in the world. There is, naturally, a large shopping mall, built as part of the project. Also in this area is the spanking new railway station, the Gare do Oriente, and the 17km-long Ponte Vasco da Gama, which links Lisbon with Montijo, on the southern bank of the Tagus.

Lisbon is in many ways a dazzling city, blessed with fabulous light and an enviable location. Whether you live there or go to visit, it has a wealth of possibilities – in terms of things to do and see – that suits all tastes, and a surprise awaits you practically every time you turn a corner. The city also presents many of the contradictions and contrasts to be found all over Portugal, all concentrated into one city. Dilapidated and tumbledown in parts, furiously modern in others, Lisbon lived its heyday many centuries ago and went into an apparently terminal decline thereafter. Now it is once again revitalising itself, a process that began with the Expo '98 project and has continued with the construction of the new stadia and associated infrastructures for the Euro 2004 football tournament. The quaint yellow electric trams, many of them built around 1900 in the Black Country, still clank up and down the impossible slopes of Alfama and Mouraria, while only a couple of kilometres away is the brashly ultramodern Amoreiras shopping mall.

On the north side of town, shanty towns huddle in the shadow of glass-fronted office blocks; there is even one within sight of the new stock exchange. The narrow streets of the Bairro Alto are quiet by day; where women in dressing gowns and slippers hang out washing and kids play. At night these same streets are taken over by a throng of up-for-it clubbers, bar-hoppers and diners. The dining experience in this city runs the whole gamut from shabby little family-run *tascas* to trendy, post-modern joints that would hold their own in London or New York. There are quaint, quirky museums near the state-of-the-art Expo '98 site with its impressive aquarium. Pensioners eke out a living on a paltry amount of money while yuppies drive around in flash cars, of which there are too many for the city's narrow old streets. For all this, Lisbon is a thoroughly attractive destination for foreigners coming to Portugal to live and work.

West of Lisbon

The city of Lisbon is not everybody's ideal of a place to live, however, as its noise, traffic and cramped conditions are far from the peace and quiet sought by many who move to Portugal precisely to get away from big city living. The suburbs and the coastal areas to the west are very attractive indeed.

About 20km west of Lisbon lies the resort of **Estoril**, nowadays a little faded but once a magnet for aristocrats and dethroned royal families. Ian Fleming based his 007 novel *Casino Royale* on the town's gambling house, and during World War Two, owing to Portugal's neutrality, the town was crawling with spies, working both for the Allies and the Axis. A little further up the coast is the former fishing village of **Cascais**, now a smart resort complete with a new marina, an abundance of restaurants, watering holes and nightlife and a few architectural gems too. Beyond Cascais is the **Cabo Raso**, just past which is the popular **Praia do Guincho** and then the **Cabo da Roca**, Europe's most westerly point. Further on are more fine beaches and coastal villages favoured by sun-seekers, bathers and surfers alike. **Praia da Adraga**, **Praia Grande** and **Praia das Maças** are among the most popular.

The inland part of this coast has many other pleasant towns and villages. **Sintra**, another world heritage site, described by Lord Byron as 'this glorious Eden', was once the summer residence of the Portuguese royals and before that of the Moorish rulers. The surrounding vegetation and landscape are exuberant, and the town has a series of mansions and palaces, many of which could well have served as inspiration for Disney cartoons. Of particular interest is the Palácio da Pena, at the top of the hill, in pink and yellow, built in a pastiche of the various styles employed during the Romantic period. Nearby is the Palácio Nacional, easily spotted thanks to its two massive white chimneys. It dates from the 14th century when it was built for Dom João I and his wife, Philippa of Lancaster. Closer to Lisbon itself is **Queluz**, a slightly shabby town that boasts a wildly rococo palace built for Prince Dom Pedro in the mid-18th century.

Overall, the area to the west of Lisbon has much to recommend it as a place to live – it is close enough to the capital to be able to take advantage of it but seemingly miles away from the sometimes maddening traffic and noise of the big city. Apart from the more tourist-type attractions and the beaches, there are plenty of golf courses and a sprinkling of English schools. There is a fair-sized but well-heeled English-speaking expat community firmly established here.

South of Lisbon

About 50km to the south of Lisbon, across the Tagus estuary and past the Serra da Arrábida, lies the city of **Setúbal**, Portugal's third port and industrial centre. Setúbal is not of itself particularly interesting for expatriates, though its economic importance inevitably gives rise to a foreign presence. The surrounding area has a lot to recommend it, though.

West of the city is **Sesimbra**, a picturesque fishing village complete with medieval castle. **Palmela,** in the nearby **Parque Natural da Arrábida**, also has a splendid castle. To the south is the Rio Sado estuary and natural park, which includes the Tróia peninsula, Setúbal's own beach resort, nowadays a little overrun with high-rise developments. More attractive, to the west, is the **Costa da Caparica**, much favoured by Lisboetas at weekends, a continuous row of beaches and clapboard houses. Anyone wishing to drop out could do a lot worse than settling here.

Further South

From the Tróia peninsula on the Sado estuary, going south to Sines, the Costa de Lisboa is administratively part of the Baixo Alentejo. Here towns are small and resorts tend to be low-key, though the beaches are extremely fine and almost totally unspoilt. The pleasant little town of **Santiago do Cacém** has a Moorish castle that was later rebuilt by the Knights Templar and, nearby at Miróbriga, some interesting Roman ruins. Santiago do Cacém is inland but the coast is close and there are two lagoon beaches at **Santo André** and **Melides**. Beyond that are the Atlantic-facing beaches themselves, which stretch in a continuous swathe between **Comporta**, in the north, and **Sines**, in the south. This is not an area that has been of particular interest to expats so it is probably worth looking into if what you want is to live away from them.

Costa de Prata (The Silver Coast)

The Costa de Prata earns its name from the silvery hue of the sun when it reflects on the Atlantic Ocean. The region stretches from a little to the north of Ericeira, the northern limit of the Lisbon Coast region, almost all the way to

Case Study: Anne Bartlett – The Good Life in the North

Anne Bartlett, 68, and her husband took early retirement from their jobs as primary school teacher and electrician and moved to a village close to Aveiro, in northern Portugal, in 1990. One of their daughters was already living there with her first child. They bought a plot of land in order to grow vegetables but found it difficult to make a going concern of it. Since her husband's death Anne allows a neighbour to use half of the land but continues to grow for herself and her family, giving away surplus produce to neighbours. She still enjoys teaching and does occasional language coaching, sometimes for pay but usually in exchange for other services or goods, such as maize for her hens or manure.

Q What brought you to Portugal originally, and why did you choose this particular area?

AB Retirement, and the fact that my daughter and baby grandson were already living here. We had thought of France but Portugal was cheaper. We chose the north because it has more rain and less heat so is better for growing vegetables. It is also a lot cheaper than Lisbon or the Algarve, where foreigners can be exploited. I like mountains and the sea; here I have both and this was the first suitable property of many viewed between Coimbra and Aveiro. I have also joined ecological and bird-watching groups and enjoy outings with them.

Q What do you consider the good points and the bad points of life here?

AB The living is easy, cheap lunch in cafés, cheap coffee and booze, local shops are open all hours and hypermarkets are ever-better stocked. I don't drive but public transport is cheap, especially for the over-65s. I also cycle a lot. People are friendly and helpful. The downside is perhaps the bureaucracy and the fact that those in authority do not always know the rules concerning non-national residents. For dealing with red tape, time and persistence are essential though the 'loja do cidadão' is helpful, with almost all the authorities under one roof. They also do not shut for lunch!

Q Do you live mainly in the expat community or have you integrated?

AB I am integrated; the language is the only problem though after doing some initial classes I began to use it daily in cafés and shops. After six years here I attended a course for foreign residents at the University of Aveiro. Also, not many expats live here so you have to use Portuguese. My two grandchildren here are half Portuguese so I speak the language with their father's side of the family.

Oporto. It is made up of most of the provinces of Estremadura and Ribatejo as well as that of Beira Litoral. This area is thus a sizeable chunk of central Portugal, which encompasses a long stretch of coastline, with pleasant resorts and quaint fishing villages, and an inland area that is largely forest-clad and mountainous. It is also well endowed with historic monuments, castles, palaces and monasteries, and has a great many pretty towns and cities. Economically it is relatively well developed and has good communications, both by road and rail – it is easily reached both from Lisbon and Oporto.

The region is popular with holidaymakers, who come from Portugal itself, neighbouring Spain and further afield. It has also begun to attract foreign property-buyers, either second-home-owners or permanent residents. This is largely because of its attractions and the fact that it is a cheap alternative to the Algarve and the Lisbon Coast regions, though it still enjoys many of the advantages offered by those areas. Infrastructures are good and the weather, thanks to the Gulf Stream, is not especially harsher.

The main urban centre is **Coimbra**, the capital of Portugal in the 12th and 13th centuries and also one of Europe's oldest university towns. The university is an important part of Coimbra life. The campus overlooks the city, and boasts an old tower and a sumptuous Baroque library, though most of the faculties now standing were built in the Salazar period in a bombastic fascist style. Salazar was a graduate of the university and later an economics professor there until he became a minister in 1928. Other illustrious alumni were the poet Luis de Camões and Egas Moniz, winner of the Nobel Prize for Medicine. The presence of a large student population, many of whom still wear the traditional black capes, makes the café scene and nightlife very animated indeed during the academic year, though at weekends and out of term-time the city takes on a quieter, more provincial air.

The male students keep alive the *'fado de Coimbra'*, a northern variant of the soulful song form that those not in the know only associate with Lisbon. An important ritual is the *Queima das Fitas* (the Burning of the Ribbons), a boisterous celebration of the end of the academic year. Surrounding the university is the old city, with narrow, ancient streets, archways and medieval walls, and the Sé Velha, the old cathedral, built in a mixture of Romanesque and Gothic styles. Another attraction is the Museu Nacional Machado de Castro, housed in a former archbishop's palace, one of the most important in the country. It exhibits Portuguese and Flemish art from the 15th to the 18th century and other treasures. Many other old churches are dotted around the city. and 16km to the south is Conímbriga, the largest pile of Roman remains in Portugal.

There are many other towns and cities of historical interest in the region. One is **Viseu**, to the north of Coimbra. This city maintains part of its Gothic walls, its 15th-century gates, evidence of Roman fortifications, a Romanesque cathedral and several other ecclesiastical buildings of importance. Due west, on the estuary of the Vouga river, is **Aveiro**, famous for its lagoon and the canals that crisscross the town. These fluvial channels earn the city its sobriquet, 'Portugal's Venice', and there are good many religious buildings of importance too.

A little south of Aveiro, and due west of Coimbra, is the pleasant resort town of **Figueira da Foz**, with long, sandy beaches and plenty of facilities for water sports. Going south from here, resorts alternate with fishing villages all the way down the coast to the beginning of the Lisbon tourist region. **Nazaré** is an attractive spot with fishing boats painted in bright colours that still ply their trade, though they now dock in the new port instead of being dragged into shore by oxen as was always the custom. Fishermen's wives can still be seen wearing the local costume, consisting of several layers of skirts.

To the south of Nazaré is **São Martinho do Porto**, a charming little town with one of the safest beaches on the whole coast, an enclosed bay, protected by two headlands that practically meet at the entrance. Further south still is the fishing port of **Peniche**, home to a large fleet. Though not especially attractive itself, Peniche is the departure point for the **Ilhas Berlangas**, an island nature reserve 12km out into the sea. Close by is a new resort, **Praia do Rei**, a golf and country club development with villas arranged around the championship-level course, rated second in the country. Just inland from here is the living picture-postcard village of **Óbidos**. This wonderfully preserved medieval village, completely walled-in and with whitewashed walls framed in deep blue, was traditionally the wedding present that Portuguese kings gave to their brides.

Inland, in the southern part of the region, there are many other places of note. Some 6km to the north of Óbidos is **Caldas da Rainha**, a spa resort first put on the map by queen Dona Leonor, who was impressed by the sulphuric waters in 1484. The town reached its peak in the 19th century. Two World Heritage monasteries are close by, at **Alcobaça** and **Batalha**.

The natural beauty of inland Costa de Prata is an added attraction. Typical are the Atlantic pine-clad hills, which give way to the beginnings of the more forbidding mountain ranges (*see* 'Montanhas', below).

The Costa de Prata has much to recommend it as a place to settle in. Apart from the vast amounts of tangible history, in the form of castles, churches, monasteries and palaces, its Atlantic coastline has a temperate climate and white, sandy beaches. Rural countryside is beyond. Local cuisine, crafts and festivals and customs are varied and give the feeling of being authentic.

Costa Verde (The Green Coast)

Two small provinces make up the Costa Verde tourist region. The northernmost province of Minho takes its name from the river that flows through Galicia, in Spain, before forming the international frontier between Portugal and its neighbour. Directly south is the minuscule province of Douro Litoral, which includes the city of Oporto, Portugal's second, and Braga, the country's ecclesiastical capital. There are many picturesque fishing villages and inland market towns. The greenness to which the region's name alludes comes from the rains that come in off the Atlantic. The beautiful coastline, thanks to a combination of luck and prompt action on the part of the Portuguese authorities, remains beautiful having been practically untouched by the several thousands of tonnes of filthy low-grade crude that spilled from the tanker *Prestige*, which sank off the Galician coast in November 2002.

Oporto is the English translation of Porto, the city that was the cradle of the modern Portuguese state and from where the Christian reconquest began in the 8th century. The city's origins go back much further, however, to the times of a Lusitanian settlement called Cale on the left bank of the river Douro, and a

Alfacinhas vs Tripeiros – or Inter-city Rivalry, Portuguese Style

Although Lisbon and Oporto ostensibly have much in common, there is also much that sets them apart. Both are hilly. Both are ports, situated on a major river that has shaped the destinies of each. Both have spectacular bridges connecting to their neighbouring municipalities on the southern bank. Both cities, owing to Portugal's seafaring history, have long enjoyed contacts with foreign cultures and become cosmopolitan as a result. Both have been European Cities of Culture – Lisbon in 1994 and Oporto in 2001.

But there, really, the similarities end. In terms of their inhabitants, customs, cuisine and way of life, Lisbon and Oporto are quite different. Like Glasgow and Edinburgh or Madrid and Barcelona, there is a fierce rivalry between the capital and the second city. Lisboetas refer to Portuenses as tripe-eaters (*tripeiros*), a reference to the northern preference for offal. Portuenses refer to the capital city-dwellers as lettuce nibblers (*alfacinhas*), alternating that insult with Mouros – Moors – a term with more than a hint of racism that is slung at southern Portuguese people in general. Portuenses are proud of their work ethic and prosperity, and claim, 'Lisbon shows off, Porto works.' Lisboetas, on the other hand, can boast a longer tradition of liberal and progressive ideas, especially during the first republic and during the 1974 revolution, and see their northern rivals as materialistic, conservative and archly religious. The first city's arrogance is summed up in the old expression, 'Portugal is Lisbon, the rest is countryside.' Whichever of the two cities you are in, you will probably stop a conversation by saying how much you like the other.

This rivalry nowadays expresses itself chiefly through football. In the eternal three-way tussle between FC Porto and either Benfica or Sporting, the northern city has had more to cheer about of late. Of the last 20 '*Superligas*' that were disputed, Porto have carried off no fewer than 13, including five consecutive titles in the late 1990s. The two Lisbon giants, between them, have managed six, four for Benfica and two for Sporting. Even Porto's city rival, modest Boavista, got its name on the trophy in 2001, another northern triumph. At the end of the 1999–2000 season, when Sporting broke Porto's five-year stranglehold on the title, some Benfica fans grudgingly turned out to applaud their city rival's triumphant homecoming, such was the pleasure of seeing their northern neighbours beaten at last. The joy has been short-lived. Porto are currently European champions, won the UEFA Cup in 2003 and have conquered the last two domestic leagues at a canter.

later one on the other side called Portus. Thus, Portus-Cale became the capital of the fledgling country that was first known as 'Portucalia'. From there to 'Portugal' is but a short phonetic leap.

Though Oporto is Portugal's second city, in many ways it leads the field in terms of commerce, sophistication and economic development. The city has certainly always known that its prosperity depended on its maintaining its historical role as a crossroads for world trade and as a manufacturing centre. By and large it has managed it. The port wine trade is another mainstay of the local economy and one of the main tourist attractions. Nobody should visit is Oporto and fail to visit one, or several, of the wine lodges in Vila Nova de Gaia (a separate municipality), on the southern bank of the Douro.

Traditions apart, Oporto is also forward-looking and dynamic. In 2001 it was European City of Culture, acquiring in the process a gleaming new arts centre, the Museu de Arte Contemporânea, designed by the prestigious Oporto-born architect Álvaro Siza. The city presents many monumental buildings from former times, most notably the Sé, the Romanesque cathedral, the Torre dos Clérigos, an 18th-century tower attached to a church, and the neoclassical, glass-domed Palácio da Bolsa, formerly the stock exchange. There are two historic bridges – the two-tiered Ponte de Dom Luis I, completed in 1886, and the Ponte de Maria Pia, designed by Eiffel to carry rail traffic. Across the river in Vila Nova de Gaia is the impressive Mosteiro da Serra do Pilar. Architecturally, Oporto is a mix of the old and the ultra-modern, though the former still prevails. The city's proximity to the coast is an added attraction, as there are beaches practically in the city, though they are not especially clean, and better ones just up and down the coast.

Three other towns set the tone for this charming area. **Braga**, founded by the Celts in 300 BC, became a Roman administrative centre in 27 BC, going by the name of Bracara Augusta. Its importance as Portugal's ecclesiastical capital is evident in the cathedral, dating from the 12th century but with additions as late as the 18th. There is also a museum of sacred art, churches such as the Renaissance period Misericórdia, the 17th–18th-century Pópulo and the 18th-century Nossa Senhora Branca. There are also sanctuaries and monasteries here. Nearby is **Guimarães**, which also has a claim to being Portugal's birthplace, with a medieval castle and walls and magnificently well-preserved historic centre. It includes a couple of ecclesiastical museums, housed in churches and convents, the 15th-century palace of the Dukes of Bragança, the Romanesque church of São Miguel and the monastery of Santa Marinha da Costa, nowadays converted into a *pousada*. Nearby is the early settlement of Briteiros. Finally, **Viana do Castelo** spreads along the northern bank of the Lima estuary. This town is famous for its handicrafts and colourful regional costumes but also has an impressive collection of Gothic churches. Dominating the city is the sanctuary of Santa Luzia, which provides fantastic views of the town, the river and the sea.

On the coast there are many pretty fishing villages. Worth visiting are **Caminha**, on the banks of the Minho, sheltered from the sea, and **Esposende** and **Ofir**, either side of the mouth of the Lima river. As well as this there are several resort towns on the coast, among them **Espinho**, site of Portugal's first-ever golf course, **Póvoa do Varzim**, a fishing port that has turned into a resort, and **Vila do Conde**, practically next door.

The region as a whole is without doubt one of the country's most colourful, and few would disagree that it is among the most beautiful. It is traversed by four east–west-flowing rivers, the most important being the Douro, which crosses Castilla-León in northern Spain and reaches the sea at Oporto. Then there is the Cavado, which flows just past Braga, coming out at Esposende. The Lima, which meets the sea at the coastal town of Viana do Castelo, and the Minho, part of the border between northern Portugal and Galicia, Spain, are the two northernmost rivers. They all have many tributaries, so the terrain is hilly and carved by deep, verdant valleys. The area is dotted with villages, many of which have hardly been touched by modern development, where age-old agricultural methods are still used. The rural areas are poor but proud and traditional village festivities can, in many cases, trace their roots back to pre-Christian times. For lovers of hill-walking, bird-watching and other similar pursuits in a gorgeous natural setting, this area is unbeatable.

As a region that has long engaged in international trade, Oporto and the surrounding area has also had an important foreign community for many years, one that is well integrated into local society. French, German, Belgian, Dutch, German and English traders and residents have all left their mark on the city. In Oporto, for English-speakers, there is a highly prestigious international school Anglican and Methodist churches, a cricket and lawn tennis club, and a mothers' club that meets at the Anglican church.

Montanhas (The Mountains)

Occupying the northeast corner and about a quarter of Portugal's surface area, Montanhas (the Mountains) is the country's poorest, most backward region. It comprises the provinces of Trás-os-Montes ('Behind the Hills'), the Alta and Baixa Beiras and the upper part of the Douro. It is a large, sparsely populated area, the least-known part of Portugal, but offers some fantastic, rugged countryside, ancient traditions, hearty cuisine and a level of unspoilt peace and quiet hard that is hard to find anywhere else in Europe nowadays.

Trás-os-Montes itself is a place that time seems to have forgotten, though it is probably more accurate to say that it is central government that has forgotten it, rather than time. It is hemmed in by three mountain ranges, a factor that has enhanced its isolation, and has a climate that locals describe as 'nine months of winter and three months of hell'. Farms are rarely mechanised, and the land is more commonly worked by hand and wooden-wheeled ox carts. Animals are slaughtered in the traditional way and no scrap is wasted. You can still see women washing out pigs' entrails in a stream before smoking them in wine and garlic and mixing them with meat to make *chouriço*, a form of sausage. The region's local costumes, dances and songs give an idea of its pre-Roman, pre-Christian, Celtic past, which locals hold on to. Religion here is deeply felt. Though Catholic rituals were adopted, they were grafted on to a much older pagan heritage and people here prefer to consult medicine men about life's important issues. While city types see *transmontanos* as primitive, the proud, fiercely independent locals, whose dialect is closer to *Galego* (Galician), spoken on the other side of the Spanish border, carry on without a care.

The name 'Montanhas' is easy to understand. The region offers some absolutely stunning mountain scenery, much of it in protected natural parkland. Consult a map and you will see the word *serra* (mountain range) dotted about all over the place. The **Parque Natural da Peneda-Gerês**, which continues over the border into Galicia, encompasses four mountain ranges, the Serras da Peneda, do Soajo, do Gerês and do Larouco, and there are several more *serras* on the borders of the park. In Portugal's far northeastern corner, close to the provincial capital of Bragança, is the **Parque Natural de Montezinho**, comprising the Serras de Montezinho and da Caroa. The river Douro, watched over by the Serra do Mogadouro, for many kilometres forms Portugal's eastern border with Spain (where it is called the 'Duero') and on either side lies the **Parque Natural do Douro Internacional**, jointly managed by the Portuguese and Spanish authorities. Further south, and to the east of Coimbra, is the **Parque Natural da Serra da Estrela**, more accessible and therefore popular with walkers, canoeists, climbers and anglers than the parks further north. Here, Portugal's only winter sports facilities are to be found.

The region has some fine cities, towns and many unspoilt villages, which like much of the rest of northern Portugal contain a wealth of architecture – especially ecclesiastical architecture – in all manner of styles, including Gothic, Romanesque, Baroque and Manueline. **Bragança**, a majestic city, with a medieval castle and walls was the seat of the royal family that occupied the throne from the mid-17th century until the declaration of the Republic in 1910. It boasts a *domus municipalis*, a unique example of civic Romanesque architecture in Portugal. **Vila Real** also has impressive ecclesiastical architecture.

Montanhas remains, for the moment, off the map for most expatriates, and few foreigners live here. This is obviously to do with the region's remoteness, economic backwardness and a perceived lack of business opportunities. Like some of the other less favoured regions, though, it could be just the place for those seeking solitude, authenticity, and relatively cheap property. For the enterprising, there is always the possibility of living an independent life cultivating food or turning a stone farmhouse into a rural tourism business. A trip here might turn any idea you had about living in Portugal completely on its head.

Portugal touring atlas

50 km
20 miles

N

①

SPAIN

Viana do Castelo
MINHO
Braga
Chaves
Bragança

Mirandela
TRÁS OS MONTES
ALTO DOURO
Vila Real
**Miranda
do Douro**

**Oporto
(Porto)**
DOURO
LITORAL
BEIRA
ALTA

Aveiro
Viseu
RIBACÔA

Guarda

COSTA VERDE

COSTA DE PRATA

②

ATLANTIC

Covilhã
Coimbra
BEIRA LITORAL
BEIRA BAIXA

Leiria
Serta
Castelo Branco

Caldas da Rainha
Abrantes

ESTREMADURA
RIBATEJO
Santarém
Portalegre

Torres Bedras

Sintra
ALTO ALENTEJO
Badajoz

SPAIN

③
LISBON
Setúbal
Évora

OCEAN

Grândola

Sines
Beja

BAIXO ALENTEJO

Castro
Verde

Odemira

BARROCAL

ALGARVE
Vila Real de Santo
António
Lagos
Tavira
Albufeira
Faro

GOLFO DE CADIZ

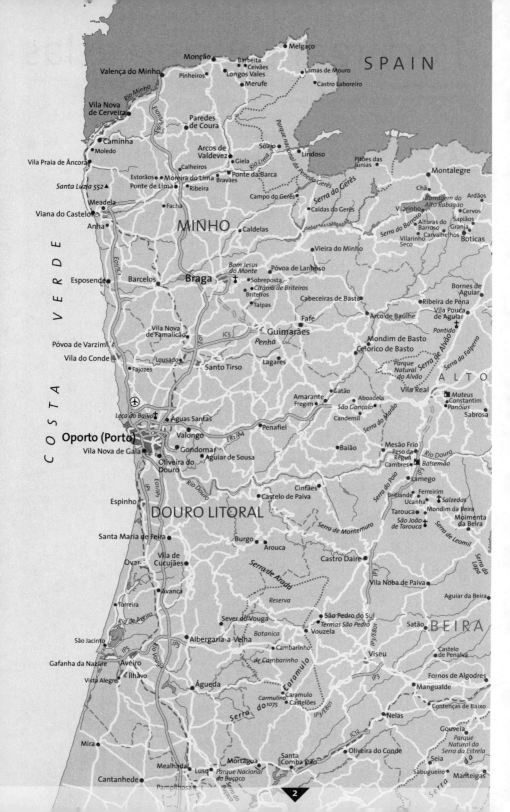

SPAIN

Melgaço
Monção
Barbeita
Ceivães
Valença do Minho
Pinheiros
Longos Vales
Lamas de Mouro
Merufe
Castro Laboreiro

Vila Nova
de Cerveira

Paredes
de Coura

Caminha
Moledo

Arcos de
Valdevez
Soajo
Lindoso
Pitões das
Junias

Vila Praia de Âncora
Giela
Montalegre

Calheiros
Ponte da Barca
Estorãos
Moreira do Lima
Bravães
Chã
Ardãos
Santa Luzia 552▲
Ponte de Lima
Ribeira
Campo do Gerês
Barragem do
Alto Rabagão
Cervos

Meadela
Facha
Caldas do Gerês
Vilarinho
Sapiãos
Granja
Viana do Castelo
Serra do Gerês
Alturas do
Barroso
Vilarinho
Seco
Carvalhelhos
Boticas
Anha
Caldelas

MINHO
Vieira do Minho

Esposende
Póvoa de Lanhoso
Bornes de
Aguiar

Barcelos
Bom Jesus
do Monte
Sobreposta
Ribeira de Pena

COSTA VERDE
Braga
Citânia de Briteiros
Briteiros
Cabeceiras de Basto
Vila Pouca
de Aguiar

Taipas
Arco de Baúlhe
Pontido

Vila Nova
de Famalicão
Fafe
Mondim de Basto
Serra do Alvão
Serra da Folgeira

Póvoa de Varzim
IC5
Guimarães
Penha
Celorico de Basto

Vila do Conde
Lousado
Santo Tirso
Lagares
Parque
Natural
do Alvão
Vila Real
ALTO

Fajozes

Amarante
Gatão
Aboadela
Mateus
Constantim
Panóias

Fregim
São Gonçalo
Sabrosa

Leça do Bailio
Águas Santas
Candemil
Serra do Marão

Oporto (Porto)
Valongo
Penafiel
Baião
Mesão Frio
Peso da
Régua
Rio Douro

Vila Nova de Gaia
Gondomar
Aguiar de Sousa
Cambres
Balsemão

Oliveira do
Douro
Lamego

Cinfães
Serra do Poio
Britiande
Ferreirim
Ucanha
Salzedas

Espinho
Castelo de Paiva
Tarouca
Mondim da Beira

DOURO LITORAL
Serra de Montemuro
São João
de Tarouca
Moimenta
da Beira

Santa Maria de Feira
Burgo
Arouca

Ovar
Vila de
Cucujães
Castro Daire
Vila Nova de Paiva

Avanca
Serra de Arada
Reserva
Aguiar da Beira

Torreira
Sever do Vouga
São Pedro do Sul
Satão
BEIRA

Rio de Aveiro
Botânica
Termas São Pedro
Vouzela

São Jacinto
Albergaria-a-Velha
de Cambarinho
Cambarinho
Castelo
de Penalva

Gafanha da Nazaré
Aveiro
Viseu

Vista Alegre
Ílhavo
Fornos de Algodres

Águeda
Caramulo
Mangualde

Carmulino
Caramulo
Castelões
Contenças de Baixo

Serra
do
1075
Nelas

Mira
Gouveia
Parque
Natural da
Serra da Estrela

Oliveira do Conde
Seia

Mortágua
Santa
Comba Dão
Sabugueiro
Manteigas

Mealhada
Lusã
Parque Nacional
do Buçaco

Cantanhede
Pampilhosa

2

25 km

10 miles

N

Verin

Serra da Coroa

Serra de Montezinho

França

Rio de Onor

Rio Sabor

Varge

Parque Natural de Montezinho

Vinhais

Sanjurge

Águas Frias

Pedra Bulideira

Castro de Avelãs

Gimonde

Bragança

Seara Velha

Santo Estêvão

Chaves

São Julião de Montenegro

Rebordelo

Outeiro

Vidago

Vilarandelo

Torre de Dona Chama

Valpaços

Lamas de Podence

Vimioso

Tresminas

Macedo de Cavaleiros

TRÁS-OS-MONTES

Mirandela

Algoso

Miranda do Douro

Murça

D O U R O

Sendim

Mogadouro

Serra do Mogadouro

Vila Flor

Sampaio

Alijó

Castelo Branco

Carrazeda de Ansiães

Rio Sabor

Pinhão

Torre de Moncorvo

Mata Nacional do Reboredo

Lagoaça

Quintana do Vale do Meão

Serra do Reboredo

São João da Pesqueira

Pocinho

Rio Douro

Vila Nova de Foz Côa

Freixo de Espada a Cinta

Freixo de Numão

Rio Douro

Penedono

Rio Côa

Barragem de Vilar

Barca de Alva

S P A I N

Marialva

Sernancelhe

Figueira de Castelo Rodrigo

Ponte de Abade

Castelo Rodrigo

Serra da Marofa

Trancoso

Pinhel

ALTA

Vila Franca das Naves

Freches

Almeida

Celorico da Beira

Ratoeira

RIBACÔA

Cavadoude

Vilar Formoso

Linhares

Faia

Estrela

Guarda

Rio Mondego

Valhelhas

Belmonte

Sabugal

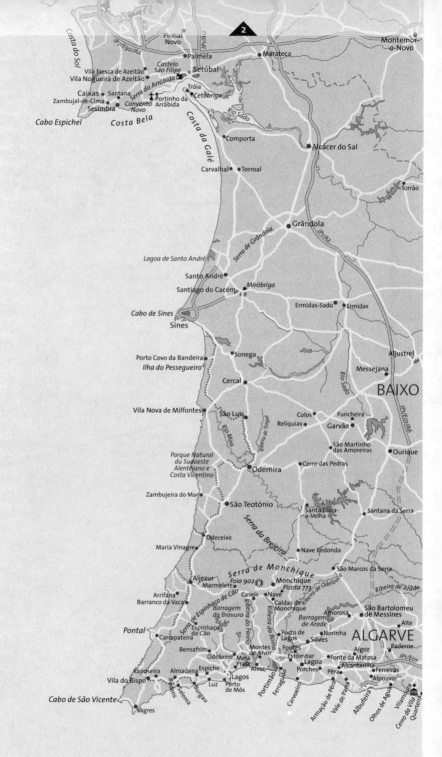

Pinhal
Novo
Palmela
Marateca
Montemor-
o-Novo

Castelo
São Filipe
Vila Fresca de Azeitão
Vila Nogueira de Azeitão
Setúbal
Tróia
Cetóbriga
Caixas
Santana
Zambujal-de-Cima
Convento
Sesimbra
Novo
Portinho da
Arrábida
Rio Sado

Cabo Espichel
Costa Bela

Comporta

Alcácer do Sal

Carvalhal
Torroal

Torrão

Grândola

Serra de Grândola

Lagoa de Santo André

Santo André
Miróbriga
Santiago do Cacém
Ermidas-Sado
Ermidas

Cabo de Sines
Sines

Aljustrel

Porto Covo da Bandeira
Sonega
Messejana
Ilha do Pessegueiro
BAIXO

Cercal

Rio Sado

Vila Nova de Milfontes
São Luís
Colos
Funcheira
Reliquias
Garvão
São Martinho
das Amoreiras
Ourique
Parque Natural
du Sudoeste
Alentejano e
Costa Vicentina
Odemira
Cerro das Pedras

Zambujeira do Mar
São Teotónio
Santa Clara-
a-Velha
Santana da Serra

Serra da Brejeira
Odeceixe

Maria Vinagre
Nave Redonda

Serra de Monchique
São Marcos da Serra
Aljezur
Foia 902
Monchique
Marmelete
Picota 773
Ribeira de Arade
Arrifana
Caseis
Nave
Barranco da Vaca
Caldas de
Monchique
Amorosa
São Bartolomeu
de Messines
Barragem
da Bravura
Barragem
de Arade
Alte
Pontal
Espinhaço
de Cão
Porto de
Lagos
Norinha
ALGARVE
Carrapateira
Silves
Algoz
Paderne
Bensafrim
Montes
de Alvor
Fontes
Fonte da Matosa
Odeáxere
Mela
Estômbar
Lagoa
Alcantarilha
Raposeira
Almadena
Espiche
Praia
Alvor
Porches
Pêra
Ferreiras
Vila do Bispo
Lagos
Porto
de Mós
Portimão
Alpouvar
Luz
Burgau
Ferragudo
Albufeira
Vilamoura
Cabo de São Vicente
Salema
Canoeiro
Armação de Pêra
Vale de Pêra
Olhos de Água
Cerro da Vila

Quarteira
Sagres

ATLANTIC OCEAN

Offshore Portugal

Madeira

Madeira and its neighbouring islands are some 1,000km to the southwest of Lisbon and about 800km from Africa's northwest coast. The name Madeira is Portuguese for 'wood' or 'timber', as the main island was totally wooded over when the first Portuguese navigators landed there in 1419. The archipelago does have several nicknames, alluding to the outstanding natural beauty and the year-round subtropical climate, which always feels like spring. Commonly used ones are 'Pearl of the Atlantic', 'Ocean Flower' and 'Garden of the Atlantic'.

The archipelago comprises Madeira itself, the largest and most populated island and where the capital Funchal is situated, plus the island of Porto Santo, and two groups of uninhabited islands – the Ilhas Desertas (the Deserted Isles) and the Ilhas Selvagens (the Wild Isles). Both these groups are bird sanctuaries. The archipelago's exceptional climate, with temperatures ranging between 16°C (61°F) and 25°C (76°F), and their legendary natural beauty long ago made it a popular holiday destination, and the local authorities have made sure that sufficient infrastructure is in place to handle it. Two international airports receive flights from Lisbon and many other European capitals – London is 3–4hrs away – and also provide an easy connection between the main island and Porto Santo, with its 9km of white sandy beaches.

The population is nowadays about 250,000. About half of them live in Funchal, the rest are scattered in small towns and villages throughout the main island and, in much smaller numbers, on Porto Santo. Politically, Madeira has enjoyed a certain level of autonomy since 1976 and some sectors of society have flirted with the idea of total independence, but apart from a few hand grenades tossed at institutional buildings during the 1974 revolutionary period there has been no violence to speak of since. The current tax regime makes Madeira a magnet for offshore investment, adding to its prosperity. However, as part of Portugal it is also a full member of the EU, with all the advantages this implies for locals and residents alike.

Considering its tiny size, just 57km long and 22km wide, Madeira offers much for the visitor and an incredibly relaxed lifestyle for the potential resident. Activities that are available and popular with visitors tend to be of a gentle nature, which is possibly why it has become known as a spot for the retired, though the serious hill walker is well catered for also – no serious walker should miss making a trek along the *levadas*. Beach lovers, on the other hand, are not well served on the main island, where there aren't any beaches. They have to go to Porto Santo to laze around on the soft white sand. This takes 15mins by plane or 3hrs by the boat service, for which foot passengers do not need to make a reservation. Golf is also available: there are two championship standard courses on Madeira.

The expatriate community in Madeira is large enough to warrant two international schools (*see* **Living in Portugal**, 'Education', p.178) and a monthly English-language newspaper, *The Madeira Island Bulletin*.

The Azores

The Azores archipelago, consisting of nine islands in three groups, has few foreign residents. This is hardly surprising given their remote location, some 1,460km from the European coast and 3,750km from North America. The islands were colonised in the 15th century and their name, Açores in Portuguese, means 'vultures', which the first colonist erroneously thought was what the birds circling overhead were. Actually they were hawks but the name stuck. The islands owe their existence to volcanic activity. The 'Grupo Oriental', the eastern group, comprises two islands – São Miguel and Santa Maria; the 'Grupo Central', the central group, consists of five – Terceira, Graciosa, São Jorge, Pico and Faial; the 'Grupo Occidental', the western group, is made up of Corvo and Flores. Access from continental Europe is not easy, though there are international airports on Santa Maria, Ponta Delgada (on São Miguel) and Angra (on Terceira). The regional airline SATA operates flights to all the islands and there are boat services between all of them.

The Azores were once believed to be the remains of the lost continent of Atlantis. Though that myth was long ago debunked, the archipelago still has an aura of mystique and legend. In addition to the natural attributes – sapphire-blue and emerald-green lakes, fertile prairies, volcanic cones and craters, colourful hydrangeas and azaleas – the intervention of humans in the form of 15th-century churches and majestic manor houses increases the attractions. Temperatures year-round range between 14°C (57°F) and 22°C (71°F) and the quarter of a million souls who inhabit this mid-Atlantic paradise do not know the meaning of stress and pollution. Like Madeira, the Azores has enjoyed a degree of autonomy and its own tax regime since 1976, though it is part of the Portuguese Republic and therefore an EU member with full rights.

However, the Azores are poor, a fact that has impelled many Azoreans to emigrate over the generations. Aggressive agricultural practices, especially the intensive cultivation of tea, tobacco, red peppers and fruit, without crop rotation, has spent much of the once highly fertile land; cattle-raising is now the main agribusiness. No longer an important stop-off point for transatlantic shipping, the islands also lost a major source of income with the demise of the whaling industry in the mid 1980s – though some boat owners now make money taking tourists whale watching and big-game fishing. Large communities of Azoreans live in the United States and Europe and the tourist boom that has brought so much prosperity to continental Portugal has yet to reach the islands. This may not be a bad thing, as the authorities have the opportunity of avoiding mistakes made elsewhere and fomenting a type of environmentally friendly tourism. Tour operators have begun to show an interest, though for the moment it is specialist travellers or people seeking solitude who come. There are few large groups on package deals, but plane loads of golfers fly in from Boston in the spring.

For the potential resident, job and business opportunities are limited and any venture requires serious thought before putting it into practice. That said, if you are enterprising and prepared to rough it a bit, rural or ecotourism are areas that could be exploited successfully. Similarly, anyone wanting to buy a plot of land and be self-sufficient and isolated might find this is just the place to live.

Portugal Today

04

It is something of an understatement to say that Portugal has changed greatly in the last three decades. When the (almost) bloodless coup took place on 25 April 1974, ridding Portugal of western Europe's longest-lasting and most entrenched dictatorship, few could have imagined how profound the ensuing transformation would be. The changes have affected all aspects of life in Portugal and are generally seen as positive, despite the many still unresolved problems that exist in Portuguese society. The country now has a solid democracy, albeit with a political class that many feel has become insensitive to the needs and aspirations of ordinary people. The economy, integrated into that of the EU, has prospered, and the Portuguese are nowadays not so far behind the rest of Europe. However, during the last few years there has been a slowdown and prospects are not overly bright at present; Portugal remains one of the EU's poorer nations. Infrastructures have improved, if somewhat patchily, and services, still far from perfect, are much better than they were. As important as all this is the fact that the revolution empowered many people who previously had no voice, and it seems no one desires a return to the dark old days of Salazarism. Portugal, at last, has stopped living in the past and has embraced the present, and the future, with great gusto.

Major Political Parties, Alliances and Elections

Recent History

Portugal is nowadays a stable parliamentary democracy and has been a member of the European Union since 1986. The current political system is a relatively recent development, as from the late 1920s until the early 1970s Portugal was run in a dictatorial, autocratic fashion. Dr Oliveira Salazar, an arch-conservative economics professor from Coimbra, held power for most of that period, from 1932 until 1968, and his Novo Estado (New State) was corporative in nature and modelled on fascism. Parliamentarians were elected from a single party; trades unions were vertical and controlled by industry bosses; censorship was rife; the education system fomented the Catholic religion; a political police force, the PIDE, kept a close watch on everybody; and economic development was characterised by gross inequality.

On 25 April 1974 the so-called 'Carnation Revolution' marked the end of this period and paved the way for the current system. Salazar himself had retired in 1968, having become incapacitated after a fall – a deckchair collapsed under him – but his system remained in place. His successor, Marcelo Caetano, timidly attempted to make certain concessions towards democratisation, but it was too late and the cracks that had begun to show in the regime became ever more evident with the passing of time.

The rot had in fact begun to set in earlier, in the 1960s, when pro-independence ideas had taken root and flourished in the colonies, forcing the government into highly unpopular military campaigns in Angola, Mozambique and Guinea Bissau. Fighting three guerrilla movements for over a decade proved to be an enormous strain for a small country which was poor in labour and financial resources. At the same time, social changes brought about by urbanisation, emigration, the growth of the working class and the emergence of a sizeable middle class put new pressures on the political system to liberalise. Instead, Salazar increased repression, and the regime became even more rigid and ossified. The 1973 oil crisis also played its part in the debilitation of the regime.

The military became divided between those who wanted to keep hold of the colonies at any price and those in favour of a more autonomous federation of Portuguese-speaking countries. The split was hierarchical and generational. Younger, lower-ranking officers adopted increasingly radical positions, supporting first of all the progressive General Antonio Spínola, and later Major Otelo Saraiva de Carvalho, who became leader of the **Movimento das Forças Armadas (MFA)**. Saraiva de Carvalho masterminded a (relatively) bloodless coup against the regime and the more intransigent sections of the military. One of the most enduring images of the revolution is the famous photograph of a young woman placing a carnation in the barrel of a soldier's gun.

A year after the revolution, on 25 April 1975, elections were held for the Constituent Assembly to draft a constitution. The elections took place in a period of revolutionary ferment – indeed, it seemed for a time that Portugal was headed towards Marxist–Leninism, especially during the 'hot summer' of 1975 when many large estates in the Alentejo were confiscated and collectivised and there was a coup attempt in November of that year by radical military units. Yet most Portuguese voted for middle-class parties committed to pluralistic democracy. The **constitution of 1976** was proclaimed on 2 April 1976 and a few weeks later, on 25 April, elections for the new parliament, the **Assembly of the Republic**, were held. These elections spelt the definitive end of the revolutionary period, and moderate democratic parties received most of the vote. Not all revolutionary achievements were discarded, however, as the first constitution pledged the country to construct socialism and declared the extensive nationalisations and land seizures of 1975 to be irreversible. The military supported these commitments through a pact with the main political parties that guaranteed its guardian rights over the new democracy for four more years. Two successive revisions of the text, in 1982 and 1988, have since removed that terminology, but the right to strike and to assemble are enshrined in the constitution, while the death penalty and censorship are completely proscribed.

The colonial issue was settled by granting independence, and a huge number of colonial Portuguese returned home, later to be followed by thousands of former colonial subjects. Partly as a result of this, but also owing to the costly colonial wars prior to the revolution and the chaos that ensued after it, the economy was in disarray for many years. It was entry into the European Union in 1986 that helped further stabilise Portugal's political system, as well as bringing the much needed investments to put the economy on a sounder footing.

The Government

Portugal is now a **parliamentary republic** with a **president**, elected by direct and universal suffrage for a five-year term. Government is formed by the **council of ministers**, headed by the **prime minister**. The prime minister is politically responsible to the president and parliament. Legislative power is exercised by parliament, which is made up of a single **house of deputies** of 230 parliamentary seats. Members of parliament are elected by proportional representation for four years. Within the limitations prescribed by the constitution, the president is responsible for dissolving parliament, appointing a prime minister and dismissing the government. One of the features that makes Portugal's system a little different from that of its neighbours is its dual presidential–parliamentary nature, which effectively means there are two centres of power. This is to avoid the dangers of an excessively strong executive, as was the case during Salazar's times, and the weaknesses of parliamentary instability, as was the case in the First Republic.

Political Parties

There are a great many political parties on the scene but only a handful have any electoral clout. The longest-established is the **Communist Party of Portugal (PCP)**, which had gone underground during the Salazar years. Despite the collapse of the Soviet Union and Eastern Bloc, the party remains doggedly Stalinist in outlook and still exerts a certain influence among the industrial working class and in rural Alentejo. This, though, is generational, and Portuguese communism will probably die of old age. It has already lost much influence on the left to a **Bloco da Esquerda** (Left Block) coalition, a relative newcomer to the scene. The **Popular Party (PP)**, heir to the conservative CDS, is conservative in a classical sense and has its power base in the north among the professional classes, the propertied upper middle classes and right-leaning Catholics. The **Socialist Party (PS)** is a much younger grouping, founded by Mário Soares in 1974 and characterised by its moderate, anticommunist, social democratic ideology. The **Social Democratic Party (PSD)** leans more to the centre right, despite its name.

A coalition of the PSD and the PP won the 2002 elections, with a total of 48.9 per cent of the overall vote and a controlling 119 out of 230 seats in the Assembleia. The **prime minister** was José Manuel Durão Barroso until June

2004, when he resigned in order to preside over the European Commission in Brussels. His resignation caused a political crisis, which was resolved within a month by the nomination of the populist mayor of Lisbon, **Pedro Santana Lopes** – described as 'Portugal's Berlusconi' for his political, media and sporting ventures – to succeed Durão Barroso as PSD leader and prime minister. The **president** of the Republic is **Jorge Fernando Branco de Sampaio** and it was he who nominated Santana.

The PS is now the chief opposition party, with 96 seats (having received 37.9 per cent of all votes). Also present in the parliament is the coalition formed by the Communists and the Greens (12 seats) and Bloco da Esquerda (3 seats).

Religion

Around 95 per cent of Portuguese people are nominally Roman Catholics, though people express their faith with different degrees of fervour. Congregations nowadays are less packed than they used to be; an estimated one-third of all Portuguese people attend Mass more or less weekly, though in the deeply Catholic north figures are much higher, and in the traditionally anti-clerical south they are much lower. For centuries the Roman Catholic Church was the foundation of Portuguese society. Traditional notions of authority, hierarchy and accepting one's station in life all stemmed from Catholic teachings, and many holidays and festivals have religious origins, as do the country's moral and legal codes. Similarly, education and health care were long the preserve of the Church, and even public works projects, on being inaugurated, received the blessing of the clergy. The prominent location of churches or chapels in practically every Portuguese village or town shows the historically dominant role of the Church. Portugal, it could be said, has long been a Catholic country, not only in a religious sense, but also socially and culturally.

That said, the Church has had to go on the defensive several times throughout history. During an 18th-century wave of anticlericalism, Marquês de Pombal expelled the Jesuits, broke with Rome and brought education under state control. These reforms were later undone, but in the early 19th century the Inquisition was abolished, religious orders banned and much Church property expropriated. And during the First Republic there was more resurgent anticlericalism – church properties were seized and education secularised again, and there were prohibitions on church bellringing and the public wearing of clerical garb.

The backlash came with Salazar's right-wing regime, which restored many of the Church's privileges. The new constitution of 1976 once again separated Church and state and provided for religious freedom. By the early 1980s the Church had accepted this situation, and desisted from trying to influence politics as it had done in the late 1970s, when it called on people to vote against the

Communists. While the Church has had to accept the liberalisation of divorce laws, abortion remains an issue in which the Catholic ethos still looms large. Pregnancies may only be terminated legally within the first 12 weeks and even then only in strictly limited medical circumstances.

Interestingly, throughout history much of Portugal's religious life has taken place outside the strict domain of the Church. This was especially so in rural areas, where people believed God to be remote and inaccessible and therefore established a close personal relationship with their saints, petitioning them to act as intermediaries. The official Church did not approve of such practices but tolerated them as a way of maintaining popular adherence to Roman Catholicism. The official Church was less tolerant of practices such as witch-craft, magic, sorcery and pre-Christian pagan rituals, the result of formal religion, folk beliefs and superstition all being jumbled together in the popular mind-set. This was common, and still carries on, in remote villages in the north, and the Virgin Mary and the Virgin of Fátima are still widely venerated.

A church is never far away. Attending mass and confession is easy, and for those interested in ecclesiastical architecture and popular forms of religious expression, Portugal is a feast. Non-Catholics have no need to worry, as the Portuguese constitution guarantees them religious freedom. Various Protestant churches, of differing denominations, have been established, espe-cially in expatriate areas; and in Lisbon there is a mosque, a synagogue and active Buddhist and Hindu communities.

The Family and Role of Women

Until the reforms that came in the wake of the 1974 Revolution, women in Portugal enjoyed considerably fewer rights – political, economic or personal – than women elsewhere in Europe. In family matters they were subordinate to their husbands, having to bow down to their decisions about children's upbringing and education, and until 1969 married women could not apply for a passport or travel abroad without their husband's permission. The 1976 consti-tution gave Portuguese women full equality for the first time ever, the result of many years of timid advances and severe setbacks.

In the late 19th and early 20th centuries, enlightened sectors of society perceived the need for women's equality and emancipation. At this time a Portuguese suffragette movement emerged and a small number of young women began to enter higher education. When the First Republic was proclaimed in 1910, laws were passed establishing legal equality between spouses, making civil marriages legally possible, permitting women to leave their husbands, and allowing for divorce. Women could still not manage property or vote.

Salazar's Novo Estado did an abrupt U-turn. The 1933 constitution made every-body equal before the law – except for women. Though the regime did permit women with a secondary education to vote (men only needed to be literate), it once again forced women to remain with their husbands. In 1940, an agreement signed by the Portuguese government and the Roman Catholic Church made church weddings legally valid again and forbade divorce. The civil code was amended on several further occasions, and as late as the 1960s the husband's dominant position was enshrined in law.

The 1976 constitution changed all this. Anyone aged over 18, male or female, was entitled to vote from then on. In addition, full equality within marriage was guaranteed. A state-run body, the Commission on the Status of Women, was established, and in 1977 it became an arm of the prime minister's office. Its objectives were to improve the situation of women and to ensure that their rights were protected. In 1991 it was renamed, becoming the Commission for Equality and Women's Rights (Comissão para a Igualdade e Direitos das Mulheres).

The Position of Women Today

As a result, the position of Portuguese women improved significantly. By the early 1990s women had begun to occupy prominent posts in many professions. For example, some 37 per cent of doctors were women by this time, and women had also made inroads into the legal profession. As well as this, over half the students in higher education were women. There were also tangible improvements in the situation of working-class women, partly as a result of legislation but also thanks to an increasingly modernised economy, which provided job opportunities in offices and factories. The number of women in the labour market has risen from 15 per cent at the time of the revolution to 48 per cent today. By the end of the 20th century most women could claim to have a better standard of living than their mothers had had, and considerably more rights.

Despite these positive gains, Portuguese women have yet to reach full equality socially and economically and continue to be under-represented in the upper levels of the administration, private enterprise, political parties and the parliament. Women judges, cabinet ministers and trade union leaders are still far outnumbered by men. Women's wages, at about 75 per cent of men's, continue to lag behind, unemployment affects women more than men, and job opportunities available to women are often at the unskilled, poorly paid end of the spectrum.

Though divorce may have become easier to obtain, often it is only educated, middle-class, urban women who take advantage of the laws. Lesser-educated rural women are not so likely to stand up for their rights and are also more prone to domestic violence and sexual assault. Rapes and beatings often go unreported, as women are likely to be treated with indifference by the police officers on duty and it can take an eternity for the case to come to court. Even then, a male-dominated judiciary does not guarantee that women's rights will be defended. On the positive side, recent changes to the Penal Code give prosecutors the right to file charges independently of the victim when prosecution is judged 'in the victim's interest'. There is now also a free hotline for victims of domestic violence.

Abortion

Another unresolved issue is abortion, permitted only in extremely limited circumstances – if the pregnancy endangers the mother's life or was the result of rape – and no intervention is possible after the 12th week. A referendum on the issue in 1998 maintained the legal status quo. Intensive campaigning by the Church and conservative groups meant a turn-out of only 32 per cent, of whom 51.2 per cent voted against changes in the law. Many poor women are thus forced into back-street clinics, risking prosecution – and their lives.

The Family

Although the family is still a revered institution, an important factor in most Portuguese people's lives, its role has changed lately. With so many women now working, and family planning available, birth rates have dropped. In 1980 the number of children born per woman stood at 2.2; by the end of the decade the figure was down to 1.5 and it continues to drop. Even so, Portugal's demographic structure shows that it has one of the youngest populations in Europe.

Major Media

Newspapers

For those who can read Portuguese, a wide range of national and regional daily newspapers is available. This may seem surprising considering Portugal's small population and relatively high illiteracy rate of around 10 per cent.

Among the best are the *Correio da Manhã*, a serious general news daily, and *Público*, a quality paper with good national and international news coverage plus a Friday arts supplement. Its sister papers, *Diário de Notícias* and *Jornal de Notícias*, are slightly old-fashioned in layout but have good regional sections, and the *Diário Económico* focuses on finance and economy. There is also the weekly *Expresso*, a bulky publication with countless supplements. The serious newspapers have all-embracing classified sections, useful if you are searching for a job, accommodation or a bargain.

Sports fans, football followers particularly, are catered for by *A Bola*, *Record* and *O Jogo*, three dailies with about 90 per cent given to '*o futebol*' and the rest to other sports. Biased towards Benfica, Sporting and FC Porto respectively, together they constitute Portugal's most widely read press.

In all expat areas and in major cities, most English-language dailies as well as major European newspapers, and international ones such as the *Herald Tribune*, are available. As a rule, the international editions of the *Guardian*, the *Times*, the *Independent* and the *Telegraph* are available from late midday onwards, somewhat later in more remote areas. As they are printed in Spain, the main British tabloids arrive earlier. In mainland Portugal there are two regular English-language newspapers, the weekly *The News*, and the *Anglo-Portuguese News*, known as the APN. In Madeira there is the monthly *Madeira Island Bulletin*.

The News focuses mainly on the Algarve, and its listings and classified sections are useful for jobs and property. The online edition(**www.the-news.net**) offers Lisbon and Oporto news plus business and sports sections. Regularly published specials, downloadable in PDF format, deal with property and travel, and periodically there are supplements covering subjects such as English-language schools. The *Anglo-Portuguese News*, published in Estoril, is more amateur in its presentation and has no online version, but does provide local and foreign information of interest to the expatriate community and useful classifieds too. Few magazines cater specifically for the foreign community, though Algarve residents have the glossy *Essential Algarve*, published in English and German, featuring fashion, lifestyle, music, travel, wine, motor and so on plus regular features, listings and restaurant and nightlife guides. Its competitor is *Algarve Good Life*, a glossy monthly with news, features, a pull-out financial supplement and events listings that include Lisbon, Oporto and Andalucía.

Television

The Portuguese, studies reveal, watch a lot of TV. The fare served up ranges from the banal – trashy game shows, soaps, reality shows, *Big Brother* and in-your-face docudramas with titillating content – to the serious and highbrow – well-researched documentaries, news programmes with good foreign coverage, classical music and quality movies (which are not dubbed). The less serious end of the range gets higher ratings, while quality TV caters to a small minority.

Until the mid-1990s just two public channels existed, **RTP1** and **RTP2**, and these broadcast for a limited number of hours a day. Since then two private channels, SIC and TVI, have become available. **SIC**, with capital from the Brazilian Globo group, quickly won an audience share with a diet of Brazilian soap operas and other undemanding content but, realising the importance of news, launched SIC Notícias, a cable channel, in 2001. **TVI**, run by the Catholic Church, failed to gain audience shares and needed desperate injections of foreign cash to survive. This helped take TVI to the number one spot as content changed in search of a wider audience, competing with SIC at its own game and offering a cocktail of soaps, game shows and masses of football. RTP1 and RTP2, costly and not competitive, continue, but the first channel has downgraded content to attract viewers. The second continues to offer highbrow content, subtitled films, programmes of regional interest and other sports and gives exposure to minority religions.

Cable television is now widely available in the major cities, with about 30 channels on offer, among them **CNN**, **MTV**, and the 24-hour **SIC Notícias** news channel. Watching Portuguese TV can be enlightening, not least for the insights it gives you into Portuguese culture and as an aid for learning the language. Note that no TV licence is necessary in Portugal – they were done away with in 1991, though the cash-strapped government has talked of reintroducing a licence scheme some time soon.

Of interest to many resident foreigners is **satellite television**, which offers a huge range of programming in many languages. English-language viewers with the right equipment can watch **CNN**, **Sky** (Premium, Cinema, News, Sports), **Eurosport**, the **Disney Channel**, the **Discovery Channel**, **TNT** and plenty more besides.

For information on bringing your own TV set or buying locally, as well as subscribing to Sky, *see* **Living in Portugal**, 'TV, Video and DVD', pp.130–31.

Radio

There is a very wide range of radio stations in Portugal, many of them local, and people listen to a lot of radio. Local stations often broadcast just to one region or even one town and its surrounding area, and the content is highly localised and often good-quality. On a national level there are three state-run stations, Antena 1, Antena 2, and Antena 3, the first broadcasts on both FM and MW, the other two on FM only. **Antena 1** (95.9 FM) is good for news and football, **Antena 2** (94.4 FM) for classical music and **Antena 3** (100.3 FM) plays a wider range of music. **Rádio Renascença**, owned by the Church, is also national and has several stations, all of them somewhat staid in content.

Other stations worth tuning into are **TSF** (89.5 FM) for news and current affairs interspersed with pop music and live football commentary, and **Nostalgia** (104.3 FM), for classic pop from the 1960s to the 80s. The **BBC World Service** is widely available on several wavelengths. To tune in you need a good short-wave radio; look in the *Anglo-Portuguese News* for the wavelengths (which may change) and programme details.

In Lisbon and the Algarve, play around with your dial and you are likely to come across an English-language station (or slot on a Portuguese station) with news, views, chat and music aimed principally at the expat population. One is the **BIG FM** (92.4 FM), a mixture of music spanning four decades and a talk show, Mondays and Fridays, from 7.30 until 10pm in the south.

Listening to Portuguese radio will help your Portuguese greatly. What at first seems like a stream of sound will after a time break down into more meaningful chunks, and eventually you will be able to understand it.

The Economic Background and the European Union

Portugal has long lagged behind the rest of Europe economically and, after the decline of the once-mighty overseas empire, dwindled to become a poor backwater, a state from which it has only recently emerged. At the time of the 'Carnation Revolution' Portugal was Europe's poorest nation, a situation worsened by the colonial wars, which absorbed some 40 per cent of the national budget. In those days, exports of canned fish, textiles, footwear, cork and wood were the mainstay of the economy. The years immediately after the revolution were not easy either. In a context of international recession, political uncertainty in Portugal discouraged outside investors, while potential domestic investors took their money out of the country (or funded right-wing parties), awaiting a more propitious environment. Throughout much of that period there were austerity budgets, and the successive governments of the late 1970s and early 1980s were continuously negotiating IMF and European Bank loans to keep the country afloat.

The turning point came on New Year's Day 1986 when Portugal joined the European Union, or EEC as it was then, after a long period of arduous negoti-ations. At that time, Portugal's per capita GDP, in purchasing power parity terms, was as low as 53 per cent of the EU average. Governments since that time have striven to reduce the gap and progress has been made – GDP is now 75 per cent of the European mean. No other recent member of the European club – neither the big next-door neighbour, Spain nor even Ireland, the 'Celtic Tiger' of the 1990s – can boast of having gained so much ground in its first few years of membership.

The Prodigious Decade

The period from the late 1980s to the late 1990s was known as the 'prodigious decade'. During those years Portugal witnessed an unprecedented consumer boom, evidenced by glittering malls on the outskirts of Lisbon and other major cities, intense traffic on the roads and the number of mobile-toting yuppies driving the new cars. As well as this, EU funding provided for major infrastruc-ture projects such as motorways, bridges, dams and the Expo '98 showground. Other areas of the economy that witnessed substantial growth were the telecom and financial sectors. Tourism has maintained its important role throughout this period, though it has begun to change in qualitative terms, with the emphasis moving from mass-market beach holidays towards higher-spending cultural tourism. During these years the Portuguese economy grew at rates higher than the EU average, around 3.7 per cent per annum, and unemployment dropped to around 4 per cent in 2001.

Agriculture and the Fishing Industry

The picture is not all rosy, however. It is true that, even before joining the EU, Portugal had slowly begun to develop a service-based economy, a process that was of course accelerated after its admission to the EU. As a result of this, by 2001 agriculture and fishing accounted for just 3.3 per cent of GDP, whereas in 1960 they represented 24 per cent. But 12 per cent of employment was still in the primary sector, illustrating how unproductive Portuguese agriculture is, how slow it has been to adapt to more productive farming methods and its inefficient system of land tenure. As a result it faces difficulties when competing with neighbours such as Spain or France. Spanish produce is much in evidence in Portuguese supermarkets.

Industry

Industrial restructuring has also been slower in Portugal than elsewhere, and therefore the industrial base often lacks economies of scale. Traditional exporting industries such as clothing and textiles are, however, slowly modernising in the face of competition from lower-cost Asian economies. It is true that, owing to unrestricted access to the EU market and, particularly, its low labour costs, Portugal was able to attract investors throughout the 1990s. A 2001 Eurostat study revealed that labour costs in Portugal averaged as little as €7 per hour compared with a staggering €26.7 per hour in Germany and €21.4 EU-wide. Investment has been significant in new manufacturing projects, especially in the automotive and electronics sectors. This situation, however, is now changing as the geographically well-placed central and eastern European countries, the EU's new members, have become increasingly appealing to investors. They too have well-qualified labour and, except for Slovenia, even lower costs. Since 2000 or 2001 Portugal has been increasingly unable to rely on its low wages as bait for investors.

It is also significant that most of Portugal's progress in making up the gap with its EU partners happened between 1987 and 1991 when Portugal narrowed the gap per capita GDP with the EU by 10.7 per cent. In the two five-year periods that followed, the gap was narrowed only by 6 per cent and 3.4 per cent respectively. It seems unlikely that Portugal will ever close the gap completely. As has been mentioned, Portuguese wages are low, so per capita income remains low for a developed country, with GDP per head standing at around €15,000 (in terms of purchasing power parity) in 2001, the second lowest in the EU after Greece.

It was about that time that the underlying problems were beginning to emerge. Before prime minister José Manuel Durão Barroso of the centre-right Social Democratic Party (PSD) entered office in 2002, Portugal had received a formal reprimand from the European Commission for the size of the country's budget deficit, which reached 4.1 per cent in 2002, breaching the 3 per cent

Photo essay
by John Miller

1 Torre de Belém, Lisbon

2 Alentejo, Monsaraz

3 Tram, Alfama district, Lisbon

4 Praia do Camilo, Lagos

5 Carvoeiro

6 Villa near Lagos

8

7 Tavira, Algarve
8 View from Largo das Portas do Sol, Lisbon

10

13

15 Palacio Nacional, Sintra
16 Tavira, Algarve
17 Life in the sun doing the washing

18 Moorish archway, Lagos

19 Monsanto, Beira

ceiling allowed by the EU's Stability and Growth Pact. The austere fiscal policy, combined with weaker global growth, has made it difficult for Portugal's economy to recover. Real GDP growth for 2002 was estimated at 0.5 per cent and the economy actually shrank by an estimated 1.3 per cent in 2003.

Government spending has been reined in and is expected to total 46.6 per cent of GDP throughout 2004, down slightly from 2002's figure but still high. The unemployment rate, though, has increased from 4.1 per cent at the end of 2001 to 5 per cent in 2002 and 6.2 per cent in 2003. The government hopes that labour reform legislation and corporate tax cuts, proposed as part of the 2004 budget, will lead to renewed growth by the end of the year. Since Portugal will be forced into greater self-sufficiency from 2006, when EU funds are likely to be cut, the government sees the changing of the country's economic development model from one based on public consumption and public investment to one focused on exports and private investment as the only way forward. The social cost of this will predictably be high. This is especially so given that income disparity, both between higher and lower earners and wealthier and poorer regions, is one of the most serious issues still to be tackled in the country. This question is considered in the next section.

Internal Issues in Portugal

Poverty and Wealth Disparities

In 1999, on the occasion of the anniversary of the Carnation Revolution, Rui Bebiano, a historian and lecturer at the University of Coimbra, wrote the following in an article about Portugal's achievements and failings in the post-revolutionary period: 'There are social problems still to be solved: inequalities between interior and coastal areas, blackspots of poverty and intolerance, unemployment, an insufficient health system, a creaking judicial system and instances of corruption. All the problems that other European nations share...'

Bebiano rightly pointed to poverty and inequalities as two of the main issues still to be addressed in post-revolutionary, modern, democratic Portugal. While he also rightly says that these problems are faced by all other European nations, in Portugal they are more pronounced. Income disparity, for example, is indeed acute in Portugal, which also has a greater proportion of poor people than other EU countries. While, as was seen above, average Portuguese purchasing power rose from 53 per cent of the EU mean on entry to its current level of approximately 75 per cent, progress has not been even for all of its citizens. *Lisboetas*, residents of Lisbon, earn on average as much as 90 per cent of the European mean. In the Alentejo region the figure is much lower, 60 per cent, and in the Azores it drops even further, to 50 per cent. It is hardly surprising that

Alentejanos and Azoreans tend to emigrate, either to Portugal's more affluent areas or to other EU countries and even the United States.

Portugal has been described by the Director of the Social Sciences Institute at Lisbon University as being the opposite of most EU countries or the USA in the sense that, while in New York or London there may be pockets of poverty, Portugal is poor with pockets of wealth. This is shown by a European Commission study published in the autumn of 2003, which found that one in five Portuguese residents lives below the poverty line, the highest rate in the pre-expansion EU. Some 21 per cent of the population gets by on less than €3,168 per year. In the other 14 member states before the recent expansion, an average of 15 per cent of citizens live below the poverty line.

The problem is not just one of a high proportion of people living at that level; Portugal also has the EU's largest income disparity. According to the same study, the average income of the wealthiest 20 per cent of the population was 6.4 times that of the poorest 20 per cent; throughout the EU, the richest one-fifth of the population earn only 4.6 times more than the poorest one-fifth.

There is also disparity between male and female earnings, as was mentioned above in the section dealing with women. Wages earned by women, who make up almost half of the active population nowadays, still lag behind those of their male co-workers, who earn between 25 per cent and 30 per cent more on average. As well as this, the stark contrasts between the elderly, many of whom eke out a living on pitifully low pensions, and the confident young urban professionals who wear designer clothes and flash their money, is all too apparent.

To what extent these problems are the legacy of decades, or centuries, of government by and for the few, or whether they have simply been exacerbated by Portugal's mad rush for development in the last few years, is a question that is too complex to discuss within the scope of this book. Anyone planning to live and work in Portugal, though, can see for themselves tangible proof of their existence. On the outskirts of Lisbon there is a gleaming new stock exchange; a short distance away there is something resembling a shanty town. Similar contrasts may be seen close to many of the major infrastructure projects carried out in recent years, be they the impressive Vasco da Gama Bridge over the Tagus estuary or the state-of-the-art football stadiums constructed for the Euro 2004 Football Championship. As an *Economist* report published in spring 2003 put it: 'Portugal is still only halfway there.'

Reducing poverty and the disparity of wealth remains a challenge for the government, though it seems unlikely that the current agenda of fiscal austerity and reforms aimed at making the labour market more flexible will lead to a more egalitarian society. In March 2004, in a speech to mark his second anniversary in office, Former prime minister Durão Barroso pledged to focus more on social issues and said, 'I am absolutely certain that in 2006 Portuguese workers and families will be much better off than they are today.' It remains to be seen if his prediction is correct.

The Health Service

When Professor Bebiano mentioned the 'insufficient health system', he was also rightly pointing to a serious problem that affects quality of life in Portugal. State-run health care, despite improvements in recent years, is still deficient in many areas of Portugal and in several aspects of its organisation and practice. Described by the Minister of Health as a 'national shame', the system is badly in need of reform. Waiting lists for operations are long and there is a shortage of doctors and nurses in some areas (although in Lisbon, Oporto and some other areas, doctor–patient ratios are comparable with other European countries). Lack of specialists in certain important areas of medicine is another problem.

The government has begun to address the issue and is beginning to overhaul the system, with measures affecting all operational aspects. An ambitious initiative on public–private partnerships has been launched, allowing the private sector to take part in the management and financing of hospital units, and new laws will allow for the setting-up of partnerships. A new Hospital Bill, presented in late 2002, provided for state hospitals to be managed by private entities while remaining under state ownership. Under this bill, state hospitals will be transformed into public companies and, where they have accumulated debts, creditors will be able to acquire capital in the hospital companies. From 1 January 2003, approximately 30 per cent of Portuguese public hospitals (representing almost 50 per cent of bed capacity) became 'public enterprises'.

Increased hospital services are also to be contracted out to the private sector. Further reforms announced include reduction in waiting lists, reform of prescription procedures, reduction of spending on drugs and greater use of generics. Other plans include the construction of 10 new hospitals and the refurbishing and replacement of several others, mostly with mixed public–private funding. This programme will cost somewhere in the region of €1.6 billion. Public and private sector partnership is to be extended to other aspects of health service. Time will tell if these changes really bring about improvements for users of the system.

See also **Living in Portugal**, 'Health and Emergencies', pp.138–41.

The Judicial System

The 'creaking' judicial system to which Professor Bebiano also referred is another serious issue. The constitution guarantees every citizen, on paper at least, access to the judicial system. Theoretically judges and courts are independent, but the system 'creaks' because it is under-resourced, understaffed, underfunded and overstretched. It is in serious need of an overhaul. Prisons are bursting at the seams with remand prisoners and cases can take months or even years to come to court. There are many reported cases of cases being declared null because they are heard once the statute of limitations had passed.

Corruption in High Places

These problems should be seen against a backdrop of falling institutional credibility, something that certainly concerns many ordinary people. Over the last two years the country has been rocked by a series of scandals: government ministers have resigned over allegations of embezzlement, favouritism, nepotism and tax evasion; the chairman of the football league was charged with corruption and match-fixing; and in the now infamous Casa Pia case, several public figures (politicians, diplomats and a TV presenter) were accused of taking part in a paedophile ring. While charges have recently been dropped against some of those implicated in the Casa Pia case, others remain under suspicion and there is a feeling that Portugal is witnessing an establishment cover-up. Many believe that public life is becoming tainted and that there is a growing culture of cronyism among the political class, at a time when unemployment is on the rise and people are expected to tighten their belts and hope for prosperity at some time in the future. The bright optimism so apparent in Portugal at the end of the 1990s seems to have given way to a crisis of confidence.

The Euro 2004 Football Championship

One more issue, not unrelated to the above, of great importance to Portuguese people was the Euro 2004 Football Championship. Of course, one of their main concerns was that the Portuguese team should do well and perhaps carry off the trophy. As it turned out, the *selecção* reached the final, knocking out England on the way, but lost to Greece. The overall success of the tournament, which UEFA said was the best-organised ever, did a great deal for the collective self-esteem of the Portuguese. This was possibly more important than the eventual success or failure of the national squad on the playing field. Before the tournament some people thought the amount spent on new stadiums and related infrastructures had been excessive, given the need for hospitals and so many other facilities. But UEFA officials had demanded 10 new or revamped grounds and that is exactly what they got – seven spanking new stadiums and three completely rebuilt ones. Total costs were estimated to be around €640 million when the price of commercial areas and clinics were included, and in excess of €800 million when the cost of new access roads were factored in.

However, the fact that the tournament put Portugal on to hundreds of millions of television screens worldwide, and that it showed the country's capacity to provide the infrastructure for and organise a major event, in many people's view compensated for the huge outlay. National self-confidence, which has taken some dents in recent times, depended on the Championship going off smoothly and without incident, which, largely, it did.

For more about football itself, *see* **Living in Portugal**, 'Football', pp.183–4.

Culture, Arts and Entertainment

To say that Portuguese culture is relatively unknown outside Portugal is something of an understatement. Very few people, apart from lusophiles, are familiar with Portuguese literature, music, cinema or visual arts. Geographical and political isolation from mainstream Europe has played its part and during the Salazar period the atmosphere in the art world was stifling.

Though Portugal's cultural output is proportionately smaller than other countries, however, the country has thrown up some excellent writers, film-makers, musicians and painters. There are many names that can hold their own with the best produced by other countries, but Portugal has not promoted itself culturally, so many of them are unfamiliar to outsiders.

Music

It is not surprising that a country with as long and complex a history of involvement in other continents such as Portugal's should have imbibed forms of musical and dance expression originally from its former colonies. Portugal's former empire included modern-day Brazil, Angola, Cape Verde, Goa, Macao and Mozambique. All of these countries' cultures have, to some degree, resurfaced in Portugal either parallel to or fused with native Portuguese art forms.

Fado and Popular Music

Portugal's best-know musical genre is *fado*, a mournful, melancholic type of song which has become known as Portugal's blues. Otherwise, it is always possible to hear many other types of music in Portugal. The major cities have long been melting pots for a rich array of urban music forms. In them, urban musical genres and styles have developed, rural traditions have been reinterpreted and foreign traditions have been transplanted. The 1960s was a period of expansion and innovation that has continued until today. Rock and jazz were introduced, political song developed, Lisbon *fado* and its cousin, the Coimbra style, were revitalised, and Portuguese pop and rock evolved.

The 1980s and 1990s saw something of a boom in musical production, and the musical styles that were produced and consumed in Portugal were increasingly global in outlook. Music from the former African colonies and Brazil have occupied an increasingly important place in musical life, particularly in Lisbon, where local styles of rap and hip-hop have emerged in more recent times. Another musical style has also emerged, one that vindicates its Portugueseness by drawing upon various musical elements that musicians and audiences alike identify as Portuguese and emphasising the Portuguese language. **Madredeus** is the group that perhaps most exemplifies this tendency, though **Rodrigo Leão**, formerly a member of Madredeus, should not be overlooked.

Tempting Fate?

The most distinctly Portuguese of musical genres, *fado*, takes its name from the Latin *fatum*, fate. *Fado* is to the Portuguese what flamenco is to the Spanish and the blues to Afro-Americans. Songs are usually about lost or unrequited loves, betrayal, past glories and despair. Though its origins are disputed, few doubt its emergence in Lisbon's poor, working-class Moorish quarter during the early 19th century. It is still heard at its best in the smoky *fado* houses of the Mouraria, Alfama and Bairro Alto neighbourhoods. Here, *fado* became associated with mid-19th century lowlife though it later gained upper-class adepts and eventually intellectuals and poets provided lyrics that helped it become more sophisticated.

The *fadista* usually sings solo, accompanied by a 12-stringed *guitarra portuguesa* and a four-stringed *viola* (Spanish guitar). The guitar sometimes highlights the singer's melody, at other times plays solo, while the viola provides the rhythm for both.

With the spread of radio and the gramophone record, *fado* became Portugal's national music form, though Salazar and his regime hijacked it and gave it a mythic status, inextricably linked to national identity, while effectively decaffeinating it by censuring the more satirical lyrics. This association of *fado* and Salazarism lost the genre much popularity and many young people nowadays prefer pop, rock and other imported music.

A recent revival has seen it reaching audiences outside Portugal. There is a new generation of *fadistas*, among them **Mariza**, Mozambique-born, Mouraria-raised, who won a BBC radio award in March 2003. Other current performers are **Mísia**, whose fusion of *fado* and other styles causes purists to wince; **Ducle Pontes**, who also does a modern take on the genre; the more classical **Camané**; **Mafalda Arnuth** and **Argentina Santos**. The most famous *fadista* ever was **Amália Rodrigues**, who started life as a humble fruit seller (so the legend goes) and went on to became *fado*'s most internationally known exponent, singing at the Olympia in Paris and on Broadway. She died in 1999, during the general election campaign. Prime minister António Guterres suspended campaigning for three days, saying the country had 'lost its voice and part of its soul'.

Classical Music

While most readers would be hard put to it to name a Portuguese classical composer, there have been many. Music written by **Dom Dinis**, the medieval king, early Renaissance composers like **Pedro de Escobar** and later ones such as **Manuel Cardoso**, **João Rebelo**, baroque composers **Carlos Seixas** and **Sousa Carvalho** are all available nowadays on CD. Domenico Scarlatti was brought to Lisbon by Dom João IV to teach music, and Italian taste long dominated Portuguese musical output, much of it sacred. Mozart and Beethoven were influences in the 19th century; the greatest Portuguese composer working then was **João Domingos Bomtempo**. During the 20th century there were many talented and highly imaginative composers at work such as the innovator **Luis de Frietas Branco**, the influential **Fernando Lopes-Graça** and **Joly Braga Santos**, and *avant-garde* figures **Emmanuel Nunes** and **Jorge Peixinho**.

Theatre and Dance

Theatre and dance, like all other aspects of the arts, suffered greatly under the Inquisition and later under Salazar, but things changed in 1974. At that time many independent theatre groups emerged, the new air of freedom brought audiences flocking to theatres, and funding was increased. A financial and artistic crisis curtailed this during the 1980s, but in the 1990s new drama schools and venues emerged. Funding remains tight, however, and independent performing groups struggle to get by. Despite this, in Lisbon, Oporto and other large cities there is a fair selection of work being performed at any given time and theatregoers can expect a diet of plays by **Gil Vicente**, the father of Portuguese drama, Shakespeare and many contemporary playwrights, as well as plenty of street theatre. Lisbon also hosts several theatre and dance festivals throughout the year.

Portuguese dance these days is characterised by the African influences, a somewhat disdainful attitude towards classical dance forms and much use of theatrical techniques. Two leading companies for contemporary dance are the **Ballet Gulbenkian**, highly respected on the international scene, and the **Companhia Portuguesa de Bailado Contemporâneo**. Classical dance is represented by the **Companhia Nacional de Bailado**, which unfortunately for purists has also begun to produce work that embraces some contemporary elements. Interesting new work may be seen by choreographers such as **Clara Andermatt**, **Olga Roríz**, **Silvia Real** and **Vera Mantero**.

Cinema

Apart from serious movie buffs, not many non-Portuguese cinemagoers get to see Portuguese films. The Portuguese cinema industry is small – during the 1990s an average of 10 full-length feature films per year were made. The approximately 100 movies made during that time were directed by almost 60 different people, so film-makers who direct more than one film a decade are the exception. Portuguese cinema survives thanks to state grants and, nowadays, financing from TV channels. The internal market is also small and domestic consumers tend to prefer imports over home-grown produce. Only a couple of films a year enjoy success, and a total audience of 150,000 is considered a box office smash. Portuguese critics are also frequently scathing of Portuguese-made films, few of which ever make it on the international commercial circuit.

In the last few years Portuguese film-making has moved in two different directions. Since 2000, when the private TV channel SIC started pumping money into the production of films for TV and then into films for screening in cinemas, there has been an increase in the number of films being made that are of an unabashedly commercial bent. The other main path that Portuguese cinema continues to tread is that of art-house films, the so-called '*auteur cinema*'. Movies coming from this vein are often extremely well received by critics who frequent the principal European film festivals such as Cannes, Venice, Berlin and Locarno. Many of them see Portuguese cinematography as having a very special constancy and quality, one that is free from constraints, innovative and surprising.

The main exponent of this current is the nonagenarian **Manoel de Oliveira**. Considered the great master of Portuguese cinema, Oliveira was born in 1908 and is the only living director to have begun his career in silent movies. He débuted in 1931 with *Douro, Faina Fluvial*, a silent documentary about life in the Douro region, which was slammed at home and praised abroad. His first feature film, the 1942 *Aniki-Bobó*, a tale of poor children in Oporto, was similarly criticised in Portugal but lauded elsewhere and is nowadays considered a classic. He then made no more films for 30 years, another victim of the Salazar regime's cultural barrenness, but returned in 1972 with *O Passado e o Presente* (The Past and the Present), a theatrical *œuvre* that marked the beginning of a period of great activity, partly spurred by the new freedom that came with the 1974 revolution. Fame and prestige on the international scene soon followed, Oliveira became the reference point for Portuguese cinema abroad, and French and Italian critics discovered him through *Amor de Perdição* (Love of Perdition) in 1978. Oliveira remains active and continues to create at an impressive rate. Since 1990 he has made an average of one film a year and has directed many major international stars, among them Catherine Deneuve, John Malkovich, Marcello Mastroianni, Michel Piccoli and Irene Papas.

Another major figure is **João César Monteiro**, who began during the so-called 'New Portuguese Cinema' movement in the 1960s, although it was only from the mid-1970s on that his work achieved its full expression. He is now one of Europe's most original directors, making extremely provocative films in which the base meets the sublime and in which he frequently appears himself.

A new figure to emerge is **Teresa Villaverde**, who started out as an actress but who moved to the other side of the camera in the 1990s. Her films are full of suffering, often concerning adolescent characters in conflict with society around. Her 1994 film *Três Irmãos* (Three Sisters) won Maria de Medeiros the best actress award at Venice. Medeiros herself is probably Portugal's most international actress, often working in France and Italy.

Going to the cinema in Portugal these days almost invariably involves going to a multiplex as old-style picture palaces are a dying breed. There are cinemas in most cities of any size but not in smaller towns and villages. As a rule films are subtitled, except of course for Portuguese productions. Listings may be found in main daily, weekly and local newspapers and in magazines such as *Visão*.

Literature

Portuguese literature dates from the 13th century when lyric poetry, courtly love poems, were the main form of literary expression. Provençal language and literature influenced these early attempts but the Portuguese language, and Galician, then a dialect of Portuguese, gave the work a flavour of its own. **Dom Dinis**, king during the late 13th and early 14th centuries, was himself an accomplished poet and troubadour who, like his father, Afonso III, encouraged poetic activity in his court.

Prose-writing emerged later, largely in the form of religious and historical texts, one of whose progenitors was **Amadis of Gaul**, a writer of chivalrous romances. Other medieval prose writers were the chroniclers **Fernão Lopes** and **Gomes Eanes de Zurara**. Poetry from the 15th century was largely influenced by Spanish writing.

The Renaissance had an important impact on Portuguese writing, particularly in the fields of poetry and drama. The work of **Gil Vicente**, considered the father of Portuguese theatre, was imbued with the Renaissance spirit and humanist ideals. Another humanist, **Francisco de Sá de Miranda**, was also heavily influenced by the Italian school and he, along with **Diego Bernardes**, successfully explored the new forms of lyric poetry as well as introducing prose comedy and tragedy into Portugal. The high point of Portuguese literature from this period was **Luis de Camões'** epic 1572 poem *Os Lusíadas* (*The Lusiads*). Camões is considered the Portuguese Shakespeare and was also an incorrigible womaniser who had to flee Portugal to escape from the vengeful husbands of the court ladies he had seduced.

Renaissance writers chronicled the age of discoveries and Portugal's expansion into Africa, Asia and America. Novels and poetry at this time also showed a clear influence of Spanish style and form. The poet **Francisco Rodrigues Lobo** and the prose writer **Francisco Manuel de Melo** were particularly influenced by Góngora.

During the 18th century, the romantic movement and imported liberal ideas affected every branch of Portuguese letters, and the leading light at this time was **João Baptista de Almeida Garret**, who inspired a whole generation of poets, novelists and playwrights. Another key figure was **Alexandre Herculano de Carvalho e Araújo**, who wrote historical novels and a history of Portugal, dabbled in journalism and pamphleteering and helped inspire the liberal, romantic and anticlerical movements that emerged in the 19th century. At the

José Saramago – O Prémio Nobel

So far Portugal's only Nobel Prize winner, José Saramago is known as 'O prémio Nobel', since Portuguese makes no distinction between award and winner. Now 82, Saramago was born poor and did not finish school, as he had to go out to work. He trained as a mechanic, then did several manual jobs before becoming a journalist, translator and writer. A long-standing, though critical, member of the Portuguese Communist Party, Saramago is given to holding forth on many issues, among them globalisation, the crisis of values in the modern age or the situation in the Middle East, though he has also not bitten his tongue when it comes to the treatment of dissidents in Castro's Cuba. His books often upset Portuguese conservatives, who discard them as simple vehicles for his left-wing views. This may be true, but does not make them any less worthy. His often sweeping generalisations on political issues contrast starkly with the complex interplay of ideas in his novels, in which he employs fantasy, the supernatural, and symbolism to explore his favourite theme, the conflict between the individual and authority.

Fame came late to Saramago when, aged 60, he published *Baltazar and Blimunda*. This playful if blasphemous fantasy is set in 18th-century Portugal with the Inquisition in full swing, and tells the story of a priest who wanted to build a flying machine. *The Year of the Death of Ricardo Reis*, in which the protagonist engages in a dialogue with the ghost of the poet Fernando Pessoa, is considered one of his best novels, as is *The History of the Siege of Lisbon*, in which a proofreader inserts a simple 'no' to completely change the interpretation of history. In the early 1990s he angered the Catholic establishment with his bitterly sarcastic *The Gospel According to Jesus Christ*, in which he interprets the Gospels in an ironic tone, inventing new miracles and prophesies. The resulting hostility towards him prompted his move to Lanzarote in 1992. His writing may seem a little inaccessible owing to his refusal to use punctuation, but it is worth sticking at it as Saramago's books (available in excellent English translations) contain, in his own words 'the possibility of the impossible, dreams and illusions'.

same time a group of poets, including **Antero de Quental**, **Teófilo Braga** and **Abilio Manuel Guerra Junqueiro**, revolted against romanticism and expounded social and philosophical ideas in their work. Realism was introduced into the novel by **José Maria Eça de Quieroz** around this time.

With the establishment of the Republic in 1910 came the modern period of Portuguese literature. 'Saudosismo', a current of writing that looked back nostalgically to an irrecoverable and mythical past, was one of the main early developments. One of Portugal's greatest-ever writers, the poet **Fernando Pessoa**, was also active at this time, though was not recognised until after his death. Otherwise, key names from this time were poet and playwright José

Régio and novelists **Aquilino Ribeiro, J.M. Ferreira de Castro, Alves Redol, Fernando Namora, Agustina Bessa Luís** and others.

In the early 1970s the publication of a volume of collected notes, stories, letters and poems by **Maria Isabel Barreno, Maria Teresa Horta** and **Maria Velho da Costa** was to shake literary circles. The book was banned owing to its erotic and feminist nature, but allowed to circulate after the collapse of the Salazar dictatorship and was published as *The Three Marias* in the United States. The best-known contemporary writers are the 1998 Nobel Prize winner **José Saramago, António Lobo Antunes** and **José Cardoso Pires** as well as the poets **Sophia de Mello Breyner Andresen** and **Eugénio de Andrade**.

A simple search on **www.amazon.co.uk** using portuguese + literature or portuguese + writers as keywords will throw up a good selection of work that is currently available in translation. *See also* **References**, 'Further Reading', p.229, for a list of recommended books by Portuguese authors.

Visual and Decorative Arts

Despite never having had a particularly strong tradition in the field of fine arts, Portugal has produced some artists of excellence over the centuries and has excelled in the field of decorative art.

Painting

Portuguese painting began in the 15th century and was greatly influenced by the long and close relationship between the Portuguese crown and Flanders. From the Flemish, Portuguese artists learned technique and composition and also religious painting and portraiture. The panels executed by court painter **Nuno Gonçalves**, between 1458 and 1464, depicting the *Adoration of St Vincent*, a true masterpiece, illustrate these trends and may be seen in Lisbon's Ancient Art Museum.

During the 16th century, when Manueline architecture was at its height, a school of painting known as the **Northern School** emerged. Naturalist themes with detailed background landscapes were a characteristic of this school, whose most famous exponent was **Vasco Fernandes**, nicknamed 'Grão Vasco'. The **Lisbon School**, active at the same time, produced several excellent painters, among them **Gregório Lopes**, one of the best-known artists of the late 16th century. Possibly Portugal's most acclaimed painter was **Amadeo de Souza Cardoso** (1887–1918) whose techniques would later inspire the French Impressionists.

Sculpture

Sculpture has also been an important facet of Portuguese artistic output. During the early 16th century immigrant French master sculptors worked in

Tile Style

One aspect of Portuguese culture that visitors cannot fail to notice and which they are usually highly taken with, is the *azulejo*, the tile. For centuries, patterned tiles have adorned façades of Portuguese buildings, public and private, monumental and humble. In Lisbon there is the Museu Nacional do Azulejo (National Tile Museum), though the whole city sometimes seems to be one big tile museum.

Historians argue about the origins of the word *azulejo*. Some say it comes from *azul* (blue), the colour most favoured, or even from the Persian word for the same colour, *zulej*. It is more likely derived from the Arabic *az-zuleycha*, which means 'smooth-polished stone'. Whatever the etymology, the tilework tradition was undoubtedly introduced to the Iberian peninsula by the Moors. They themselves had learned the art from the Persians who had, in turn, inherited the techniques from the Assyrians.

During the 14th century, Islamic-style tiles with abstract designs were produced in great quantities at a factory in Sevilla, Spain. Although the Portuguese had by this time largely freed themselves from Moorish domination, a certain number of the tiles produced found their way into Portugal and can be seen on the walls of the Royal Palace in Sintra. European tilework was improved by the Italians who developed majolica techniques during the 16th century. When the *mudéjar* (local Moorish) artists were expelled from Spain after the completion of the reconquest, many settled in Portugal, where they established factories and incorporated majolica techniques into their work. As they worked for local clients they were forced to break with the Islamic tradition, depicting humans and animals and even lascivious scenes, anathema to their Muslim beliefs. By this time, and into the 17th century, Portugal had found its own identity and money was available as the country rose to maritime superpower status. Churches, cloisters and private homes all over the country commissioned 'tile tapestries', and the fashion was for grandiose scenes of battles, crowds and hunts. The preference for blue seems to stem from this period, influenced by Chinese porcelain, which was fashionable all over Europe at the time.

By the 18th century, Portugal was the European leader in tile production, but many factories were destroyed in the 1755 Lisbon earthquake. Then, in 1767, the Marquês de Pombal established the Real Fábrica and mass-production techniques were employed. In the early 19th century, with the Peninsular Wars and the exile of the Portuguese court to Brazil, the popularity of tilework waned and the Royal Factory closed in 1835. Since then the craft has staged a comeback and modernised itself, and has become not just part of Portugal's heritage, but part of the fabric of modern Portugal too.

Portugal in the Renaissance style, mainly employing marble and alabaster. **Joaquim Machado de Castro** was Portugal's most famous 18th-century sculptor – he made the bronze equestrian statue of Dom José which still stands in Lisbon's Praça do Comércio. Other fine examples of neoclassical Portuguese sculpture are on show in royal palaces such as those at Queluz and Ajuda, just outside Lisbon. The **Romantic School** would also influence Portuguese sculpture in the 1800s; one of the best artists working at that time was the Oporto-based **António Soares dos Reis**.

Woodwork and Tiles

Carved woodwork, especially in church interiors, was one of the most popular art forms throughout the whole Iberian peninsula from the 15th to the 18th centuries. Coimbra's Sé Velha has some superb late Gothic woodcarving and the reliquary chapel in the monastery at Alcobaça exemplifies the early Baroque style. The later Baroque style, known as **Joanine** (named after Dom João V who was on the throne from 1706 to 1750) can be seen in the retables of the high altars in Oporto and Viseu cathedrals. Also, splendid examples of late Baroque and rococo work exist in Tibães and Falperra, both near Braga in Northern Portugal.

As well as this, another important decorative art form that has long been cultivated in Portugal is the patterned tile (*see* box).

Artists Today

In modern times, politics has made its presence felt in the art world. While during the 19th century Paris and the romantic, naturalist and realist movements were plainly influential on Portuguese artistic output, the 20th century was a more difficult time for artists. The shadow of Salazar was long and the early 20th-century *avant-garde* manifestations, more or less in step with the rest of Europe, would soon be curtailed by the dictatorship. It was not until the freer atmosphere after the 1974 revolution that Portuguese artists had a chance to catch up.

The last couple of decades have seen Portuguese art absorbing global trends and generally taking more part in the worldwide cultural dialogue. Possibly the three best-known and reputed contemporary artists working today are **Pedro Cabrita Reis**, **Julião Sarmento** and the London-based **Paula Rego**. Cabrita Reis' creations question the architectonic spaces of the collective memory and emotional intimacy. Sarmento works in various idioms, painting, sculpture and video installations among them, exploring secrecy, voyeurism and the female body. Rego, acclaimed in the UK as much as in Portugal, focuses on a critical figurative portrayal of the female condition and life in Portugal.

Architecture

Roman, Moorish, Romanesque and Gothic

Portuguese architecture, properly speaking, began with the start of the monarchy, though there are a number of buildings which pre-date this, among them the Visigoth temple of Balsemão, the Mozarab church of Lourosa, built in 912, the basilica of Santo Amaro at Beja and the church of São Frutuoso near Braga, considered the purest example of Byzantine architecture in the Iberian Peninsula. The finest Roman building is without doubt the Temple of Diana (AD 2–3) at historic Évora in the Alentejo.

Few Moorish structures survived the Christian reconquest, but the Moorish influence on Portuguese architecture would continue to influence architecture in the country for many centuries. Even now, modern buildings may have more than a hint of Moorishness about them, and the Portuguese obsession for using tiles on the façades of buildings is clearly of Arab inspiration.

During the second half of the 11th century, the Romanesque style was introduced into Portugal by Cluniac monks and was in vogue until the early 13th century. While this period left fewer examples of remarkable buildings than in neighbouring Spain, there are nevertheless a few fine churches and cathedrals, especially in the north, dating from this period. The cathedrals in Braga, Oporto, Lamego and Coimbra, especially the Sé Velha, are fine examples.

After this came Gothic architecture, which Cistercian monks introduced later in the 13th century. Characteristics of this style are the use of the Latin cross, immense naves with high vaulting and side walls which are illuminated by large windows with precious stained glass. Two of the best examples are the monasteries at Alcobaça and Batalha, in the Tagus Valley tourist region.

The Manueline Style

Towards the end of the 15th century a style emerged that was unique to Portugal. The Manueline style, as it became known, is thus called because it surfaced during the reign of Dom Manuel 'the Fortunate'. The emergence of this style coincided with Portugal's overseas expansion, and it employed much imagery that was inspired by the country's maritime importance. Francisco de Arruda, the builder of the famous fortified tower in Belém, popularised the use of knotted cables, chains, anchors, sails and coral as decorative forms for cathedrals. Some of the best examples of the Manueline style may be seen at Tomar, the Unfinished Chapels at Batalha and the great church and cloister of Jerónimos Monastery in Belém.

The Renaissance and Baroque Style

French architects were responsible for the Renaissance flair apparent in Portuguese architecture from the early 1500s, though they themselves showed clear Italianate influences. The cathedrals of Leiria and Portalegre, the Jesuit college in Évora and the São Roque church in Lisbon's Bairro Alto district are fine examples of this style.

The Baroque style had also became predominant throughout Portugal from the 15th century onwards, though it took on a Portuguese flavour of its own, in the variant known as the **Joanine style**. Extravagant examples are to be seen in the interiors of the Santa Clara and São Francisco churches in Oporto and in other churches and civic constructions in Lamego, Viana do Castelo, Braga and other towns in the north. Granite is the main building material and decorative material, and the lines are mostly curved. Brilliant whitewashing sets off the granite trim on the façades of the buildings in this elegant style. The convent of Mafra is considered the best example of Baroque architecture in Portugal, with its imposing dome and magnificent 88-metre-long library.

The Pombaline Style

The last style of note before modern times was that instigated in Lisbon by the Marquês de Pombal, who took charge of rebuilding the city after the great earthquake of 1755. The 'Pombaline' style is civic architecture that is rather severe by Portuguese standards. Pombal was a practical, no-nonsense man who ordered several fine, geometric squares to be built and connected by straight roads. His Praça do Comércio is without doubt one of Europe's finest squares.

The 19th and 20th Centuries

The 19th century, with the Napoleonic wars followed by the industrial revolu-tion, saw a mixture of engineering projects that embodied the spirit of the age and no little nostalgia, harking back to the Moorish and the Manueline periods. The Rossio station in Lisbon, built at the end of the 19th century, is a good example of this. Art Nouveau was a style used in the early 20th century and there were timid attempts at modernism, but with the rise of Salazar and his Novo Estado architecture took on a pseudo-fascist style, particularly noticeable in certain public buildings such as the Biblioteca Nacional (National Library) in Lisbon or some of the faculty buildings in the University of Coimbra. Salazar's regime also fostered a style known as **Portuguese Modern Traditional**, which made use of romantic touches on apartments, houses and public buildings.

Architecture Today

The post revolutionary period and the prosperity of the 1990s have encour-aged much new public- and infrastructure-building in Portugal, some of it excellent and some of it appalling. The problem was that, when EU funds started flowing towards Portugal, awareness of public planning was still almost non-existent, so many post-modern projects were executed without respecting historical surroundings. That said, architects such as **Álvaro Siza**, particularly, **Eduardo Souto de Moura** and **João Carrilho da Graça** have rightly gained respect internationally. Siza was responsible for the redevelopment of Lisbon's historical Chiado district, destroyed by fire in 1988, and his Pavilhão de Portugal, a Bauhaus-like structure built for Expo '98 held in the capital was highly acclaimed. Other Expo '98 constructions of note were Spanish architect **Santiago Calatrava**'s Gare do Oriente station, the 17km-long Ponte Vasco de Gama over the Tagus estuary, and the expanded metro system.

The most recent architecture of note in Portugal has been the new football stadia built for the Euro 2004 competition.

First Steps

05

This chapter looks at what potential settlers in Portugal might expect to find if they move there. It is a 'warts-and-all' overview of living in Portugal and points out some of the shortcomings of daily life in the country as well as describing the good side. This all comes in the first section, 'Why Live and Work in Portugal?', below. Most of the content of this section has been extracted from the interviews completed by the people who agreed to be the subject of case studies. The overall impression given is that, while Portugal offers excellent quality of life, and residents are generally happy there, the excessively bureaucratic administration is something that detracts from this. But not enough to make them want to leave.

We also describe the various ways of getting to Portugal. As will be noticed, cheap travel is heavily biased towards the Algarve, which is not necessarily where those planning to work in Portugal – as opposed to retiring or living in private-means splendour – would necessarily go.

Why Live and Work in Portugal?

Working and living in Portugal, like anywhere else, has its good points and its bad. In general, most of the residents interviewed for the case studies in this book pointed out more positive aspects than negative ones. What follows is an overview of the upsides and the downsides, based on many sources but particularly on their comments.

Portugal's Main Attractions

Few would disagree, however much of a cliché it might be, that one of the foremost attractions of Portugal is its climate. As was seen in **Getting to Know Portugal**, apart from the inland mountainous areas of the north, the weather throughout most of Portugal compares favourably with that in northern Europe. In the far south, the Algarve, 'winter' is an almost meaningless word, and Madeira offers superb weather practically all year round. Added to this is the picturesque beauty of many parts of the country, its coastline, the astonishing variety of landscapes inland and its charming cities, towns and villages.

Most people consulted also had many good things to say about the host community. Portuguese people, they agree, are friendly, hospitable, polite and kind to strangers. In addition, Portugal is not a country where you feel especially threatened as, despite the perceptions of some, crime rates are relatively low, if rising. By taking a few precautions you can usually avoid trouble, and violent crime is in fact quite rare.

The cost of living in Portugal, though rising, is still noticeably lower than in northern Europe, particularly when it comes to leisure and pleasure, as eating and drinking remain within the reach of most pockets.

In all, this adds up to a general picture of a high quality of life in a relaxed, beautiful setting. As the journalist whose case study appears overleaf, who has lived and worked in several countries, put it, 'Portugal is far more liveable-in overall, in my experience, than the UK, Mexico, Brazil or the USA.'

Apart from all of these points, there are a few others which, objectively, make Portugal an attractive destination. One of the most important is the country's membership of the European Union. The significance of this is often overlooked but, as will be shown in **Red Tape**, British, Irish and other EU citizens enjoy rights in all other member states that are practically the same as those they have in their own countries. Briefly, these include the right to reside, to travel to and from the chosen country of residence without hindrance, to seek work, to engage in trade union activity, to practise a profession, to study, to move money, to own property, to enrol children in schools, to make use of the health services available and so on. Having these rights, of course, implies fulfilling certain obligations, but only the same ones as locals have to comply with.

As so many expatriates have chosen Portugal before, it is a well-trodden path. Going to live and work there is not entering virgin territory; nobody needs a frontier spirit, unless of course they want to take over a semi-ruined farmhouse in an isolated location. There are many services available, English-speaking lawyers, relocation agencies and more besides, to make life easier for the newly arrived. For those who want them, there are in some places ready-made communities to slip into, in which there may be people with similar interests and no language barriers.

Maybe the above all sounds too good to be true. It is all true but, while nobody disputes the benign nature of Portugal's climate, its picture-postcard prettiness or the kindly disposition of its people, there are some less positive aspects that should be pointed out to give a balanced picture.

Negative Factors

Government-run Services

Most of the interviewees mentioned the poor, at times abject, functioning of government-run services. This is clearly something that affects quality of life both for natives and foreign residents. The health, judicial and tax systems were all singled out for criticism, as were the procedures for obtaining a residency card. The general impression is that public services and administration is overly bureaucratic, slow, insensitive to users' needs and inadequate overall. One of the interviewees spoke of a 'feeling of insecurity, not yet in the streets, but on the level of hospital care, fiscal changes that translate into huge queues, lack of information'. Another put it more succinctly: 'The simple often proves complicated' and goes on to say that 'most government information is written in difficult-to-understand Portuguese. There is also the assumption that the

Case Study: Martin Roberts, Travelling Journalist

Liverpool-born Martin Roberts, 43, a journalist with an international news agency, was transferred to Lisbon in December 1999. Having previously lived in Brazil, he already spoke Portuguese when he arrived. He moved on again, to Washington DC, in January 2004.

Q What took you to Portugal originally? How did you find your first job and flat?

MR I went because my company transferred me there, so I arrived with a job already set up. I found a flat advertised in *Público*; it was well within my budget, despite agencies telling me 'Ooh, you'll get nothing for that.'

Q How do you find working here compares with working at home?

MR I haven't worked in Britain since 1986. Compared to Mexico and Brazil, the Lisbon office is smaller and more isolated from the company mainstream, which made working more difficult. But I found settling in and living there a doddle and, were it not for my work, I could have happily stayed.

Q What are the good and bad points of life in Portugal?

MR On the good side, the picturesque countryside and cities, low crime, relatively low living costs (though food and petrol are cheaper in Spain), people being kind to strangers (with notable exceptions), the Multibanco system, which doesn't charge if you withdraw from another bank and allows you to pay bills. Portugal is far more liveable-in overall, in my experience, than the UK, Mexico, Brazil or the USA. The bad points are reckless drivers and inconsiderate smokers. Lisbon also lacks the vibrancy of other European capitals.

Q How did you find dealing with red tape? Has it got any easier in recent times?

MR Getting *segurança social* and residency cards took a very long time, but were not urgently needed. Tax returns could have been difficult had I not had free help. And finding out about how reciprocal agreements for UK National Insurance benefits work in practice is difficult, both in Portugal and the UK. Now, in the USA, though, I have found it *far* more difficult to open and run a bank account, get a mobile phone, etc. than in Portugal.

Q Did you mix mainly with expats or did you integrate?

MR I saw little of British expats but, being single, I often found it easier to mix socially with expats from other countries rather than Portuguese people. My Portuguese workmates would only socialise at Christmas dinners or weddings. Women are reserved about socialising alone with men, many would bring friends to innocuous occasions. That said, my Portuguese friends are some of the nicest people I know, I really miss them.

Q Any tips for would-be residents?

MR I would be wary of turning up without work or not knowing conditions.

citizen should inform him/herself rather than being informed by government. If you consider all the hype around e-government, the reality is yet to come close.' And this is despite government attempts to streamline and rationalise bureaucracy in recent years! For more on red tape, see Chapter 06.

Unemployment

Another problem, crucial for those planning to go to live and work, is the job situation. Unemployment has risen since the boom finished in 2001 and currently sits at around 7.2 per cent. Foreigners, even EU citizens, should be aware that work has become increasingly hard to find and in the current recession there are fewer business opportunities than before. One of the interviewees put it this way: 'It is not a good place to be looking for work. EU funding has been important for economic growth and development; what happens when that runs out remains a post-2006 question', adding that you should 'go to Hungary for professional or business opportunities!'

In addition, salaries are among the lowest in the EU, even if you do find a job. It is only the high-fliers with executive and management jobs in large companies, usually multinationals who really earn decent wages. Job-seeking for foreigners may be restricted to certain, well-defined sectors, for example, teaching, which are not especially well paid.

See **Working in Portugal**, pp.189–224, for more on working and employment.

Other Negative Factors

So, while Portugal may be cheaper than other EU countries, lack of job and business opportunities and low wages mean it is difficult to prosper. It should also be pointed out that Portugal is not that cheap. Another interviewee said, 'Utility and phone costs are the highest in the EU, and petrol is expensive'. Imported goods are also expensive. Another negative aspect that is also worth mentioning, as it may be life-threatening, is traffic danger. Driving habits in Portugal were described in ascending order by the interviewees as 'reckless', 'very dangerous' and 'suicidal' and one resident says, 'I have seen the most stupid driving that I have ever come across since we have been here.' This is something to bear in mind when taking to the road.

In short, Portugal offers a pleasant, relaxed lifestyle in an enviable climate and surroundings, but is not a place for the ambitious or the impatient.

Travelling to Portugal

If you are planning to go and work in Portugal, where you live will be dictated by the job or work you find. If you are lucky enough not to have to work, then your choice of where to live will be determined more by your needs and tastes.

Some long-term residents stay put and only make home visits from time to time. Others go back and forth with a certain frequency. Ease of travel to and from your Portuguese home to the 'old country' may, in the latter case, be an important issue.

Most of Portugal is quite accessible these days, and not only from London, as there are flights from a number of UK and Irish airports, especially to the Algarve. Central Portugal is well served by scheduled flights to Lisbon, and most of the northern end of the country is fairly easily reached from Oporto, which is also on several major airlines' regular itineraries. Inland and mountain areas can harder to reach, though, as communications are not universally good and road improvements have not extended to the entire country.

Madeira, though much further away, does have regular connections both from continental Portugal and northern Europe and only the remote Azores are relatively poorly served; even they can be reached easily from Lisbon if not from many places in continental Europe. Few people, it should be said, choose the Azores to live in and only a small community of foreign residents is based there.

By Air

Portugal has international airports at Lisbon, Oporto and Faro in mainland Portugal, as well as Funchal, in Madeira, and Ponta Delgada, on the island of São Miguel, Azores. Lisbon airport, nearly 3hrs from London, is the main Portuguese hub for international air traffic into and out of Portugal and has road, rail and coach connections with the rest of the country. Oporto takes marginally less flying time than Lisbon and is well situated for travellers making for north and central Portugal. For most of central Portugal it is much of a muchness whether you fly to Oporto or to Lisbon. Faro, just under 3hrs from most British Isles airports, is the only Algarve airport but is well connected, so few Algarve destinations are more than 1–2hrs away and the southern Alentejo is also close. Madeira is 3hrs 40mins from London and getting anywhere on the island is quick, as it is small. Flying time from continental Europe to the Azores is over 4hrs and few major airlines go there. The best bet is to go from Lisbon on the Azorean local airline SATA.

Scheduled Flights

The main airlines that operate regular flights from the British Isles to Portugal's three mainland international airports, at Lisbon, Oporto and Faro, and Funchal in Madeira, are **British Airways**, **TAP Air Portugal** and **Aer Lingus**, the national airlines of the three countries concerned. TAP flies five times daily between London and Lisbon, three of them from Heathrow and two from Gatwick. The company also flies twice daily from Heathrow to Oporto and once a day from Manchester to Lisbon. Anyone travelling from Manchester to Oporto can take this same flight but must go via Lisbon, where there is a short stop, before proceeding to the northern city without changing planes. TAP also flies once a day from Heathrow to Faro.

For other Portuguese destinations, such as Funchal, it is necessary to change planes in Lisbon, and TAP only flies to Terceira, in the central Azores group. For other Azores islands the local airline SATA is the one to choose.

British Airways flies daily from both Heathrow and Gatwick to Lisbon, from Gatwick to Oporto. BA also has a daily flight from Gatwick to Faro and six flights a week from Gatwick to Funchal. Travelling from other UK airports to Portugal with BA invariably involves changing planes at one of the London airports. Aer Lingus, for its part, operates three scheduled flights a week each from Dublin to Lisbon and Faro but does not fly to Oporto or Funchal. It is also worth enquiring either online or at a travel agency as to whether Lufthansa, Swiss Airlines, Alitalia or Air France have any flights available, special deals or offers.

Several factors come into play to make any prices for fares quoted here almost meaningless. These are seasonal variations; availability of seats at any given time; and different prices depending on whether you purchase at a travel agent or online, whether you book ahead or buy at the last minute and whether there are any offers at a given time. When consulted, BA gave some sample fares: expect to pay upwards of €150 for a return flight to Lisbon or Oporto, as little as €99 to Faro and back and upwards of €199 to Madeira. Cheaper deals may be found online and there are occasional special offers. Aer Lingus said to expect fares from Dublin to Lisbon starting at €148 and €280 to Faro. As always, there is no substitute for shopping around, either using the Internet, travel agencies, the travel sections of the main daily or Sunday newspapers such as the *Sunday Times*, or magazines with good travel pages such as *Time Out*.

No-frills Budget Airlines

Several cut-price airlines operate regular services to Portugal and, during the holiday season, schedule charters too. From the UK some fly from major airports such as London Gatwick, Luton or Stansted as well as from some of the bigger regional airports such as Birmingham, Manchester or Glasgow. In addition, it is nowadays possible to travel to Portugal from a growing number of UK regional airports. Some also operate from the Irish Republic, also either from Dublin or, again, Ireland's regional airports. The main drawback is that they fly almost exclusively to Faro, such is the allure of the Algarve, to the detriment of other parts of Portugal. This is fine if you are planning to live in the Algarve or some easily reachable part of southern Portugal, but not much use if you wish to settle elsewhere. This trend evidently reflects the importance of the tourist and holiday home markets.

The main players are **easyJet**, **Ryanair**, **MyTravelLite**, **BMIBaby**, **Jet2** and **Monarch Airlines**. If the Algarve is your destination then there are any number

Main Airlines

Aer Lingus	t 0845 084444	www.aerlingus.com
Air France	t 0845 359 1000	www.airfrance.co.uk
Air2000	t 08702 401402	www.air2000.com
Alitalia	t 0870 544 8259	www.alitalia.co.uk
BMIbaby	t 0870 607 0555	www.bmibaby.com
British Airways	t 0845 773 3377	www.ba.com
easyJet	t 0870 600 0000	www.easyjet.com
GB Airways	t 0845 773 3377	www.gbairways.com
Jet2	t 0870 737 8282	www.jet2.com
Monarch	t 0870 040 5040	www.monarch-airlines.com
MyTravelLite	t 08701 564564	www.mytravellite.com
Ryanair	t 0818 303030	www.ryanair.com
TAP Air Portugal	t (020) 7828 0262	www.tap.pt

of cheap deals available at any given time and it is worth looking at their websites, listed above. Budget airlines, it should be pointed out, are not always quite so 'budget'. Be careful to read the small print; what looks like an unbeatable offer may actually be the price only for the first handful of customers, and late-comers may find that the real price they are expected to pay is much higher than that advertised. Booking well ahead usually guarantees the best fares.

By Sea and Road

Portugal is a long road trip from the UK or Ireland. When moving there you may choose to do your initial trip by car, especially if you are taking a lot of possessions that would be impractical if flying. If you entrust everything to a removals firm it is easier to arrive by air. You may in any case find it better to buy a car locally, rather than taking a foreign-registered one with you, thus avoiding paperwork. This would also mean that you do not face the additional dangers of driving a right-hand drive car on the relatively dangerous Portuguese roads. For more on both of these issues and others, see **Living in Portugal**, 'Driving', pp.161–7.

If you really want to drive, there are two options available. The first is to cross the English Channel and then drive through France and Spain. From the Channel ports, depending on the route you take, Oporto is about 1,800km, Lisbon over 1,900km and Algarve 2,200km. The second option is to sail to Santander or Bilbao and bypass France completely. The drive at the other end is thus reduced considerably; it is about 650km from Santander to Oporto, for example, 840km to Lisbon and 1,000km to the Algarve. From Bilbao add on another 50km or so.

Choosing between these two options involves factoring in cost, distance, time and fatigue. Sailing to Spain is pricier but avoids petrol, tolls, food and accom-modation expenses while travelling through France. Travelling to a French

Channel port is cheaper but means a much longer haul once on the continent. Time spent sailing to Bilbao or Santander could be spent driving through France, or vice-versa. And fatigue is the result of the time spent driving, more in the case of the first option or less in the case of the second.

The two direct ferry services available between Britain and northern Spain are: **P&O Ferries**, twice weekly from Portsmouth to Bilbao (Portsmouth–Bilbao, Tuesday, Saturday; Bilbao–Portsmouth, Monday, Thursday) and **Brittany Ferries**, also twice weekly from Plymouth to Santander (Plymouth–Santander, Monday, Wednesday; Santander–Plymouth, Tuesday, Thursday). To Bilbao, sailing time is approximately 27hrs, to Santander about 24hrs.

As this is an ocean crossing, both companies attempt to make the trip feel like a leisurely cruise. The ships are larger and more comfortable than Channel ferries, with more restaurants, entertainments and other amenities. Fares, despite variations, are quite high, maybe around £550–750 for a standard (over five days) return for a car and four people in summer. Even so, these routes are popular, so book well in advance if travelling in summer.

If going via the Channel ports and through France and Spain, set aside at least three days for the trip. P&O, Brittany Ferries, Hoverspeed and Transmanche offer a huge choice of routes, or you can go through the Channel Tunnel with Eurotunnel. If you are in no hurry you may decide to make a pleasant, relaxed trip of it and do some sightseeing en route. If cost is an issue, remember that France and Spain have many toll roads (*autoroutes* in France and *autopistas* in Spain), which can work out to be expensive. You might like to travel on other roads, look at the scenery and have some nice meals. What you spend on this might work out to be more or less what you save on tolls.

For Portugal, it is best to head southwest through France to the northern end of the Pyrenees, entering Spain at Irún. From there you pass San Sebastián, go south of Bilbao and head down towards Vitória-Gasteiz and Burgos, after which a number of options are available depending on whether you are going to northern, central of southern Portugal.

Both the French and Spanish road authorities have websites with regularly updated information about the state of the roads, weather conditions, road-works in progress and tolls. For France, one is **www.autoroutes.fr**, the *autoroute* concessionaire's site, with information about toll charges and maps. There is also **www.bison-fute.equipement.gouv.fr**, the French National Traffic Centre's

Ferry Operators

Eurotunnel	t 08705 353 535	**www.eurotunnel.com**
Hoverspeed	t 0870 240 8070	**www.hoverspeed.com**
P&O Ferries	t 08705 20 20 20	**www.poferries.com**
Seafrance	t 08705 711 711	**www.seafrance.com**
Transmanche Ferries	t 0800 917 1201	**www.transmancheferries.com**
Brittany Ferries	t 08705 665 333	**www.brittany-ferries.com**

Railways

Eurostar	**t 0870 186 186**	**www.eurostar.com**
Rail Europe	**t 08705 848 848**	**www.raileurope.co.uk**

(Reservation and information service run by French Railways in the UK.)

SNCF (French Rail)	**www.sncf.com**
RENFE (Spanish Rail)	**www.renfe.es**
CP (Portuguese Rail) **t 808 208 208**	**www.cp.pt**

site, which has information on hold-ups, alternative routes and so on. The Spanish site, **www.dgt.es**, provides information in English, but a better route planner is to be found on **www.viamichelin.com**.

By Train

Travelling by train to Portugal involves passing through Paris, France and Spain, with different options along the way depending on your final destination. Wherever you are heading, it is a long trip (about a day and a half) but a pleasant one for train buffs. From the UK to Paris the Eurostar is recommended, followed by the high-speed train (TGV) from the Gare d'Austerlitz to the Basque border at Irún/Hendaye. There you have to change trains as Spanish trains run on a wider gauge. From Irún, the Rápido Sud-Expresso takes you across northern Spain and enters Portugal at Vilar Formosa and goes on to Pampilhosa (where you can change for Oporto) just southeast of Coimbra and then on to Lisbon. Allow about 18hrs.

From Lisbon there are train and coach links to the rest of Portugal. An alternative is to go via Madrid and take the 8hr overnight Lusitânia Express to Lisbon. Another possibility, from Madrid to the Algarve, is the high-speed AVE, to Sevilla, 2hrs, 25mins, and the Eva Bus coach to Faro. Fares from the UK to Portugal are likely to be more than a budget flight; expect to pay over €150 just from Paris. It is more an option for the nostalgic train-traveller.

By Coach

Not many residents choose to travel by coach from northern Europe to Portugal. First, the journey is incredibly long. From Victoria Coach Station to Lisbon takes almost 40hrs. To the Algarve it is almost two days. Second, the fare is likely be more than a budget flight. Add to this the cost of food and drinks consumed on the way, and it turns out to be an expensive trip.

• **Eurolines**, Victoria Coach Station, Buckingham Palace Road, London SW1, **t** (020) 7730 0202, **www.eurolines.co.uk**.

Red Tape

06

Without exception, everybody who was interviewed as a case study for this book had something to say about bureaucracy in Portugal. In most cases their comments were negative. 'I don't even want to talk about red tape in Portugal,' said one. 'Getting residence permits, driving licences and tax-paying status is still slow,' said another. The 'total inflexibility' of administrative procedures was another's complaint while a fourth interviewee pinpointed the problem as being 'the assumption that the citizen should inform him/herself rather than being informed by government'.

Sclerotic administrative procedures are the legacy of several centuries of authoritarian and unrepresentative government. It is, however, only fair to say that, since entering the EU, in 1986, successive Portuguese governments have made attempts to simplify and streamline bureaucratic procedures. The results of these attempts have been mixed, and some of the interviewees expressed the opinion that things are slowly getting better. Overall, new residents can expect to find fewer hassles than, say, a decade ago, but should still be prepared for seemingly unnecessary paperwork and civil servants who are not overly efficient or helpful.

This chapter looks principally at red tape in so far as it affects becoming a resident, being able to work and applying for Portuguese nationality. It should be stated that, for EU citizens at least, things are not nearly as onerous as they used to be; in order to work as employees, ply their trade as freelancers, set up in business or study, only a residency card is needed. Non-EU citizens, on the other hand, can expect rather a rougher ride, involving applying for a visa from a Portuguese consulate in their home country before taking up residence.

An important point to bear in mind, as is highlighted elsewhere in this book, is the need to speak Portuguese to a reasonable level of proficiency when coming face to face with administrative procedures. The reasons for this are obvious – you cannot expect to walk into a government office and assume the functionaries who attend you to be able to speak English, though you might be lucky. If your Portuguese is not up to it, take somebody with you who can act as an interpreter.

Visas, Permits and Other Paperwork

EU Citizens

Not all would-be Portugal residents are aware of the extent to which EU legislation now allows for citizens of any member state to live and work in any other member state, while enjoying practically the same rights as nationals of the country they choose to live in. What follows applies to British and Irish citizens (the most likely readers of this book) who choose to go to Portugal to live. But it equally applies to the German who chooses to reside in Spain, the Spaniard

Citizen's Shops – Cutting Red Tape

One recent step in the right direction, in terms of streamlining and simplifying bureaucratic procedures, has been the establishment of the *loja do cidadão* (literally, citizen's shop), a kind of one-stop administrative department store. Most government departments are present in the *lojas*, so anybody who has two or three different bits of paperwork to do need not traipse around town from one ministry or department to the next.

A comprehensive range of procedures can be dealt with at the *lojas*, including all civil registry matters, enquiries and payment of bills to utilities companies, postal services, social security, taxes, pensions (for Portuguese pension entitlement), road tax and driving licences and more besides. For the moment there is only an information service for questions relating to foreigners' matters and residency; actual applications must still be made at the Serviço de Estrangeiros e Fronteiras (Service for Border Control and Aliens). The *loja* has also opened many mini-branches known as *postos de atendimento ao cidadão* (PAC) in these cities and others too. The Algarve, the Alentejo and the Azores still do not have the benefit of their services.

There are *lojas* at the following addresses:

• Aveiro: Rua Orlando Oliveira, 41–47, Forca Vouga 3800-004 Aveiro.

• Braga: Rua dos Granjinhos, 6, 4710-352 Braga.

• Coimbra: Avenida Central, 17, 18–20, 3300 Coimbra.

• Lisbon: Laranjeiras, Rua Abranches Ferrão, 10 1600-001 Lisboa.

• Lisbon: Restauradores, Praça dos Restauradores, 17–22 1250-187 Lisboa.

• Madeira: Avenida Arriaga, 42-A, 9000-064 Funchal.

• Oporto: Avenida Fernão de Magalhães, 1862, 1° 4350-158 Porto.

• Setúbal: Avenida Bento Gonçalves, 30-D 2910-431 Setúbal.

• Viseu: Quinta das Mesuras, Lotes 8, 9, 10, Est. de Ranhados 3500-643 Viseu.

Most *lojas* are open from 8.30am to 7.30pm, Monday to Friday and from 9.30am to 3pm on Saturdays. There is a call centre dealing with enquiries concerning services at all *lojas* (t 808 241 107, **lojadocidadao@lojadocidadao.pt**, **www.lojadocidadao.pt**). The website is currently in Portuguese only and there is no sign of when services will be available in English. There are links to the web pages of the different arms of the administration that are represented at the *lojas*; some of these now have information and downloadable forms available in English, though their information can sometimes be inadequate or completely out of date. The Finanças (Inland Revenue) English pages, for example, quoted information in *escudos* as late as summer 2003.

who takes up residence in Holland or the Dutch person who decides to relocate to Italy. Give or take a few procedures specific to some countries, and the greater or lesser levels of bureaucracy to be dealt with in each, the criteria and the underlying concepts are the same throughout the EU. All EU citizens, theoretically, belong to the same continent-wide labour market. EU directives are very clear on this issue, and as job-seekers in any EU country, citizens of any member state enjoy the following rights:

- **The right to employment in any member state under the same conditions as nationals – nationals cannot be favoured over you solely on the grounds of their nationality.**

- **Where incentive measures for recruiting national workers exist, to be counted as a national worker in the application of such measures.**

However, access to employment may depend on the possession of certain qualifications, diplomas, experience or the knowledge of the local language.

In terms of the type of work to which you have right of access, EU guidelines are also very clear:

- **You may apply for any job for which you feel you are qualified, except for certain public service posts, for example, the diplomatic service, the police, judiciary or the armed forces.**

- **Most public sector jobs in health, education, commercial services and research for civil purposes are open to all EU nationals and are not restricted on grounds of nationality. This varies from one country to another – ask the national authorities for specific information as contained in the fact sheet 'Right of Access to Employment'.**

- **You may also apply for vocational and professional training anywhere in the European Union, again, ask for the fact sheet 'National Education Systems'. As well as this you may conduct research anywhere in the EU; there is fact sheet available called 'Training and Mobility of Researchers'.**

Call the UK freefone number t 0800 581591 to request these fact sheets.

The system of mutual rights and obligations between member states guarantees all EU citizens four fundamental rights:

- **To move freely and to stay in the territory of member states.**

- **To vote and to stand as a candidate in local and European Parliament elections in the member state of residence.**

- **To protection, in a non-EU country in which a citizen's own member state is not represented, by the diplomatic or consular authorities of any other member state.**

- **To petition the European Parliament and to apply to the European ombudsman.**

The only grounds on which you may be refused the right to reside in another member state is if you are considered to be a danger to public health or order. HIV-carriers and those with AIDS are not refused on grounds of their condition. Residency brings with it the following rights:

• To take up any kind of paid employment, register as a jobseeker, and claim unemployment benefits, if you are entitled to them; this also brings the same rights over working conditions, pay, sick leave, holidays, redundancy, trade union membership and access to vocational training. There are exceptions: the armed forces or police are not an option, and certain public posts are excluded; *see* Chapter 08, **Working in Portugal**, for more details.

• To enrol your children in Portuguese state schools and, provided you fulfil the entry requirements, to study at a Portuguese university.

• To open a bank account, move money in and out of the country as nationals do, or apply for mortgages.

Rights, of course, imply obligations. Residents, like nationals, are subject to the law of the land and must pay their taxes. Many residents seem conveniently to forget this, but penalties for tax evasion are getting heavier in Portugal. *See* **Living in Portugal**, 'Taxation', pp.135–8. In practice, finding work may be more difficult – *see* **Working in Portugal**.

Documents

There are certain documents that anybody who is going to reside in Portugal, whether from an EU country or outside, must obtain. The most essential ones are the tax or fiscal card and the residency card.

Tax or Fiscal Card

The tax card, or fiscal card (*cartão de contribuinte*) is obligatory for residents and non-residents who have financial dealings in Portugal. If you are planning to stay in the country to live and work, run a business or simply live off your own means, you need this card. Even if you only plan to buy a holiday home and visit more or less frequently, you must still obtain the card beforehand, as you will be liable for taxes on your property and must therefore have a fiscal number (*número de identificação fiscal/NIF*). The card is very easy to obtain – just go to your local tax office (the Portuguese Inland Revenue is the Ministerio de Finanças, generally just known as Finanças), taking your passport and a photocopy of the identification pages. The *cartão de contribuinte* and its number will be quoted in all dealings and is necessary to open a bank account and to register your property.

Residency Card

A residency card (*cartão de residência*) must be applied for by all those European Union, European Economic Area and Swiss citizens who are paid workers (*trabalhador por conta de outrém*), wish to act as a sole trader (*empresário em nome individual*) or become self-employed (*trabalhador por conta própria*). Similarly, those who wish to live off their own means (*vivendo de outros rendimentos*), students (*estudantes*) or family members of any of the above (*familiares*) must also apply for the residency card.

The paperwork involved is not too excessive and you must make your application at the Serviço de Estrangeiros e Fronteiras (Foreigners' Department) closest to your place of residence; *see* pp.97–8 for a list..

Employed Workers

Present these documents:

• An application form; this form (model DR 0002) is printed in Portuguese, English and French so is easy to fill in and can be requested on an initial trip to the office or downloaded, in PDF format, from **www.sef.pt/pdf/ pedido_titulo_residencia.pdf**.

• Two recent and identical passport-type photographs in colour.

• The original and a photocopy of a work contract, in which the starting and finishing dates must be stated.

• The original and a photocopy (of the relevant pages) of your passport.

• €2.54, the fee charged on making the application.

Sole Traders and Self-employed Persons

Present these documents:

• An application form, as above.

• Two recent and identical passport-type photographs in colour.

• Documents proving that you have established a company as a sole trader or a declaration of having begun self-employment.

• The original and a photocopy (of the relevant pages) of your passport.

• A document proving that you are covered for health care, which may be an insurance policy or a social security card.

• €2.54, the fee charged on making the application.

Living Off Your Own Savings

Present these documents:

• An application form, as above.

• Two recent and identical passport-type photographs in colour.

• Documents proving that you have sufficient means to support yourself (normally proof of a pension being paid by bank transfer or of some other means of income or savings).

• The original and a photocopy (of the relevant pages) of your passport.

• A document proving that you are covered for health care, which may be an insurance policy or a social security card.

• €2.54, the fee charged on making the application.

Students

Present these documents:

• An application form, as above.

• Two recent and identical passport-type photographs in colour.

• Proof of sufficient means to support yourself, equivalent to or higher than the national minimum wage.

• Proof of being a registered student in the institution where you are studying.

• The original and a photocopy (of the relevant pages) of your passport.

• A document proving that you are covered for health care, which may be an insurance policy or a social security card.

• €2.54, the fee charged on making the application.

Family Members who are EU Citizens

Present these documents:

• An application form, as above.

• Two recent and identical passport-type photographs in colour.

• Spouses: marriage certificate issued less than one year ago.

• Children: birth certificate.

• Document proving that you are covered for health care, which may be an insurance policy or a social security card.

Family Members who are Citizens of Third Countries

Present this document:

• A residency visa (*visto de residência*), applied for at a Portuguese consulate in the country of origin or current residence.

Non-EU Citizens

Things are a lot tougher for citizens of non-EU countries, who normally need a visa to enter Portugal even on a visit. For purposes of work and/or residency a visa will almost certainly be necessary, and many other requirements are made by the authorities. The best source of information is the Portuguese consulate in your own country. Information may also be found, in Portuguese, on the web page of the *Serviço de Estrangeiros e Fronteiras* (**www.sef.pt**). On the site it is also possible to download an application form for residency at **www.sef.pt/pdf/ YY_pedido_aut_residencia_ing.pdf**. This form (model DR 0001) comes in Portuguese and English.

Getting Portuguese Nationality

Given the now relatively privileged position in which EU citizens find themselves and the wide-ranging rights enjoyed on taking up residence in any member state, there seems little point in taking Portuguese citizenship as there is not really much to be gained from doing so. If you can reside, work, run a business or live as a retiree, without hindrance, in any member state, why go through the rigmarole of changing nationality?

However, if one so wishes, it *is* possible to acquire Portuguese nationality. Non-EU citizens, in fact, may well have more pressing reasons to follow the process, as obtaining residence status is tedious and a longish stay outside the country (or the EU) may mean losing it anyway. Americans, Canadians, Australians or New Zealanders may find that obtaining citizenship is a definitive solution if their aim is to stay permanently. A Portuguese passport also entitles them to live and work anywhere else within the EU.

By Express Desire or through Naturalisation

The basic criteria to be met in the case of a 10-year resident who wishes to take up citizenship by desire or through naturalisation are:

- **To be at least 18 years old (or emancipated under Portuguese law).**

- **To have lived in Portuguese territory with a valid residence permit for at least six years, for citizens of Portuguese-speaking countries, or 10 years for citizens of other countries.**

- **To be able to show sufficient knowledge of the Portuguese language.**

- **To be able to able to prove that 'a substantial link' exists with the national community (being integrated).**

- **To have civic responsibility.**

- **To have the means to provide for one's livelihood.**

When making the request, a request form will be required. It must be completed and signed by the applicant and have all personal details such as full name, date of birth, marital status, place of birth, parental information, nationality, current and previous place of residence, professional activity carried out and the reasons for wishing to become naturalised (in the case of those choosing naturalisation). This form is also available in PDF format on the SEF website (**www.sef.pt/pdf/naturalizacao.pdf**). Otherwise you can pick it up at any branch or regional office of the SEF. In this case the request form should be signed in the presence of a public notary.

As well as the application form, the following documents should be attached:

- A photocopy of your residence permit.

- An original and photocopy of your birth certificate (include a photocopy of the certificate because you will need the original later on when you register your new nationality at the Central Registry Office).

- Documentation proving competence in the Portuguese language, which can be obtained through:

  - an exam certificate issued by an official Portuguese educational institution.

  - a document written, read and signed by the applicant in the presence of a notary.

  - a document written, read and signed by the applicant in the presence of the office manager of the local council in your area of residence or, in the case of Lisbon and Oporto, in the presence of the director of the Central Cultural Services, or a suitably delegated person, who can attest to the facts contained within the document, and authenticate the signature with an official stamp.

- Proof of the existence of a substantial link to the national community, through documentary or any other legal means – proof of long-term residence, photocopies of children's birth certificates, property deeds, etc.

- A criminal record certificate issued by the Portuguese authorities within the previous three months.

- A criminal record certificate issued by the relevant authorities in the country of origin within the previous three months, authenticated by the Portuguese consulate and, if not in Portuguese, with a translation attached; in the case where such a document is not issued, a declaration to this effect issued by the relevant authority should be attached.

- Documentary evidence that the applicant is capable of looking after him or herself, such as a declaration from an employer including the starting date of work, type of employment, the monthly salary, photocopy of the previous salary slip and a photocopy and the original income tax (IRS) declaration from the previous year, giving details of any income.

- A declaration from social security proving registration in that service, and detailing the date of admission, and details of social security salary deductions including the actual amounts.

- Documentary evidence showing that the applicant has completed military service in the country of origin or a statement indicating the nonexistence of any such requirement.

- Complete photocopies of any passports used in the previous five years.

Through Marriage to a Portuguese Citizen

Those who are married to a Portuguese citizen may apply once the following conditions are met:

- Having been married for more than three years.

- Making a statement expressing the wish to acquire Portuguese nationality, based on the stability of the marriage (this statement may be made in any civil registry office, if the interested party resides in Portuguese territory or territory under Portuguese administration, or, if the residence of the interested party is abroad, through diplomatic and consular services, which is then sent, along with the other relevant documentation, to the Central Registry Office. This statement of intention can be made by the applicant or by proxy, if capable, or by legal representatives, if unable to make the declaration him or herself.

- Providing proof, using relevant facts, that the person has a substantial connection with the national community.

- Not having committed any crime which is punishable under Portuguese law by a prison sentence of greater than three years.

- Not being a civil servant of a foreign state.

- Not having carried out voluntary military service for a foreign state.

The documents that must be handed in along with the request are:

- A marriage certificate.
- A birth certificate of the foreign spouse.
- A birth certificate of the Portuguese spouse containing an annotation of the marriage.
- A certificate of foreign nationality.
- A criminal record certificate issued by the Portuguese authorities, the authorities of the country of the interested party, and the authorities of the country where the person has resided.
- Proof that a substantial link exists with the national community (this may be done through documentary means, witnesses or any other legal means).

The request, along with any necessary documents, should be handed in at the local office of the Serviço de Estrangeiros e Fronteiras or, if there is no delegation nearby, to the civil governor. The SEF informs the applicant, within 8 days, whether the request has been formulated correctly, the right information given and if all the necessary documents are there. The applicant has 30 days to reply, which may be extended if this is justified. Once this period of time has expired, SEF will, within 8 days, ask the Ministry of Justice and the Ministry of Foreign Affairs for the necessary information to process the request for naturalisation. Within 15 days of the last information furnished, SEF will issue a decision (*parecer*) regarding the request.

Useful Contacts

Serviço de Estrangeiros e Fronteiras (SEF)

The Service for Border Control and Aliens is the body that deals with all matters concerning residence and obtaining Portuguese nationality. There are offices at the following addresses.

Lisbon and Vale do Tejo

For administrative purposes, this region also includes the Alentejo.

- **Head Office:** Rua Conselheiro José Silvestre Ribeiro, 4, 1649-007 Lisboa, t 217 115 000.
- **Lisbon Regional Office:** Avenida António Augusto de Aguiar, 20, 1069-119 Lisboa, t 213 585 500.
- **Central Lisbon Registry Office:** Rua Rodrigo da Fonseca, 198, 1099-003 Lisboa, t 213 817 600.

In Lisbon there is an SEF at the *loja do cidadão* in Praça Restauradores. Otherwise there are offices Beja, Cascais, Elvas, Évora, Portalegre, Santarém and Setúbal, as well as one jointly operated with the Spanish authorities in the border village of Caya (Caia in Portuguese), in Badajoz, Spain.

Central Portugal

- **Coimbra Office:** Rua Venâncio Rodrigues, 25–31, 3000-409, Coimbra, t 239 824 045/t 239 823 767, f 239 823 786.

There are also offices in Aveiro, Castelo Branco, Espinho; Figueira da Foz, Guarda, Vilar Formoso and Viseu, as well as in the *lojas do cidadão* in those cities where this service exists.

Algarve

- **Faro Office:** Rua Luis de Camões, 5, 8000-388, Faro, t 289 805 822/ t 289 888 300, f 289 801 566.

There are also offices in Albufeira, Portimão and Vila Real de Santo António.

Northern Portugal

- **Oporto Office:** Rua D. João IV, 536, 4000-299 Porto, t 225 104 308, f 225 104 385.

There are also offices in Braga, Bragança, Viana do Castelo and Vila Real, and an office operated with the Spanish authorities at Tuy in Pontevedra province.

Madeira

- **Madeira Office**: Rua Nova da Rochinha, 1-B, 9054-519, Funchal, t 291 232 177/t 291 229 589/t 291 231 414, f 291 231 918.

There is a sub-office in Porto Santo.

The Azores

- **Ponta Delgada Office**: Rua Marquês da Praia e Monforte, 10, Apartado 259 9500-089, Ponta Delgada, t 296 302 230, f 296 284 422.

There are also offices on the islands of Angra do Heroísmo, Pico and Horta.

Portuguese Embassies and Consulates in the UK

- **Portuguese Embassy**: 11 Belgrave Square, London SWIX 8PP, t (020) 7235 5331, f (020) 7245 1287/7235 0739, www.portembassy.gla.ac.uk.
- **Portuguese Consulate General**: Silver City House, 62 Brompton Road, London SW3 1BJ, t (020) 7581 8722.
- **Portuguese Consulate (Manchester)**: Alexandra Court, 93 Princess Street, Manchester M1 4HT, t (0161) 834 1821.
- **Portuguese Consulate (Edinburgh)**: 25 Bernard Street, Edinburgh EH6 6SH, t (0131) 555 2080.
- **Honorary Portuguese Consul (Bristol)**: 4 Knoll Court, Sneyd Park, Bristol BS9 1QX, t (01272) 658 042.
- **Honorary Portuguese Consul (Belfast)**: Hurst House, 15–19 Corporation Street, Belfast BT1 3HA.
- **Portuguese Consulate (Jersey)**: 14 Conway Street, Saint Helier, Jersey, t (01534) 877188.

British Embassies and Consulates in Portugal

- **British Embassy**: Rua de São Marçal, 174, 1200 Lisbon, t 213 929 440, f 213 924 186, www.uk-embassy.pt. *Open Mon–Fri 9–11.30 and 2–4.*
- **British Consulate (Lisbon)**: Rua São Bernardo 33, 1249-082 Lisbon, t 213 924 000, f 213 924 185, ppa@lisbon.mail.fco.gov.uk.
- **British Consulate (Oporto)**: Avenida da Boavista, 3072, 4100-120 Porto, t 226 184 789, f 226 100 438, consular@oporto.mail.fco.gov.uk.
- **British Consulate (Portimão)**: Largo Francisco A. Mauricio 7-1°, 8500-535 Portimão, t 282 417 800/417 804, f 282 417 806.

Living in Portugal

07

Over the last two or three decades many people from northern European countries have taken the decision to uproot themselves, leave their cold countries and make a new life for themselves in the warmer climes of southern Europe. Portugal is one of the countries that many have chosen to move to, and they still do. The construction of a united Europe, and Portugal's integration into it since 1986, have smoothed the way for many people. The legal barriers that used to make such movements of people difficult have slowly been removed. Citizens of EU and EEA countries may now freely establish their residence in the member state of their choice, find work or practise their profession there and enjoy practically the same rights as nationals of the country.

But choosing Portugal, as anywhere, implies adjusting to a different lifestyle, learning the ways of the country, accepting that not all the same home comforts are necessarily available. It also implies many advantages, in terms of a relaxed lifestyle and a quality of life that you do not find in the country you have left behind. This learning process, and the acceptance of the differences, can take time and requires patience. It need not be traumatic, however, as the Portuguese are generally accepting of foreigners. This chapter gives many pointers as to how to 'live' and how to make life easier.

Learning Portuguese

Why Learn Portuguese?

You might be a little taken aback if you were walking along your local high street and somebody asked you for directions in machine-gun-speed Portuguese. You might, then, understand how a Portuguese person would feel if you asked for directions in English. It works both ways. While it is true that in Portuguese tourist resorts and expatriate areas many local people speak English to a reasonable, at times excellent level, this does not mean that learning the language is unimportant if you are planning to stay. Even if you end up living in a community of expats – as many do – there will still be countless situations in which a working knowledge of Portuguese will be useful or even essential. If you are working or running a business you will inevitably have to deal with work colleagues or administration, and you cannot expect functionaries to be able to attend to you in English. In emergencies, being able to make yourself understood could mean the difference between life and death. It cannot be emphasised strongly enough that the ability to communicate in Portuguese is vital. Learning a language is fun and a challenge. Despite the difficulties involved, it need not be a chore. When you finally begin to feel that you are making headway, there is a great sense of achievement.

Learning Before You Go

Once you have decided to move to Portugal, you should start learning the language as soon as possible, preferably before leaving. In the UK and Ireland there are plenty of places where you can find classes in Portuguese, though not as many as there are for its neighbour, Castilian Spanish. It is also possible to study without attending classes in person. The options available are outlined below. People who live in larger towns and cities will find more possibilities available than those living in smaller, more isolated locations.

Public Evening Classes

Generally an inexpensive option, evening classes usually coincide with the academic year and may be pitched at students hoping eventually to take GCSEs or A-levels, though there may be less structured, conversation-based classes. These can range from 'survival' level to groups for advanced speakers. You should preferably do some structured learning before embarking on a conversation course.

To find out about courses, contact your local education authority, further education college or adult education centre. In addition to this, many UK and Irish universities have Hispanic studies departments in which Spanish and Portuguese are taught. If no courses are available there for the general public, they will almost certainly be able to point you in the direction of classes in the area.

Classes in Private Language Academies

Language academies abound in the UK and Ireland. At one end of the range are large international organisations with branches both at home and abroad, which offer classes at all levels in many languages, often providing tailor-made courses (at a price) to suit individual students' needs. At the other end of the range are smaller outfits, with a more limited selection of languages and courses. Either way, look in the local *Yellow Pages*.

Some of the larger establishments are listed below:

- **Berlitz**, Paradise Forum, Birmingham B3 3HJ, **t** (0121) 233 0974, **f** (0121) 233 1236, **www.berlitz.com/local/uk**. Has six other centres around the UK. Courses in European and Brazilian Portuguese are available at their London centre, 9–13 Grosvenor Street, London W1A 3BZ, **t** (020) 7915 0909, **f** (020) 7915 0222, and at other UK centres if there is demand.

- **Inlingua**, Rodney Lodge, Rodney Road, Cheltenham GL50 1HX, **t** (01242) 250493, **f** (01242) 250495, **www.inlingua-cheltenham.co.uk**. Centres throughout the UK and Europe, including Portugal.

Canning House

A very useful source of information on both academies and private teachers is Canning House, 2 Belgrave Square, London SW1X 8PJ, **t** (020) 7235 2303, **f** (020) 7235 3587, **www.canninghouse.com**. Look for 'Portuguese courses' on the left-hand side of the home page of the website. This will direct you to the non-political, non-profit-making Hispanic and Luso Brazilian Council, founded in 1943 to stimulate understanding between Britain, Spain, Portugal and Latin America. The Council can provide you with an extensive list of academies where Portuguese is taught as well as the names of some private tutors. The majority are in London but since several are also language academies that are established nationwide the information is not exclusive to the capital. In addition, if you are London-based you can attend many of the cultural activities, talks, film showings and so on, which are of great interest to hispanophiles and lusophiles and will help you to get a grounding in Portuguese culture before you move.

• **Cactus Languages**, Suite 4, Clarence House, 30–31 North St, Brighton BN1 1EB, East Sussex, **t** (01273) 775868 or **t** 0845 130 4775, **www.cactuslanguage.com**. Tailor-made, one-to-one and group courses at all levels.

Learning with a Private Teacher

Taking private tuition is another, if costlier, option. Expect to pay between £20 and £30 per hour for individual classes. The list provided by Canning House (*see* box above) has many private tutors based in the London area. The London-based **Institute of Linguists**, Saxon House, 48 Southwark Street, London SE1 1UN, **t** (020) 7940 3100, **f** (020) 7940 3101, **info@iol.org.uk**, **www.iol.org.uk**, has a database with private Portuguese tutors all over the UK.

There is a sizeable Portuguese community in many British cities, so putting up a notice in your local library saying 'Portuguese Teacher Wanted' may also reap results.

Self-study

The BBC has some courses which you can follow online, provided you have Real Audio Player. Look at **www.bbc.co.uk** and follow the links to 'Education'; the main options are French, Spanish and German, but, if you click on 'Other Languages', you will access Portuguese. The beginners course is called 'Talk Portuguese'. You can also follow the links to the online shop, which has various materials available for sale at beginners' and post-beginners' level; choosing the book and cassette together is recommended.

Apart from following this course online, you may buy it in book form or accompanied by cassettes. Other, slightly more comprehensive courses are:

• *Discovering Portuguese*: an introduction to the language and culture of Portugal with a course book and cassette pack, both sold separately but designed to be used together.

• *Talk Portuguese*: a short course for absolute beginners; as above, there is a course book and cassette pack, both sold separately, but designed to be used to be used together.

• *Get By in Portuguese*: a book and cassette pack, this is aimed at the post-beginner who wants to travel and try out the language.

Look out for the Talk Portuguese sessions on BBC Learning Zone, late night on BBC2.

There are many other self-study courses available, some of which are listed in **References**, 'Further Reading', p.228.

Language Exchange

This is the cheapest option of all, whether you are at home or in Portugal. Look for a native Portuguese-speaker who is looking to improve his or her English, get together for an hour or two, as often as you can, and spend half of the time speaking in one language, half in the other. This can be very productive once you are past the threshold stage, as there is no pressure to push ahead and complete a course book by a certain date as there is in an academy-based class. Nor are you limited or pushed by the abilities of classmates. It is also, possibly, the beginning of a friendship, and you can learn a lot about Portuguese culture from your exchange.

Instituto Camões

Like the British Council, the Goethe Institute, the Instituto Cervantes or the Institut Français, which promote the languages and culture of Britain, Spain, Germany and France, the Instituto Camões does the same with Portuguese.

In the UK and Ireland, the universities of Belfast, Cambridge, Dublin, Edinburgh, Leeds, London, Newcastle-upon-Tyne, Nottingham, Oxford, Sheffield and Wales all have departments where there is at least a lecturer if not a chair in Portuguese studies, generally as part of a larger Hispanic, or Spanish and Latin American studies department. In most cases, these departments have some connection with the Instituto Camões.

The institute is based in Lisbon, at Rua Rodrigues Sampaio, 113, 1150-279 Lisboa, **t** 213 109 100, **f** 213 143 987, **www.instituto-camoes.pt**.

Learning in Portugal

There are many options for learning Portuguese once in Portugal, either from total beginner's level or to build upon the Portuguese learned before arriving. The Instituto Camões (*see* box, previous page) is a good place to start. If it has no courses running near where you live staff will be able to direct you towards an academy or school. Many of the larger, internationally established language-teaching organisations mentioned above also run schools in Portugal.

Finding a Home

Finding somewhere to live once you move to Portugal is clearly a top priority. Exactly how you approach it, the type of accommodation you need (and eventually find), the area you live in, whether you rent or buy and many other things will be determined by the circumstances in which you move there and what you do once in the country. Long-term plans and whether or not you have children of school age will determine your property moves, as will the priorities and importance you give to location. Your earning power will determine whether you can buy or have to stay in rented accommodation. Other factors will play their part also.

Some who go to Portugal to take up a job are lucky enough to have accommodation provided by their company as part of their overall relocation package. This is generally the case at the higher end of the job market, where companies often have access to a variety of apartments, houses and villas and offer their top management a choice. Others, while not actually having accommodation provided, may at least benefit from a list of contacts given by their employer. Others either stay temporarily with friends or acquaintances, or possibly in a *pensão*, while they look for something more permanent.

The Housing Market

The Portuguese housing market is relatively small and in 2004 is under pressure from an influx of immigration, largely an urban phenomenon, which has created a shortage of flats for rent in larger cities. As well as this, the wave of foreign second- and holiday-home buyers in certain areas has pushed prices to unprecedented levels. The tourist industry has also helped to push prices up, as many properties in resort towns are owned and managed specifically for holiday lettings, and not for residential purposes. As a result it is very difficult to find long-term rented accommodation in these places.

The serious housing shortage in Portugal affects Portuguese people and foreign residents alike, especially those who have to work and live on a salary, whether they are looking to buy or to rent. Many of these buyers go for villas,

Living in a Comunidade

If you are not in the market for a villa, then you will probably be looking for a flat or an apartment. An apartment or flat within a block of apartments is a 'community' property. In a community (*comunidade*) your responsibilities do not begin or end at your own threshold. This is because there are many areas which are the common responsibility of all the owners: the entrance hall, stairways, lifts, landings, the façade, the patio, garden or grounds, fence and gate. In a more deluxe community there may also be a swimming pool, tennis courts, play areas and parking facilities. Some fittings, too, such as a satellite dish, are common elements. Though you do not have to take personal responsibility for their maintenance, you do pay for this in your community fees, sometimes known as condominium fees.

When you buy a property that is part of a community, you are buying proportional ownership of all the common elements. The only properties that cannot be said to belong to a community are single houses on private plots of land, whether in the country or in a town or city.

By law, all apartment blocks and *urbanizações* must have an officially constituted owners' community (*comunidade de proprietários*), which must draw up and vote on its set of statutes (*estatutos*). These statutes should define very clearly what constitutes communal property and the proportion of maintenance costs corresponding to each owner. This is usually proportionate to the size of each property: if you own an apartment of 40 square metres your share of the costs should be about one-third of those of a neighbour who has an apartment of 120 square metres. Voting rights are similarly proportional. You should know exactly what your share is to be, and this should be reflected in the property deeds. If there is no legally constituted community, refrain from buying.

You are usually charged monthly, quarterly or six-monthly and should be given an annual breakdown of expenditure. The annual accounts should be approved at a members' AGM, and minutes of previous years' meetings should be made available to a prospective buyer. Fees range enormously and correspond to the level of services that are provided to the members. Community meetings can be fairly stressful affairs, especially if there are confrontational neighbours in the community.

often in the 'luxury' category, which is probably not what most readers of this book have in mind. But a consequence of this is that even if you are looking for a more modest type of property, prices have been dragged upwards. Whether the emerging markets in the new EU member states will attract buyers eastwards, reducing pressure on the Portuguese market, remains to be seen.

This section is not aimed at people buying at the top end of the market, however. Many readers who cannot afford to buy a villa will move into an apartment or flat, and therefore living in a community.

Most Portuguese families, about 60 per cent, live in rented accommodation. In the larger cities, Lisbon and Oporto, particularly, only about 20 per cent of people actually own their own homes. This is hardly surprising in view of the situation described above and with Portuguese salaries taken into account. Many families struggle even to pay the rent, let alone take on a mortgage, so are effectively excluded from the housing market. Some native Algarveans go across the river Guadiana to the Spanish town of Ayamonte to buy property, where prices are lower. Not surprisingly, the Greater Lisbon area, the Algarve, especially the coast, and Oporto and its surrounding areas, are the most expensive parts of Portugal. Madeira is also catching up.

Renting

Although you are probably better off buying a home in the long term, it is often sensible to spend some time initially living in rented accommodation. There are several good reasons for this.

If you do not intend to stay permanently in Portugal, you may not want to commit yourself to buying a property. Even if you aim to stay indefinitely, you have much to gain from a period in rented accommodation before buying. By renting for a few months, or a year or two, you can get to know the area you are living in well and see both its positive and negative sides. You also have time to get a clear view of your money-making prospects, either through your business or your job. If your business is doing well or your job looks likely to be stable, then you can maybe think about committing money to a property. If the reverse is true, and you feel you have to move on, you will not have sunk money into a property that you would then have to sell quickly, and more than likely at a loss. This is because over a short period of time properties do not usually go up in value enough to cover the costs involved in selling it again and, even if they do, you would be liable for capital gains tax.

Looking for Rented Accommodation

Look for rented accommodation in Portugal in the same way as you would in the UK. For many people the printed press is the first contact with the rental market. National and local newspapers and magazines carry classified adverts with houses and apartments for rent – look in the classifieds under '*imobiliário – aluga-se*'. These papers usually have an online version also (*see* list on p.200). Not all adverts quote a price, and sometimes foreigners are quoted higher prices than Portuguese people. The English-language press also has rental adverts, though these are more limited. You can of course place your own 'wanted' advert as well.

You may also look for a long-term rental via an estate agent. Although they are mostly are in the business of buying and selling, some handle rentals also.

How the Case Studies Found their Accommodation

The people who kindly consented to be 'case studies' for this book found their homes in a variety of ways:

- 'As I was working for Cambridge School, they provided contacts...'
- 'I moved in with my partner...'
- 'Through a local property agent...'
- 'I trailed around estate agents in the area where I wanted to live and got the reps to show me as many places as they could within my price range. It took me three days to find a flat. Everyone I dealt with spoke English.'
- 'I found a flat advertised in *Público*; it was well within my budget, whereas agencies had said "Ooh, you'll get nothing for that".'
- 'When I later came to live here (I thought I would stay here for a year) I lived with my mother who had rented a flat. Later, I found a flat of my own – through friends.'
- 'I stayed with my daughter while house-hunting...this was the first suitable property of many viewed between Aveiro and Coimbra.'
- 'My tax adviser, PWC, gave me contact numbers for two estate agents. I also found another contact from the noticeboard of one of the schools I visited. One of the PWC contacts and my own contact were all we used and they showed us a selection of houses around Estoril and Cascais. I spent four days here on my first visit...then came back for a long weekend.'

So, they used a variety of house-hunting methods that included agencies, employer help, the grapevine, the classifieds and simply driving around until the right place came up. Only one arrived with accommodation already arranged.

These are some of their comments about prices:

- 'Rents are creeping up and are higher than in Spain, but about half of those in London.'
- 'The best large villas in a good location [inland along the Lisbon Coast] could be around €1,000,000 and a small village house probably around €100,000.'
- 'Cheaper than the UK. Villages are cheaper than towns or cities. Lisbon and the Algarve are more expensive and can exploit visitors.'
- 'Salaries are low [and] house prices are high, especially close to the cities or tourist areas.'

Expect to have to pay a fee, possibly the equivalent of one month's rent. Alternatively, you may see adverts on noticeboards in workplaces and educational institutes; again, you can put up your own 'wanted' advert yourself.

Rental Terms

When looking at adverts in the newspapers there are some terms that it is useful to understand:

assoalhadas	number of rooms
casas de banho	number of bathrooms
tipologia, t1, t2, t3, etc.	number of bedrooms
antiguidade do imóvel	age of the building
aquecimento central	central heating
ar condicionado	air conditioning
arrecadação	storage space
comodidades	mod-cons
cozinha equipada	itted kitchen
disponibilidade do imóvel...	available from...
elevador	lift
estacionamento	parking space included
estado do imóvel	condition of the building
exposição solar	exposure to sunlight (south-/west-/east-/north-facing)
gás canalizado	mains gas
jardim	garden
lareira	fireplace
mobilada	furnished
montante de entrada (€)	amount of deposit required
parabólica	satellite dish
piscina	swimming pool
sauna	sauna
terraço/pátio	terrace/patio
vidros duplos	double glazing
vista	view

Sample rentals available shortly before publication were:

• Lisbon (Graça): south-facing, fully furnished, one-bedroom apartment with fitted kitchen, mains gas and views over the Tagus river; €650 per month. No central heating; the building has a lift.

• Lisbon (Bairro Alto): west-facing, fully furnished, one-bedroom apartment, 40 sq m, refurbished three years ago, with parquet flooring, fitted kitchen, double glazing and excellent views over the Santos and Estrela neighbourhoods; €430 per month, deposit €860. No central heating or lift.

• Lisbon (Odivelas, northern suburbs): east-facing, unfurnished three-bedroom apartment with fitted kitchen, mains gas, double glazing, views and a storage room on the ground floor; €540 per month. Lift.

Lastly, the grapevine is an extremely useful source of information – your co-workers may very often be the ones that put you on to the best leads.

In resort areas, especially the Algarve, there are extremely few long-term rentals as there is so much money to be made in short-term holiday lets. Out of season, a landlord or management agency might be prepared to rent from September to March at a reasonable price. You will probably have to leave before Easter, the beginning of the mid-season and the point at which rents start to go up. You may, if you are lucky, find inexpensive accommodation as a house-sitter for the owners of a holiday home, as many prefer their property to be occupied when they are not there. Finding a long-term rental through the summer months is practically impossible in any resort unless you are prepared to pay the extortionate high-season rates.

Outside tourist areas, in small towns and cities, long-term lets are more common and prices are more reasonable. There are not a great many places for rent, however. In the larger cities, Lisbon especially, rents can be quite high. What is available depends very much on your budget. As in the sales market, the range on offer goes from small, one-bedroom apartments to smart villas with swimming pools and carports. Rental properties may be **furnished** (*mobiliado*) or **unfurnished** (*sem mobília*). Though properties in tourist areas are invariably furnished, in a city you may find either. The size, expressed in square metres, the number of bedrooms, the condition and age of the property, whether it is furnished or unfurnished, and its location all determine the price.

Rental Contracts

All rentals are subject to a **contract** (*contrato de arrendamento*), which should clearly state the rights and obligations of the two contracting parties. Rental laws have traditionally favoured tenants, which has held back the development of the sector: landlords are wary of renting to anyone they fear they may not be able to get rid of. A standard long-term rental contract is for **one year** and then may be renewed for further periods if both parties wish. **Utilities bills** are usually paid by the tenant.

As with renting anywhere, it is a good idea to have an expert check over the contract before signing. This is especially advisable if your Portuguese is weak. Look out for clauses relating to repairs for damage (as opposed to wear and tear) and any community charges the landlord expects you to pay (you should not have to). Most demand a **deposit** of two months' rent as a guarantee in case of any serious damage or breakages, and the landlord may also require a **guarantor** (*fiador*) who will be liable if you fail to pay the rent.

In the case of taking a furnished flat, make sure to get a full **inventory** of all items included. Check whether the flat has central heating and/or air-conditioning (rare except in newly built blocks or renovated older properties), or any other mod-cons. Questions such as the form of payment should be made clear from the beginning.

Short-term rentals are the norm in resort areas, for the simple reason that there are so few long-term arrangements available. There are specific laws governing these agreements; the contract clearly states the rental period and as it is understood that occupation is temporary there are usually no problems on either side.

Buying

Once you are sure that you are going to stay indefinitely, and that your financial situation is reasonably buoyant, you may start thinking of buying a property. If you are not in a situation to buy outright, you will have to look at some form of financing (*see* pp.114–15). If you are living on a typical Portuguese salary and have no other savings, this might be beyond your means. As buying a property is one of the biggest decisions you are likely to take in your life, it is not something to be approached lightly and is certainly not to be rushed into. Preparation is essential.

First of all you should fix a budget based on a calculation of overall costs, not just the price you think you can pay for a property. It should also include all taxes and fees that are payable as part of the transaction plus any likely expenses for essential repair work that may be needed to make the property habitable. Be realistic, expect repair work to take longer and cost more than at first estimated. Once you have this overall budget worked out, the price you can pay for the property is the total left after fees and repair costs are accounted for.

Looking for Property

You can now start looking at properties that come within this price ceiling. As with renting a property, you can start by checking the '*imobiliário*' section of the classifieds in any **newspaper**. This is probably the best place to find private sellers if you prefer not to get involved with agencies. Local papers can be particularly useful as they tend to specialise in properties in a relatively small area. The main dailies also carry a lot of property adverts, usually organised regionally, and their online editions can be useful for these purposes because you can specify what you want and your price limit without having to wade through pages of print. One quite reasonable classifieds site is **www.classificados.iol.pt**, click on '*casas*' and you are taken to **http://casa.iol.pt**, from where you can choose apartments or houses by area, price, size and so on. The English-language press comes with property adverts, many of them placed by private individuals. You could also place a 'looking for' advert yourself, either in the English publications or Portuguese ones.

The windows of **estate agents** will give you a good idea of what is available within your budget without any commitment on your part. If you decide to enter and see what the estate agent (*mediador imobiliário*) has to offer, make sure that you are dealing with one who is professionally qualified and licensed to operate (*mediador autorizado*). They should also belong to a professional association such as the Associação de Mediadores Inmobiliários (AMI) or the Associação Portuguesa de Empresas de Mediação Inmobiliários (APEMI). Be careful, not all of them are. Most agencies display the sticker of one or more of these bodies on their shop door or window and have their certificate in a frame on the wall. This may not be guarantee enough, as the agent could have left (or been asked to leave) the association and not removed the sticker. You should not be shy about asking to see proof of an agent's registration, since if they are bona fide they will have no problems in showing it to you. The role of the estate agent in Portugal is the same as anywhere else, namely to attract potential buyers for properties that sellers have entrusted to them. As such they are working for the seller, though that is no reason for you to assume they are out to cheat you.

It is the seller who pays the estate agent's commission. It is illegal for the agent to take commission from both parties. These fees are usually between 5 and 10 per cent of the price of the property. The amount will depend on the value of the property, whether it is new or old and the area where it is located. Cheaper properties generally pay more commission than more expensive properties and properties in main tourist areas tend to pay more commission than in less sought after (and generally poorer) areas. In order to protect his substantial commission the agent may ask you to sign a document before he takes you to see the property. This is a statement that it is he who has introduced you to the property, so avoiding later arguments about who should be paid the commission due.

There are other significant differences from English practice. Generally agents are rather less proactive than they are in the UK. This is particularly true in rural areas, especially non-tourist rural areas. You will seldom find printed property particulars or be supplied with photographs. Still less will you find plans or room dimensions in most estate agents' offices. They see their role as capturing property to sell and then showing buyers around that property.

Property in Portugal can be bought at **auction**, just as in the UK. Some auctions are voluntary, others run by court order. Prices can be very attractive. A few years ago, at the height of the last recession, there were incredible bargains with prices, perhaps, 30 per cent of 'value'. Now auctions usually offer less spectacular bargains but can still be attractive because, particularly in many judicial auctions, the process is intended first and foremost to recover someone's debt. Once that and the considerable costs have been covered there is little reason to press for a higher price, even though the owner will receive the excess. Buying a property at auction is not simple for someone who does not live in the area and it is vitally important that you have taken all the normal preparatory steps – including seeing a lawyer – before you embark on the process.

The Notary Public (Notário)

The notary is a special type of lawyer. They are in part public officials but also in business, making their living from the fees they charges for their services. Notaries also exist in England but they are seldom used in day-to-day transactions. Under Portuguese law, only deeds of sale (*escrituras públicas de compra e venda*) approved and witnessed by a notary can be registered at the land registry. Although it is possible to transfer legal ownership of property such as a house or apartment by a private agreement not witnessed by the notary, and although that agreement will be fully binding on the people who made it, it will not be binding on third parties. Third parties – including people who want to make a claim against the property and banks wanting to lend money on the strength of the property – are entitled to rely upon the details of ownership recorded at the land registry. So if you are not registered as the owner of the property you are at risk. Thus, practically speaking, all sales of real estate in Portugal must be witnessed by a notary. The notary also carries out certain checks on property sold and has some duties as tax enforcer and validator of documents to be presented for registration.

His fee is fixed by law, and is modest. For each signatory to the title, he is paid b11 plus a fee for the deed of a fixed €175, irrespective of value. Notaries are challenging this level of fees and they have threatened to go on strike to secure better payment.

Notaries are strictly neutral. They are more a referee than someone fighting on your behalf. They are usually someone who checks the papers to make sure that they comply with the strict rules as to content and so will be accepted by the land registry for registration. Many Portuguese notaries, particularly in rural areas, do not speak English well enough to discuss complex issues. Very few will know anything about English law and so will be unable to tell you about the tax and other consequences in the UK of your plans to buy a house in Portugal. In any case, it is not their job to do so and the buyer will, anyway, seldom meet the notary before the signing ceremony and so there is little scope for seeking detailed advice. It is, in any case, rare for notaries to offer any comprehensive advice or explanation, least of all in writing, to the buyer.

For the English buyer the notary is no substitute for also using the services of a specialist lawyer familiar with Portuguese law and property transactions.

Independently of the estate agent, you should also seek the services of a good **lawyer** who specialises in property. For this you may choose to contract a UK lawyer who deals with property abroad or a Portuguese lawyer, though you may want one who speaks English in order to explain documents to you in your own language. You should ask other foreign buyers for a recommended lawyer; alternatively a list is available from your nearest British Consulate. Have the lawyer on board from the beginning, rather than called in to solve a mess that you have got into by not consulting one in the first place. A lawyer's services will typically cost you 1–3 per cent of the overall price of your property depending on the services provided. If you are going to spend €200,000 on a property, you will pay between €2,000 and €6,000 in legal fees. It may seem a lot, but how much might you eventually spend in lawsuits if it all goes wrong?

Sources of Information

Just as it is difficult to give accurate, general price information (*see* below), so it is difficult to point people towards good sources of information in English. The market for second and holiday homes in the Algarve is so dominant that it distorts the search capacity of Google, to the extent that information about other types of property elsewhere is seriously lacking. Simply googling 'portugal + property' is not good enough. Over 90 per cent of thousands of matches will be for sites advertising holiday or vacation apartments, villas and more villas on the Algarve unless you considerably refine your search criteria. Even if you refine it to exclude, 'Algarve', 'holiday', 'vacation' and 'villa' these adverts still come up. It can be extremely irritating if you are not looking for a holiday villa, have no desire to go to the Algarve and prefer live and to rent or buy somewhere else. Research for this book proved equally frustrating and it was found, in the end, that Portuguese-language sites are more useful.

The most useful proved to be **http://casa.iol.pt/**, which allows you to search for apartments, houses and other types of property, by region, municipality (*concelho*), price, or number of bedrooms (*T1*, *T2*, etc.). Information is provided with photos. Equally useful for regional searches is **www.imoregioes.com**.

Property Prices

It is very difficult to give an accurate picture of the range of property prices, as they vary considerably from region to region, from neighbourhood to neighbourhood in cities, according to size, type and quality, year (or century) of construction, proximity to services and so on. As well as that, anything quoted here may well be out of date by the time you read this book.

However, research carried out close to this book's publication date threw up the following results.

Lisbon

In Lisbon, prices vary hugely according to the neighbourhood. Lapa, a beautiful and salubrious neighbourhood to the west of the centre, with river views, offers apartments in old but restored buildings, with over 110 sq m of space for around €250,000. Other nearby, but less posh, neighbourhoods offer similar size and quality apartments for more than €175,000. Across town, just under the castle, similar space is available in a renovated old building for €120,000. In nearby Estoril, on the coast, a small, detached three-bedroom house with basement and garden, needing work, was going for €375,000. A little way along the coast, in Cascais, expect to pay close on €200,000 for a two-bedroom flat. Up the

Lisbon coast, in the fishing town of Ericeira, a brand new two-bedroom apartment of 106 sq m in a closed condominium development, by the beach, cost as little as €150,000.

Coimbra

In the old university city of Coimbra a small (85 sq m) new two-bedroom flat starts at €120,000 and in nearby Aveiro a brand new 135 sq m apartment costs €137,000. Further north, in Oporto, €135,000 gets you a second-hand two-bedroom apartment with 105 sq m of space, although something newly constructed can cost considerably more and gives you less space.

The Algarve

The Algarve has a lot on offer and prices vary enormously. The cheapest apartments may not be suitable for year-round living. About the absolute minimum for a small studio or one-bedroom apartment in the central Algarve is €100,000 and you may find a small townhouse costs more than €175,000. Prices have traditionally been a little lower in the western Algarve (west of Albufeira to Lagos) but are creeping up now thanks to improved road communications. The less-developed eastern Algarve has also tended to have lower prices but they may start to climb as other areas become saturated and overpriced. This area is the easiest to find out prices on the Internet.

The Alentejo

The Alentejo, still one of the least developed or sought-after areas has a small property market: village and small town houses, usually needing work, may cost as little as €40,000 but you will need to invest a lot in restoration. Farmhouses in need of conversion work cost around €75,000 to €90,000.

Financing the Purchase

This highly complex question is beyond the scope of this book other than to give some basic guidelines. As this book is also aimed at those who are living and working in Portugal, or intend to, rather than those looking for a second or holiday home, the main focus here is on Portuguese mortgages.

A Portuguese mortgage is one that you would take out to finance the purchase of your home in Portugal either from a Portuguese bank or a foreign, generally British, bank that is registered and operates in Portugal. You cannot take out such a mortgage from a UK building society or high street bank. A mortgage with these characteristics is basically a loan secured against the property. As anywhere, if you cannot keep up with payments the bank will repossess your property.

The main features of Portuguese mortgages are:

- **They are usually created on a repayment basis, being paid off in equal payments spread over a period of time.**

• There may be restrictions or penalties for the early repayment of the loan.

• The formalities involved in making the application, signing the contract and completing the transaction are more complex than in the UK.

• Most, though not all, Portuguese mortgages are granted for a 15-year period. Periods as short as five and as long as 30 years are not unknown, however, though the mortgage must usually repaid by your 70th (sometimes 65th) birthday.

• The maximum loan is usually 80 per cent of the value of the property though the bank may insist on it being no more than two-thirds of the purchase price.

• Fixed rate loans are more common than in the UK.

• Banks will not generally loan more than an amount whose monthly repayment comes to more than 30–33 per cent of your disposable monthly income. This is why if you have an average Portuguese salary you may have problems getting a mortgage to buy a house.

• There is usually a minimum loan (of maybe €20,000). Some banks will not give loans for properties below a certain value and are loath to loan for the purchase of rural properties.

• The paperwork on completion of the mortgage is different. There may be a separate mortgage contract (*contrato de mútuo com hipoteca*) or the mortgage can be reflected solely in the *escritura*, which is prepared by and signed in front of the notary public (*notário*).

When making an application to a Portuguese bank, you will be asked for various types of information, the most important being concerning your income, if you are employed on a salary, or your average net earnings over the last three years if you are self-employed. Provided bank staff are satisfied that the property is a sound investment, after seeing a survey, and that you are in a position to service the loan, if all is satisfactory you should receive preliminary approval within two to four weeks. You will then have 30 days to accept the offer, after which it lapses. Make sure your lawyer looks over the mortgage offer in detail and explains it to you point by point.

There may be problems in getting a mortgage for a brand new property – one that is still being built and therefore does not yet fully exist. Normally you have to make stage payments as work progresses and take title on completion of the building work. The bank might be loathe to grant a loan, as until you take title you own nothing that you can mortgage. A mortgage is usually only granted to cover the final payment. Banks may, however, offer a credit facility to help you with the earlier payments and once you have taken possession you may begin to make the normal monthly mortgage payments.

The Law

As you would expect, the law relating to the ownership of property is compli-cated. A basic textbook on Portuguese property law might extend to 500 pages. There are certain basic principles that it is helpful to understand.

1 The main legal provisions relating to property law are found in the civil code, which was introduced in 1867 but modified since, most notably in 1967. The analysis of rights reflects the essentially agrarian society of late 18th century Portugal and pays limited attention to some of the issues that, today, would seem more pressing. That has only partly been remedied by the later additions to the code.

2 The civil code declares that foreigners are to be treated in the same way as Portuguese people as far as the law is concerned.

3 Portuguese law divides property into two classes – moveable property (*bienes muebles*) and immovable property (*bienes inmuebles*). The whole basis of ownership and transfer of ownership depends on which classification property belongs to. The distinction is similar to the English concept of real and personal property *but it is not exactly the same*. Immovable property includes land and buildings, but not the shares in a company that owns land and buildings.

4 The sale of real estate located in Portugal must always be governed by Portuguese law.

5 The form of ownership of land is always absolute ownership. This is similar to what we would call freehold ownership.

6 It is possible to own the buildings – or even parts of a building – on a piece of land separately from the land itself. This is of particular relevance in the case of flats, which are owned 'freehold'.

7 Where two or more people own a piece of land or other property together they will generally own it in undivided shares (*pro indiviso*). That is to say the piece of land is not physically divided between them. Each owner may, in theory, mortgage or sell his share without the consent of the others – though the others might have certain rights of pre-emption – that is the right to buy the property in preference to any outsider.

8 Where a building or piece of land is physically divided between a number of people a condominium (*condomínio*) is created. The land is divided into privately owned parts – such as an individual flat – and communally owned areas. The management of the communally held areas is up to the owners of the privately held area, but can be delegated to someone else.

9 Transfer of ownership of real estate is usually by simple agreement. This must be in writing. That agreement binds both the parties to it but is not effective as far as the rest of the world is concerned, who are entitled to rely upon the

content of the land register. Thus ownership of land can be transferred between buyer and seller, for example, by signing a sale contract even if the seller remains in possession and some of the price remains unpaid. But that ownership would not damage the interests of someone other than the buyer or seller (such as someone owed money by the seller) who is entitled to take action against the person named as owner in the land registry. Ownership can also be acquired by possession, usually for 30 years.

10 Other rights – short of ownership – can exist over land. These include rights of way, tenancies, life interests, mortgages and option contracts. Most require some sort of formality in order to be valid against third parties but they are always binding between the people who made the agreements.

11 There are two land registers. Each area maintains a tax register (*registo predial*). In this all the land in the district is divided into plots and assessed for tax purposes. The second register is the deed and mortgage register (*registo de propriedade*). Not all land is registered here. The entries (size, boundaries, etc.) do not necessarily correspond in the two registries.

Property Inspection

Whatever property you are thinking of buying you should think about having it inspected before you commit yourself to the purchase.

A new property will be covered by a short guarantee running from the date of handover and covering minor but not trivial defects in a new property. The property will also benefit from a guarantee in respect of major structural defects that will last for 10 years. As a subsequent purchaser you assume the benefit of these guarantees. After 10 years you are on your own. For property more than 10 years old (and, arguably, for younger property too) you should consider a survey.

If you decide on a survey, there are a number of options available to you.

There are several things that you can check yourself. These will help you decide when to instruct a surveyor to do a proper survey and help direct him to any specific points of interest.

It may be possible to arrange for another local estate agent to give the property a quick 'once over' to comment on the price asked and any obvious problem areas. This is far short of a survey. It is likely to cost about £200. It is also possible to have a valuation (*avaliação*) carried out by an official valuer (*técnico avaliador*). This is also likely to cost about £200 for a simple property, but can sometimes be less helpful and practical than the estate agent's valuation.

The mortgage-lender, if you are having a mortgage, may arrange a 'valuation and survey'. This is no substitute for a proper survey. Many lenders do not ask for one and, where they do, it is normally fairly peremptory, limited to a check on whether it is imminently about to fall over and whether it is, on a forced sale at short notice, likely to be worth the money the bank is lending you.

If you are going to do a virtual demolition and rebuild, then it might make more sense to get a builder to do a report on the property. A reputable and experienced builder will also be able to comment on whether the price is reasonable for the property in its existing state. Make sure you ask for a written quotation for any building work proposed.

Your lawyer can also put you in touch with a Portuguese surveyor. In most rural areas there will be limited choice. If you prefer you can select 'blind' from a list of local members supplied by the surveyors' professional body. The cost of a survey is typically £500–1,500. You will find that the report is different from the sort you would get from an English surveyor. Many people find it a little 'thin', with too much focus on issues that are not their primary concern. It will, hardly surprisingly, usually be in Portuguese. You will need to have it translated and have access to a technical dictionary. Translation costs amount to about £60–100 per thousand words, depending on where you are located and the complexity of the document. Incidentally, always use an English native speaker to translate documents from Portuguese into English. An alternative to translation of the full report would be to ask your lawyer to summarise the report in a letter to you and to have any areas of particular concern translated. A few Portuguese surveyors, mainly in the popular areas, have geared themselves to the non-Portuguese market and will produce a report rather more like a British survey. They will, probably, also prepare it in bilingual form or at least supply a translation of the original Portuguese document.

In popular expatriate areas, a number of UK surveyors – usually those with a love of Portugal – have seen a gap in the market and have set themselves up in Portugal to provide UK-style structural surveys. As in this country, they usually offer the brief 'Homebuyers' Report' or the fuller 'Full Structural Survey'. This is not as simple as it would first appear. To do the job well they must learn about Portuguese building techniques and regulations, which are different from those in the UK. Without this knowledge, the report will be of limited value. Prices are generally slightly more expensive than for a Portuguese report, but it will be in English and so avoid the need for translation costs. Your UK lawyer should be able to recommend a surveyor able to do a survey in your area. Alternatively, look for advertisers in the main Portuguese property magazines.

Check they have indemnity insurance covering the provision of reports in Portugal. Check also on the person's qualifications and experience in providing reports on Portuguese property and get an estimate. The estimate will be an estimate because they will not know for sure the scope of the task until they visit the property and because travelling time means that visits just to give estimates are not usually feasible. Most surveys can be done in seven to ten days.

Contracts 'Subject to Survey'

This is unusual in Portugal. Legally, there is nothing to stop a Portuguese preliminary contract containing a 'get-out clause' (*condicion resolutoria*) stating that the sale is conditional upon a satisfactory survey being obtained. It is unlikely to meet with the approval of the seller or his agent unless the transaction is unusual. In an ordinary case, the seller is likely to tell you to do your survey and then sign a contract.

Checklist – Things You May Ask Your Surveyor to Check

- Electrical condition and continuity.
- Drains, including assessment of drain to point where they join mains sewers or septic tank.
- Septic tank.
- Rot.
- Cement quality in a property constructed out of cement.
- Underfloor areas, where access cannot easily be obtained.
- Heating and air-conditioning.
- Pool and all pool-related equipment and heating.
- Wood-boring insects. Roughly half of Portugal is infested with termites, so this is important.

Buying the Property – Step by Step

Having found a property that you wish to buy, either from a private seller or via an agency, and appointed independent legal help, you may now enter into the purchasing and conveyancing procedures.

Usually the first stage in the process, the signing of the promissory contract (*contrato promessa de compra e venda*) commits buyer and seller to the transaction. The contract states the names, addresses and tax and ID numbers of the seller and buyer, and contains a detailed description of the property in question, the land registry file number and the terms and amount of payment. It fixes a date for the signing of the deed of sale (*escritura*) and a date for the buyer to take possession, generally the date of signing. The buyer usually pays a deposit (*sinal*) of around 10 per cent (though in some cases more) of the sale price, and is given a receipt for this. In the case of the buyer's later backing out, the deposit is lost; if the seller backs out, he or she is liable to pay the buyer double the amount of the deposit paid. The contract will also state who is to pay the costs of the purchase. Before signing this contract, have your lawyer check it.

Usually a condition of sale, or purchase, is that the property must be free of any charges, debts and burdens, and all bills should be paid up to date before the signing of the *escritura*. **Any debts are inherited by the new owner.** This is a crucial phase and it is here that you will appreciate the worth of a good lawyer who should have all this checked for you (never use the services of an agent who is acting for both the buyer and the seller). You should have this checked as

False Declarations: A Warning

Changes in Portuguese tax legislation could mean homeowners face a hefty bill when they sell up. But it will be a lot worse for those who intentionally under-declared the value of their homes to pay less in property transfer and capital gains taxes. They will now face possible fines and the compulsory purchase of their homes.

The legislation came into force throughout Portugal on 1 October 2004 and is designed to combat decades of tax-evasion, traditionally rife in the housing sector and perpetrated by Portuguese citizens and expatriates alike. Under current UK regulations, infringement of the rules following the 1 October 2004 deadline would see buyers and/or sellers considered as money launderers and subject to UK legal proceedings.

Because property transfer and capital gains taxes have traditionally been so high, tax evasion has been commonplace. Property transfer tax (SISA) averaged 10 per cent, so owners would declare a lower price in their sale contract than that actually paid by the buyer. Consequently the buyer would pay property transfer tax, and the seller would pay capital gains tax only on the *declared* value.

In January 2004 property transfer tax was reduced to an average of 6 per cent on properties worth over €500,000, but for Britons investing through offshore companies it may still be as high as 15 per cent.

The Justice Department and the Finance Ministry, backed by a budget of €100 million, will work together to enforce the new regulation, starting on 1 October 2004. It obliges all notaries, judicial secretaries and judicial technical secretaries to submit all conveyance deals electronically to the Finance Ministry. It is hoped that this will help enforce the law and prevent tax-evasion.

The onus is on buyers to make sure they are buying at the correct price and pay the correct property transfer tax; if they don't, they face two penalties. The first is to pay the remainder of the real tax value, as well as a fine. The second is for those properties with a declared sale contract value that is over 30 per cent less than the actual value; in these cases the local authority will have compulsory purchase powers and may buy the property, at the *declared* contract value.

Sellers in Portugal who originally bought and under-declared are in a quandary, as they now are looking to sell and will be caught out by the huge cost of their house being subject to capital gains tax liable on its *real* value.

Adapted from a statement by John Howell & Co.,
International Legal and Property Specialists.

close as possible to the signing date. It is also important for the lawyer to make general enquiries and special enquiries: checks that find out, for example, whether there are any road building or other major schemes planned in the immediate vicinity of your desired property as these could affect your enjoyment of it, your peace and quiet and its resale value.

The culminating moment of the purchasing process, also known as completion or closing, must take place in the presence of a Portuguese notary, on the date agreed in the promissory contract. The process involves the signing of the deed of sale (*escritura*), which transfers ownership of the property, the payment of the balance of the purchasing price, paying the notary's fees and the deed registration fee. Property transfer tax (SISA) should have been paid already and the receipt should be given to the notary; keep a copy for yourself. Normally you should be able to take possession of the property there and then.

The Cost of Buying a Property

You will be liable to pay:

• **Notary's fees**: the notary is the only person authorised to approve and witness the deeds of sale of a property, therefore no sale can legally proceed without a notary's presence at the moment of signing; the fee is fixed by law and modest: €11 per signatory of the title and €175 for the deed itself, regardless of the value of the property in question.

• **Property transfer tax** (SISA): the rate for properties whose declared value is below €80,000 is 0 per cent; those with a value of €80,000–110,000, 2 per cent; those with a value of €110,000–150,000, 5 per cent; those with a value of €150,000–250,000, 7 per cent; those with a value of €250,000–500,000, 8 per cent; and those above €500,000, 6 per cent. For your own protection, make sure that the *declared* value corresponds to the *real* value of the property, if not you could be in trouble, *see* box 'False Declarations'.

• An annual **municipal tax** on property (*contribução autarquica*): the rates are based on valuations determined by tax authorities and are generally much lower for older properties than new ones. Rates are between 0.7 and 1.3 per cent on buildings (though they are fixed each year by each municipality); this is likely to go down in the near future with newer homes being charged at between 0.2 and 0.5 per cent and older ones subjected to rates varying between 0.4 and 0.8 per cent.

• **Mortgage costs**: Typically about 4 per cent of the money borrowed.

• **Land registration costs**: Normally 0.8 per cent of the price of the property. There are two land registers. Each area maintains a tax register (*registo predial*). In this all the land in the district is divided into plots and assessed for tax purposes. The second register is the deed and mortgage register (*registo de propriedade*). Not all land is registered here.

Insuring Your Home

Whether you use a Portuguese or an international company to insure your home, you are recommended to take out cover on the building, the contents and for third-party liability, and to find a policy that will cover you for likely and not-so likely types of damage. The 'likely' includes fire, flooding, burglary, storms, gas explosions, heavy rain, high winds, freezing weather and acts of vandalism. The 'not-so likely' includes natural catastrophes such as lightning, earthquakes (remember the severe tremor of 1755) and forest fires, which ravage large areas of rural Portugal every summer.

If you buy a house with garden, you should include cover for outbuildings such as the garage, the garden and any garden furniture, satellite dishes, the swimming pool and/or tennis court if you have them, fences, gates and driveways. No insurance company is likely to pay up if they can prove that your property had structural faults, which is a good reason to have a thorough inspection done before buying.

If you buy an apartment, the community will most likely have insured the whole building, and annual renewal of the policy may be a percentage of your community charges. Find this out before buying, because if the building is not insured, or if the insurance is not comprehensive enough, you should think twice about buying. You must take out another policy that will cover you for third-party damage to other properties in the block that may arise from burst pipes or a fire in your apartment.

Cover contents against the same risks. Usually, insurance companies will pay for clothing, bedding and furniture to be replaced, though not necessarily the full value if these items are old and partially worn out. A good insurance policy should cover accidental damage to plumbing and electrical installations, damage caused by burglars, loss of keys, alternative accommodation if your house is rendered uninhabitable and the value of food in a deep freeze if the electrical installations give out or you suffer a power cut. A standard policy may not include these things, so check the details and insist on it if necessary. Valuable items such as cameras, camcorders, computer equipment, jewellery or antiques should photographed, and receipts kept in a very safe place, preferably off the premises. Villas and ground- or first-floor apartments need iron bars over the windows, a reinforced door and possibly an alarm system before a company will insure.

Many factors enter the calculation of the premium: the building's size, date of construction, value, location (high burglary rates mean high premiums) and value of contents. If you have to make a claim, inform the insurance company as soon as possible, never more than a week after the event. If you are burgled, report this to the police and include the report (*denúncia*) with your claim. Finally, if you take out the policy in a country other than Portugal make sure that the policy is valid in Portuguese law.

Home Utilities and Telephones

Electricity

Electricity is expensive in Portugal compared with the rest of the EU. On renting or buying a property, one of the first things you should do is get the electricity contract put in your name or make a new one if the property is new. You do this at the local office of **Electricidade de Portugal (EDP)**, t 800 505 505 (freefone), **www.edp.pt**, which also has offices in most *lojas do cidadão*. You have to provide proof of identity and occupancy of the property. Check that the last occupant has paid bills on leaving the property or you might have to pay them, especially if you do not have the account put in your name immediately.

Liberating Energies?

The Portuguese energy sector is currently in a process of liberalisation. This follows the lead taken next door in Spain, where it is now possible for consumers to choose which company supplies their gas and electricity. Eventually, the aim is for there to be a single Iberian market, the MIBEL, or Mercado Ibérico de Electricidade. Quite how this will happen and what it will all mean in Portugal remains unclear. Together with the Italian group ENI, EDP recently acquired a controlling share of Gás de Portugal (GDP).

The company is also planning to raise capital, in a share issue, to acquire the northern Spanish electricity producer Hidroeléctrica del Cantábrico. As EDP is GDP's biggest customer, the European Commission is planning to launch an enquiry into the merger because it believes that, as EDP could make GDP its exclusive supplier to the detriment of other gas companies, it is possibly contrary to the principles of a free market. Brussels seems to fear that the move will set a precedent for mergers in other countries, which would tend to encourage less, rather than more, competition. EDP's position is that as there is an agreement with Spain to create the MIBEL, the EDP's market share should be seen in the Iberian, not the Portuguese, context. Within the peninsula, EDP only has about 19 per cent of the market in electricity and gas so it does not, the company argues, represent a 'dominant position'. That is as may be, but Portugal occupies a little less than 19 per cent of the peninsula's surface area (one-sixth) and its population is approximately one-fifth (20 per cent), 10 million compared with Spain's near 40 million. Seen that way, as EDP's effective operating areas is Portugal and not the rest of the peninsula, this looks a little like a dominant position. Across the border, in many areas, effective monopolies or duopolies continue, so to talk of a liberated market is still optimistic.

As for consumers, whether the MIBEL will bring them a greater range of supply options and lower bills or not, and how exactly it will function in practice, is as yet unknown.

Keep Warm, Stay Cool

If you live in rented accommodation you will have no choice about the system employed for heating water. Apartments invariably have either an electric boiler or a gas water heater installed. The disadvantage of electric boilers is that if they are small the hot water may not last for all your needs and you will have to wait for it to heat up again. Gas heaters, running off a gas bottle, provide unlimited hot water while the gas lasts. If you buy your own flat or house you can choose which system you prefer. Boilers are cheaper but as electricity is expensive the cheaper option in the long run may be to have a gas heater plumbed in, though this is initially more expensive.

Central heating is rare in older Portuguese properties, and it is surprising how cold it can get in winter, even in the south. If in rented accommodation you may have to buy some form of heating. Individual gas-powered heaters are a good option as they are cheap and usually come on rollers so may be moved from one room to another, though they do dry out the air and should not be used in a small space for too long. If you buy your property you can look at several options. A wood-burning stove is a popular one as firewood is still inexpensive in Portugal, especially in summer, when you can stock up for the coming winter. Electrical systems are used less, for reasons of cost, and are only viable if you install storage heaters to take advantage of cheaper night-time rates. Central heating systems that use bottled gas are quite common and not overly expensive to install in a small- to medium-sized property, and gas-fired underfloor heating is also popular, especially in older, renovated properties.

If you live in the south you may find air-conditioning essential rather than a luxury. Some modern properties are built with air-conditioning already installed but you cannot bank on it. The choice of air-conditioning systems is very wide and they range from small units on wheels that can be used to cool down just one room to large systems that cover a whole house. Air-conditioning systems that are not well maintained and kept clean can become a health hazard and may cause respiratory problems.

Voltage is 220 AC at 50 MHz and all plugs are of the European two-pin type. UK three-pin plugs will either need changing or an adaptor, so take a supply with you if you are going to use appliances brought from home. Electrical devices brought from the USA, running at 110 volts, will need a converter or a transformer. Some come with a 110/220 switch; check this and switch to 220 before plugging it in. Appliances that run on 240 volts might be slow or not work at all, as is the case with some televisions. You might find it is better to buy locally, as electrical devices are not especially expensive and may be better designed to fit into a Portuguese house. Washing machines and fridges, for example, come in standard dimensions and fitted kitchens are built to take them; imported appliances may not fit.

Modern houses and apartments are generally well wired and safe. Older properties may need rewiring or at least an inspection from an EDP-authorised electrician who will issue a safety certificate or recommend a new installation. Electricity is metered and the company will not authorise connection of the meter or installation of a new one if the wiring is inadequate. Check the wiring well before moving in, as it may take some time to get reconnected if it has to be replaced.

Bills come monthly and do not necessarily reflect actual consumption but are an estimate. Learn to read your electricity meter to see whether the amount you are paying roughly corresponds to the electricity consumed. The estimate should be lower though this is not always so and you might be paying over the odds. In this case, contact EDP; someone will read the meter and adjust your bill accordingly. You can pay by direct debit or through the Multibanco system (*see* p.134). Non-payment results in suspension of service. You can pay a fixed monthly sum, calculated on the previous year's average monthly consumption. The meter is read at the end of the year and you and EDP settle the difference.

Gas

Apart from Lisbon and the surrounding area, few people in Portugal have piped gas. Bottled butane (*butano*) and propane (*propano*) are widely used for cooking, heating and hot water. This option is far more economical than electricity and, if installations are inspected regularly, it is safe. Many Portuguese cookers have two or three gas burners and one electrical ring. This is useful as you can still heat something up in the event of a power cut or your gas bottle running out. An inspection is necessary before you can contract bottled gas from a local supplier; if all installations are in good condition the property will be awarded a safety certificate. Bottles (*garrafas*) may be picked up at stores or delivered to your home. On buying the first bottle you pay a deposit and from then on every time you need gas you swap an empty bottle for a full one. As they are heavy, it is worth having bottles of gas delivered, especially if you live on an upper-floor apartment without a lift. It is a good idea always to have a least one spare as you never know when it will run out on you, though predictably this happens when you are in the shower. Prices fluctuate, currently the 11k bottle for domestic use costs just over €12. Larger bottles of 45k are also available, which are especially useful if you live a long way from the nearest supply point.

Water

Water, or the lack of it, is a problem, particularly in the southern half of Portugal. Water shortages there are a fairly common occurrence as are restrictions in summer when supplies are low. As vast numbers of people visit the

Algarve every summer, water demand is highest in the country's driest region (along with the Alentejo). Swimming pools, showering tourists, golf courses and English-style lawns suck from an already insufficient supply. Restrictions or low reserves can mean that the supply is either cut off for several hours a day or that pressure is too low to enjoy a decent shower. These problems may or may not be solved by the massive £1.2 billion mega-dam project at Alqueva in the Alentejo, which politicians claim will end the region's perennial water problems, though environmentalists disagree.

If you are planning to go and live in a remote part of the country, do check with your future neighbours beforehand how frequently there are cuts in the water supply and whether you might need to have a well (*poço*) or a borehole (*furo*) to ensure your supplies. As well as this look at the option of installing a water storage tank (*depósito*) to cover your needs during dry spells.

As with electricity, on moving into a dwelling that is connected to the water supply you have to get the contract put in your own name and show identification and proof of occupancy at the town hall. Make sure the previous owner or occupier has paid all bills, otherwise you will have to. Water is metered and the cost can vary considerably from one area or even municipality to another, as in some places it is managed by the local council and in others it is supplied by private contractors. Prices have tended to rise recently, which at least had the effect of making people a little less wasteful. **Bills** are usually bi-monthly; you can pay them at the town hall, by direct debit from your bank account or via the Multibanco system (*see* p.134). As meters are not read frequently, the company often sends an estimate of water used. This is fine unless the estimate is far in excess of real consumption over a period of time. Be careful if the estimate is low, too, as when the company eventually gets around to reading the meter you could face a large bill. Keep an eye on your bills as there have been cases of overcharging. Charges are normally in three price bands – the more you use, the more you pay per cubic metre.

In Portugal, tap water varies in quality depending on where you are. Although it is usually safe to drink, it can sometimes taste unpleasant since so many chemicals are needed to purify it.

Telephones

The Portuguese telephone network has been profoundly transformed over recent years and state-of-the-art technology is in evidence. The monopoly formerly operated by Telecom Portugal has been broken up and, with new providers competing for a market share, the price of calls has started to lower.

Telecom Portugal remains the largest provider but subscribers can now use **Novis** and **Oni** for fixed telephone services. It can be difficult to choose which provider to use as it may appear that they offer much the same deal. But as they charge different rates for different types of call, get full information from all three, take a yellow marker and highlight the tariffs for the types of call you are most likely to make. Whichever provider you choose, you are not limited to using only their services, as there is a system of 'selection and pre-selection of operator'. This is a form of indirect access that allows you to choose another provider, other than your main one, for certain calls. If you make many more international than local calls, or more inter-provincial calls than international ones, it could be in your interest to use more than one operator.

Telecom Portugal's own cheap rate is 9pm–9am on weekdays, all day at weekends and public holidays. Other providers' cheap rate periods vary. If you are not happy with your own operator you can change to another without losing your number. This is called 'porting'. There are some very informative pages on these matters, in English, on the website of ANACOM (Autoridade Nacional de Comunicações), the national communications body that monitors fair competition (**www.icp.pt**).

If your new house already has a line, put it in your name. If the line is still live, arrange with the previous occupants to put it in your name as of the moving-in date to save confusion over bills. If the line is dead or there is no line at all, apply to Telecom Portugal, who still handle the physical network. You need the usual documents, proof of identity and occupancy, which may be the deeds or a rental contract. Expect connection to take between a few days and a few weeks, depending on where you are. It used to take forever, so do not despair.

Fixed Line Telephone Operators

- **Portugal Telecom**, Avenida Fontes Pereira de Melo, 40, 1069-300 Lisbon, **t** 215 002 000, **geral@telecom.pt**, **www.portugaltelecom.pt**.

- **Novis**, Apartado 42110, EC Telheiras, 1600-801 Lisbon, **t** 808 100 100 (new customers) or **t** 808 106 100 (existing customers), **info@novis.pt**, **www.ip.pt**.

- **Oni** (Lisbon): Lagoas Park, Edifício 12, 2740-269 Porto Salvo, **t** 210 005 300, customer service: 16 509, **f** 210 007 175; (Oporto): Rua de Santa Catarina, 663-1°, 4000-454 Porto, **t** 220 014 480, customer service: 16 509, **f** 220 014 470; **info@oninet.pt**, **www.onisolutions.pt**.

Telephone Numbers

Portugal has no area codes. Numbers begin with a 2 followed by eight more digits. Lisbon numbers all begin 21, Oporto numbers 2, Algarve numbers 28 and so on.

From outside Portugal dial **t** 00 351 followed by the nine-subscriber number. For emergencies of all types call **t** 112; English is often spoken. For directory enquiries, which are charged, call **t** 118. Most post offices have telephone directories for all regions of Portugal or check directory enquiries, **www.118.pt**.

For operator-assisted calls, dial **t** 177; this number, and **t** 179 is also for international enquiries. When calling abroad, dial 00 + the country code (44 for Britain, 1 for the USA, 353 for Ireland, etc.) then the area code (omit the first 0 in the UK and Ireland) and the number of the subscriber. All country codes appear in the information pages of the telephone directory.

Mobile Telephones

Over the last decade, almost all Portuguese people have joined the mobile revolution. Data published by ANACOM reveals that, as of 31 December 2003 there were some 9.34 million subscribers – in a country with a population of just over 10 million! Therefore you are just as likely to see a black-clad widow on a funicular train in Lisbon chatting away as you are to see youngsters furiously texting one another.

Call costs are still comparatively high compared with other countries, but are coming down. There are three operators in Portugal: **Optimus**, **TMN** (part of Telecom Portugal, the privatised national phone company) and **Vodafone** Portugal. It is rumoured that Stelios, the entrepreneur behind easyJet, is about to enter the mobile market with **easyMobile**, offering cheap calls via the Internet. It is not known when this service will be in operation.

All three operators have websites, but only Vodafone has information in English and that only for business clients. In general their websites are very heavy on information so you are better advised to go to a 'physical' shop and pick up the latest leaflets with details of offers, etc. Each operator's website has information on **sales points** (*pontos de venda*) throughout Portugal, so it is easy to find your nearest shop. As always, it pays to shop around and see what each has to offer. A typical initial deal might be a promotional pack including a telephone plus a certain amount of prepaid credit. You can top up credit via the Multibanco system and in many other retail outlets. Alternatively, you may choose the contract modality, whereby you are billed periodically for calls.

As with fixed lines, it is possible to use different operators for certain calls, to change the operator with whom you have contracted the service and to 'port' your number. You may not transport a telephone number of either a fixed operator to a mobile or a mobile operator to a fixed one.

Mobiles from other European countries generally work in Portugal, though make sure to activate the roaming service before travelling there.

Mobile numbers in Portugal all begin with either 91, 93 or 96.

Mobile Telephone Operators

• **Optimus**, Centro de Apoio a Clientes, Apartado 52121, 1721-501 Lisbon, customer service **t** 1693 (24hrs), from other networks **t** 93 1221 000, **f** 217

547 000, **1693@optimus.pt, www.optimus.pt** – for a list of dealers click on *'pontos de venda'*.

• **TMN**, Avenida Álvaro Pais, 2, 1649-041 Lisbon, customer service **t** 1696, **t** 217 914 400, **f** 217 914 500, **e 1696@tmn.pt, www.optimus.pt** – for a list of dealers click on *'pontos de venda'*; you can chose from 'Lojas TMN', TMN's own shops, or 'Agentes', authorised dealers.

• **Vodafone Portugal**, customer support (*apoio ao cliente*), Parque das Nações, Avenida Dom João II, Lote 1.04.01, E 101 Mez, 1990-093 Lisbon, **t** 16912, **f** 210 916 899, **apoiocliente@corp.vodafone.pt, www.vodafone.pt**. The website only has information in English for businesses but if you want to know where your nearest dealer is, go to **www.vodafone.pt/main/ shop/Onde+Estamos/Pontos+de+Venda**; click on the map on the province you are in for a full list of dealers.

Internet, Faxes, Post and Television

Internet and E-mail

E-mail is a rapid and cheap way of staying in touch for those with access to the Internet. In one e-mail you can send photographs and other documents as attachments. Those without facilities at home can use cybercafés and it is also possible to connect up at the local post office. Hotmail and Yahoo-type addresses are accessible from anywhere in the world, as are many other providers these days. The problem with these free accounts is that they do not allow you to store much information and you constantly have to clean out your in-box, especially if you receive a lot of attachments. Hotmail has recently started to offer a larger amount of storage space, for a fee, and Yahoo also now offers 6MB of storage space though users fear that this is the prelude to a paying service in the near future.

Telepac (freefone **t** 800 200 079, **www.telepac.pt**) is one of the most popular local providers in Portugal and offers the Netpac package for a reasonable rate. In addition, all the fixed telephone operators now offer Internet packages – just check their websites to see what deals they have.

It is also possible to send and receive e-mails from mobile telephones and access Internet pages from them.

Fax Machines

With the advent of e-mail, the fax machine is, for many, an outmoded form of communication, but it is still a fast, reliable way of staying in touch. If you take your own fax machine to Portugal, make sure it is compatible and that repairs and spare parts are available there, otherwise buy locally – they have come down enormously in price. Faxes may be sent from and received at post offices; charges are by the page and the distance.

If you find the service to be a little slow and cumbersome, alternative points for sending and receiving are travel agencies and stationers, who will provide the service for varying charges.

Postal Services

Portugal's postal service is by no means the best in the world but it is also far from the worst. Its modernised **post offices** now present a comfortable, user-friendly image even though the staff may be a little sluggish. There are offices of the **CTT** (Correios e Telecomunicações, **www.ctt.pt**) in practically every town and many small shops sell **stamps** (*selos*). In both cases look for the sign of the red horse carrying a rider blowing the post-horn against a white background.

n large towns and cities, post offices are usually open from either 8.30 or 9am until 7pm, from Monday to Friday and on Saturday mornings until 12.30pm. In smaller towns they may close at lunchtime between 12.30 and 2pm and may only stay open until 6pm.

The main central post office in Praça dos Restauradores in Lisbon has extended hours, until 10pm Monday to Friday and until 6pm on Saturdays and Lisbon airport has a 24hr branch.

Postcodes

If sending a letter within Portugal, you should be aware that postcodes have recently changed format. Previously they comprised four digits, now they are seven, made up of a group of four digits (the original number) followed by a dash and then another group of three, which narrows down the location for sorting purposes. New codes still respect the old ones, so '1070-065' Lisboa would have been simply 1070 before. This is just as well, as many people still do not use the full version. *See also* **Reference**, 'Postcodes', pp.241–2.

Sending Post Abroad

When sending a letter abroad you have four choices of service: *Azul Prime*, *Correio Azul*, *Correio Normal* and *Correio Económico*. Delivery times, if you read the information on the website, do not appear to differ greatly between one service and another. The standard first-class mail service is the *Correio Azul*, ('Blue Post'). With this service, mail sent to European destinations from continental Portugal and the Azores takes three, possibly four days. From Madeira it can take up to five. The website also claims that mail gets to the rest of the world in four days by *Correio Azul*, though five or six is possibly more realistic. The *Azul Prime* service is much more expensive – rates are almost double those of the normal *Correio Azul*, though the delivery times are practically the same.

The advantage of this service is the 'Track and Trace' function by which you can monitor the progress of your mail. If you post a letter in a rural area you may expect it to take a little longer. Rates are subject to occasional increases but those below were checked shortly before going to press.

Correio Azul rates are €1.75 for a letter up to 20g to Europe or anywhere else in the world. A letter weighing between 20g and 50g costs €2.35, from 50g to 100g is €2.75 and from 100g to 250g costs €3.75. Thereafter rates go up in bands by weight and from 250g the worldwide rate is higher than the European. Thus a package weighing between 250g and 500g costs €5 to Europe and €7 world-wide, and one from 500g to 1kg costs €7.50 to Europe and €13.50 to the rest of the world. *Azul Prime* rates are approximately double these. A cheaper option, not much slower, is *Correio Normal Internacional (Avião)*, airmail. CTT claims its airmail service will get letters to their destination in Europe in five days and to the rest of the world in seven. Rates for letters up to 20g to all of Europe excluding Spain are €0.56, to Spain €0.48, to the rest of the world €0.72. A fraction cheaper, but maybe not enough to warrant using it, is the *Correio Económico*. Full price tables can be consulted on the website, but only on the Portuguese-language pages. Click on the *'Preçário'* button and choose the service you need information for.

For fast, efficient communications, there are other options, namely **courier services** (*mensageiros*). Correios has its own messenger service, EMS, which is fast, inexpensive and reliable. Otherwise, most of the larger international couriers have offices in Portugal.

Courier Services in Portugal

- **DHL**, Lisbon office, t 218 100 099 (freephone), **www.dhl.pt**.
- **UPS**, t 800 205 020 (freefone), **www.ups.com/europe/pt**.
- **TNT**, t 218 545 050, **www.tnt.com/pt**.

TV, Video and DVD

If you are thinking of taking a TV, video or DVD machine to Portugal, check out first whether they are compatible. Portuguese television sets and videos function on the PAL/BG system, as does most of continental Europe, whereas British models use the PAL/I system. If they are not compatible, check to see if the equipment can be modified. You might find that it is not greatly more expensive to buy locally or across the border in Spain. That way you will also be sure of being able to find a repair service close to your home.

Many expats are not especially interested in what Portuguese TV has to offer. What they are mainly want to see is Sky and its multiple entertainment and sports channels, which include Premiership and Coca-Cola Championship football as well as matches from the lower divisions. This is a can of worms as, unfortunately, Sky is as yet not available to subscribers outside the British Isles and there is no sign that it will be in the near future. To get around this some people ask a private company to install all the necessary equipment, including a Sky digibox, and then register with Sky using the address of a friend or relative in the UK who then posts the card (which is inserted into the box and makes it work) out to them. This is, to say the least, irregular if not illegal, and if Sky were to find out they would cut you off straight away. By all accounts there are also small, UK-based companies that offer the full package, including the digibox and falsified documents. This amounts to straight fraud. In areas like the Algarve it seems there are also individuals and companies who tout pirated cards; again, this is illegal. By all accounts Sky, aware of this situation, has tried by legal and technical means to put a stop to these illegal practices but it seems that the crooks' technical capacities are keeping them a step or two ahead of the company.

The BBC no longer offers its worldwide TV services.

Money and Banking

Banks

One sector of the Portuguese economy that is representative of Portugal's transformation over the last 10 or 15 years is that of banking. Not so long ago, Portuguese banks were largely state-run dinosaurs, infamous for their inefficiency, staffed by an army of lethargic civil servants. After a period of privatisation, the only remaining **state-owned bank** is the **Caixa Geral de Depósitos (CGD)**, the country's largest financial group, which has on several occasions served as an instrument of government intervention in the economy, usually in defence against unwanted takeover bids from foreign investors. It retains this status owing to its privileged relationship with the state. Otherwise, the state's retreat from the banking sector was followed by a whirlwind of mergers and acquisitions throughout the 1990s. There are now just four main (very large) **private banks**. One of them, **Totta & Açores**, is controlled by the Spanish bank **Banco Santander Central Hispano (BSCH)**. The other three banks are **Banco Comercial Português (BCP)**, easily the largest; **Banco Espirito Santo (BES)**; and **Banco Português do Investimento (BPI)**. Between them, the CGD and the four leading private banks control over 80 per cent of retail deposits. Santander Central Hispano's aggressive entry into Portuguese banking in 1999 shattered the cosy climate in which banking traditionally operated. Further consolidation is likely in future, especially in the face of the economic downturn.

Foreign banks are also present in the Portuguese banking market, among them familiar names such as Barclay's and Citibank and another Spanish group,

The Euro

Portugal was among the first group of countries to introduce the Euro on 1 January 2002. The euro (symbol €), is now the official currency of a dozen EU countries. A euro consists of 100 cents or 'eurocents' with denominations of 1, 2 and 5 cents in copper and 10, 20 and 50 cents in brass. One-euro coins have a silver centre and a brass rim, two-euro coins are the other way round. The design on the European side of the coins is common to all, while the reverse side features a national symbol. The notes come in denominations of 5, 10, 20, 50, 100, 200 and 500 euros and are distinguishable by their colour and size. All euros are legal tender throughout the Eurozone. Portuguese prices are generally expressed with the € symbol after the amount. A full stop separates thousands and hundreds, and a comma separates euros from cents. In this book the standard British way of expressing numbers is used. So, while a Portuguese price might read 99.999,99€, it is expressed here as €99,999.99.

Banco Bilbao Vizcaya y Argentária (BBVA). Both BBVA and BSCH are themselves the result of the consolidation that has taken place in the Spanish banking sector. The sector has thoroughly modernised itself, as a look at the inside of any branch shows. No longer dark and musty, banks tend to be light and airy, with much hi-tech in evidence. Electronic and Internet banking in Portugal now compares favourably with that in other countries, and ATMs are to be found just about everywhere, including in supermarkets. The **'Multibanco' system** is an excellent innovation (*see* box overleaf), which allows card-holders with accounts held at any bank to make use of ATMs belonging to any other, without charge, anywhere in Portugal.

As a rule, banks are open 8.30–3pm although some branches in commercial and tourist areas may stay open as late as 6pm. Banks close at weekends and on public holidays.

Bank Accounts

It is possible to open one or more bank accounts in Portugal, though it is advisable to keep any account you may have had in your home country open too, even if you make little use of it. You have much to gain by banking locally, especially if you receive an income from abroad. Each person's needs are different. Pensioners settling in Portugal or anyone planning to run a business will almost certainly need a fuller and more sophisticated banking service than someone who is TEFLing or studying there for a short period. If your Portuguese is not very good you may want a bank that can offer you service in English – there are plenty in expatriate and tourist areas. If you are to receive money from abroad, even occasionally, you may care to find out how much commission the bank is likely to charge you for the operation. As a rule, Portuguese banks charge for most services.

Multiple Banking, Single Card

Many Portuguese banks, if you open an account with a minimum of €50, are willing to issue a plastic debit card called the 'Multibanco'. This card may be used in 95 per cent of all Portuguese shops and restaurants, road toll booths and payphones as well as to withdraw money from ATMs all over Portugal and throughout Europe. In the UK, Multibanco is associated with the Link ATM system, as used by Abbey, though many financial institutions will accept it. In addition, you may charge up the credit on your mobile, pay your social security contributions if you are a freelancer and pay all utilities bills such as electricity and fixed-line telephone. As it is a debit card you must have sufficient funds to cover the operation, but the beauty of the system is that if you use an ATM belonging to a different banking group from your own, you are not charged.

When you open an account you are given the card immediately and it comes, in the case of some banks, without your name embossed but with a white strip for you to put your signature. The cards also have no expiry date and thus can be used until they need replacing because of wear and tear. The card is issued with a PIN, which you can change as frequently as you like, just by inserting it into an ATM and following the instructions. Not all banks agree to giving out cards so easily; international banks for example usually insist on issuing a card that is personalised, with the name that appears on the ID shown on opening the account embossed on to the card.

The Multibanco is also available with a Visa or MasterCard facility built in. In this case, however, you will receive the PIN by post to whichever address you give the bank within 7–10 days of the card being issued. This is dependent on your having conducted your account in an acceptable manner over a period of time – so do not bounce any cheques!

The simplest and most widely used type of account is the **current account** (*conta corrente*). Cheques are still accepted fairly widely, though there are no cheque guarantee cards. It does seem that electronic banking will condemn the cheque to extinction. If you use this form of payment, make sure you have sufficient funds to cover the value of the cheque. If one bounces on you, you will be liable for stiff bank charges and three bounces will see you banned from writing cheques on any Portuguese bank for up to two years. Portuguese current accounts pay little interest, possibly about 0.1 per cent.

If you have any savings, move them into a **deposit account** (*depósito a prazo*). You can also arrange for a bank to transfer automatically the balance over a certain sum of a current account into one that pays interest. Euro-zone interest rates are currently low. Beyond this, for more sophisticated banking needs, look carefully at all the types of account available, and read the small print, as you might find that terms or conditions of use vary from account types that you are more familiar with. If your Portuguese is poor, get help. You should, in any case, ask other residents how satisfied they are with their banking arrangements.

Having decided on a bank and account type, go to the local branch and open an account. To do this you must be 18 or over. Take some form of ID – either your passport or your residency card, proof of an address in Portugal and your tax card (*cartão de contribuinte – see* **Red Tape**, 'Tax or Fiscal Card', p.91). It is easy to open an account on the spot in Portugal – easier than doing it from abroad. If you do wish to open an account from abroad, look for a branch of the bank in question in your country, ask for an application form and stipulate which Portuguese branch you wish the account to be held at.

Though a full-time resident in Portugal, you should still maintain at least one account open at home, especially if you move large sums of money between the two countries. Similarly, if you move back to your home country but keep on your Portuguese property, it is sensible to keep an account open there.

Offshore Accounts

Many expats keep offshore accounts and usually for a perfectly legitimate reason. Not all British banks, especially those that were formerly building societies, offer many facilities for moving money abroad, despite the free movement permitted under EU law. It may, quite simply, be easier to gain access to funds held in an offshore account. Others, however, assume that having an offshore leaves their money out of the clutches of the Portuguese taxman. It does not. Not declaring money held in an offshore account is a serious offence.

Taxation

Tax in Portugal, as anywhere, is complex, and the information provided here amounts to no more than basic guidelines. You are advised to seek professional help for dealing with all tax issues. As this book is written for people who wish to go and work in Portugal, only work-related income tax is dealt with here.

Who Is Liable to Pay Income Tax?

Anyone who is resident in Portugal is subject to tax on any income. Non-residents are only subject to personal income tax on income arising in Portugal – this would apply for example to foreign homeowners who rent out their property.

You are considered to be a resident in Portugal if, among other conditions, you meet one or more of the following conditions:

- **If you stay in Portugal for more than 183 days in any calendar year; these days may be in one block or in various shorter periods spread throughout the year.**

- If you have a dwelling, either owned or rented, in Portugal on 31 December of the relevant calendar year and the Portuguese tax authorities have reasonable grounds to assume that you intend to use it during the following year as your habitual residence.

- If your centre of economic interests (principal investments, business or other sources of income) is in Portugal and you spend most of your money in the country.

- If the head of the household is resident in Portugal, then you will also be assumed to be resident there unless you can convince the tax authorities of the contrary, in which case you will be assessed as a non-resident but the head of the household will be liable for taxes as a resident.

What Income is Subject to Tax?

Personal income tax (*imposto sobre o rendimento das pessoas singulares* or *IRS*) is imposed on the earned income of employed or self-employed individuals and those running a business.

Income is divided into categories: the more you earn the more you pay, both in terms of the amount and as a percentage of your income. If you are married, tax is usually assessed on the overall income of the household – the total of both of your incomes. Couples who are unmarried are generally assessed individually, as two households. Household income generally includes the income of any dependent children under the age of 18, though in certain circumstances 'dependent' can apply to children over this age.

Portugal is, overall, a comparatively high-tax society, though for many years many people, both nationals and foreigners, have managed to get away with under-declaring owing to the arcane and inefficient nature of the tax authorities. This situation is changing: the system is becoming more adept at catching those who do not declare all they should and severe penalties are imposed on those caught.

Income Tax Rates

The following personal income tax rates applied in 2003 and show the amounts that would have been paid in 2004:

Taxable Income	Rate	Cumulative Tax to Top of Band
Up to €4,182	12	€501.85
€4,182–6,325	14	€801.92
€6,325–15,683	24	€3,047.72
€15,683–35,071	34	€9,979.60
€35,071–52,277	38	€16,137.76
Over €52,277	40	€20,910.80

Deductions

You may deduct the following expenses from your gross income:

- **Any payments made to the Portuguese social security scheme.**
- **Your personal allowances or those of your family.**
- **Payments made to an ex-wife or child (alimony) as a result of matrimonial proceedings.**

Tax Credits

For 2003, taxpayers were able to credit the following against their tax liability:

- **A personal allowance of €213.96 for each single taxpayer or €178.30 for each married taxpayer.**
- **An allowance of €142.64 for each child.**
- **Mortgage interest and other housing costs in certain cases, usually up to 30 per cent of applicable amounts with a ceiling of €527.99, or rental payments made to the owner of the Portuguese residence, limited to €527.99.**
- **Health care, education and life insurance expenses up to certain limits, (30 per cent, 30 per cent and 25 per cent respectively).**
- **Personal income tax paid in another country, up to the amount that would have been paid on that income in Portugal.**

Payment of Tax Due

You will be sent a tax form in January. You must complete your tax form and submit it by the dates applicable in your case. If you have only a pension or income from employment it must be filed between 1 February and 15 March. If you have other income as well you must file your return between 16 March and 30 April. You will then be sent a tax bill – usually within two months – and you must pay it within one month. Late payment incurs a penalty.

The Double Taxation Treaty

The detailed effect of double taxation treaties (intended to avoid your being taxed twice on the same income) depends on the two countries involved. Whilst treaties may be similar in concept they can differ in detail. Only the effect of the Portugal–UK treaty is considered. This treaty dates from 1969 and covers income tax, capital gains taxes and corporation taxes. It does not specifically cover inheritance tax.

The main points of relevance to residents are:

- Any income from letting property in the UK will normally be outside the scope of Portuguese taxation and, instead, will be taxed in the UK.

- Pensions received from the UK – except for government pensions – will be taxed in Portugal but not in the UK.

- Government pensions will continue to be taxed in the UK but are neither taxed in Portugal, nor do they count when assessing the level of your income nor when calculating the rate of tax payable on your income.

- You will normally not be required to pay UK capital gains tax on gains made after you settle in Portugal except in relation to property located in the UK.

- You will pay Portuguese capital gains tax on the disposal of moveable (personal) property in Portugal.

- If you are taxed on a gift made outside Portugal then the tax paid will usually be offset against the gift tax due in Portugal.

- If you pay tax on an inheritance outside Portugal, the same will apply.

Double tax treaties need to be read in the light of personal circumstances.

Health and Emergencies

Portugal does not present any particular health risks to foreigners. The complaints most typically suffered are sunburn or sunstroke, or asthmatic and other respiratory complaints owing either to pollen, in country areas, or pollution in the larger cities. Expats, at times, consume alcohol to excess.

The Portuguese themselves are a fairly healthy nation. Statistics on longevity and coronary complaints are reasonably encouraging. This is in great part thanks to the Portuguese Mediterranean-style diet that makes much use of olive oil and garlic and in which fish, rice and salad are staples. Where the Portuguese let themselves down is through smoking, alcohol consumption and road accidents. AIDS statistics, especially in prisons and among the 15–24 age group, are also alarmingly high, the second highest in Europe. The Portuguese take less exercise on average than people in other European countries.

Most threats to health are easily avoided by being sensible: eat well, drink in moderation, smoke less or preferably not at all, take some exercise, drive carefully and avoid sun during the hottest hours of the day.

State Health Care

State-run health care, despite tangible improvements in recent years, is still deficient in many areas of Portugal. The Minister of Health described the system last year as a 'national shame' and it is certainly facing many difficulties. Waiting lists for operations are long, and thousands of patients do not have a doctor in their local health centre (*centro de saúde*), so they tend to rush off to emergency services, precisely what the introduction of health centres was designed to avoid. Stories in the press concerning medical blunders are common, as are complaints about disregard for the most basic rules of doctor–patient care. Another problem is that away from the big cities people have no choice but to use the public hospital, as private hospitals only exist where there is demand and the wealth to support them. There is also a shortage of specialists in certain important fields of medicine. This all points to imbalances in the system, as other areas are well provided for. The greater Lisbon area, for example, has five hospital beds for every thousand inhabitants, a figure that is on a par with other areas of Europe.

The government is beginning to tackle these issues, and plans to overhaul the health system are now afoot. An ambitious initiative on public–private partnerships has been launched, allowing the private sector to take part in the management, and financing of hospital units and new laws will allow for the setting-up of partnerships. The government plans to construct 10 new hospitals and to renovate and replace several others; most of the proposed new hospitals are to be built with mixed public–private funding. This programme will cost somewhere in the region of €1.6 billion. Public and private sector partnership is to be extended to other aspects of the health service. A new Hospital Bill, presented in autumn 2002, provided for state hospitals to be managed by private entities, while remaining under state ownership. Under this bill, state hospitals will be transformed into public companies and, where they have accumulated debts, creditors will be able to acquire capital in the hospital companies. Increased hospital services are also to be contracted out to the private sector, and further reforms announced include reduced waiting lists, reform of prescription procedures and the introduction of generic medicines.

Despite its defects, the system works to some extent. If you are an EU or EEA citizen you are entitled to use it, for the most part free of charge, whether you are working in Portugal or are retired, subject to certain limitations. If you find a job you will be issued with a **Livrete de Assistência Médica** either by your local health centre, the regional centre (*administracões regionais de saúde*) or directly by your employer. If you are not working, but living on a pension or your own means and have paid insurance contributions into your own country's system, you have the same rights as a Portuguese person.

Private Health Care

Given the problems faced by the state-run system, many foreign residents choose to use private health facilities. There are plenty of these facilities in areas where expats concentrate. It is not difficult to find English-speaking doctors or

Essential Vocabulary for Health and Emergencies

arm *braço*	skin *pele*
back *costa*	stomach *estômago*
chest/breast *peito*	teeth *dentes*
chin *queixo*	throat *garganta*
ears *ouvidos*	tongue *língua*
elbow *cotovelo*	ambulance *ambulância*
eyes *olhos*	bandage box *caixa de adesivo*
feet *pés*	bandages *ligaduras*
fingers *dedos*	blanket *cobertor*
hair *cabelo*	dentist *dentista*
hair *pêlos*	doctor *médico/a*
hands *mãos*	drugs *medicamento*
head *cabeça*	elastoplast *penso rápido*
heart *coração*	fire station *quartel dos bombeiros*
intestines *intestinos*	glasses *óculos*
kidneys *rins*	health centre *centro de saúde*
knee *joelho*	illness/disease *doença*
leg *perna*	injured *ferido*
lips *lábios*	medical post *posto clínico*
liver *fígado*	nurse *enfermeiro/a*
lungs *pulmões*	patient *doente*
muscle *músculo*	pharmacy *farmácia*
nails *unhas*	police *polícia*
nose *nariz*	prescription *receita*

I have a pain in my head/teeth/ears/spine/heart *Tenho uma do de cabeça/dentes/ouvidos/coluna/coração*
I am pregnant *Estou grávida*
I am ill *Estou doente*
Call a doctor/ambulance/the fire brigade/the police *Chame um médico/uma ambulância/os bombeiros/a polícia*
There has been an accident *Houve um acidente*
He/she is losing blood *Ele/ela está a perder sangue*
Somebody is drowning *Está uma pessoa a afogar-se*
They stole my bag *Roubaram-me a mala*
I broke my glasses *Parti os meus óculos*
I found this in the road *Achei isto na rua*

dentists and there are a good many practices, clinics and even small hospitals that exist to cater for the resident and temporary foreign population. There are also plenty of specialists in other areas such as physiotherapy, psychotherapy, aromatherapy, homeopathic medicine and even Reiki, many of whom advertise in English-language newspapers and magazines. There are rehab clinics for alcohol- and drug-abusers and the Algarve has several health farms for those wanting to lose weight, clean out their system.

You can take out private health insurance to cover the costs. Shop around and see what different companies can offer. Look closely at the small print. You may find that some services are not available for six months and that only basic treatment is covered in the period immediately after taking out the insurance. Many companies specialise in policies for foreign residents, including:

- **BUPA International**, BUPA House, 15–19 Bloomsbury Way, London WC1A 2BA, **t** (01273) 208181, **www.bupa-intl.com**.

- The **Exeter Friendly Society**, Lakeside House, Emperor Way, Exeter EX1 3FD, **t** 0808 055 6575, **www.exeterfriendly.co.uk**. This company has a policy called Interplan Euro which is tailor-made for the expatriate living in Spain or Portugal for a minimum of 180 days a year.

- **PPP Healthcare** (allied with the AXA group), Phillips House, Crescent Road Tunbridge Wells, Kent TN1 2PL UK, **t** (01892) 503856, **f** (01892) 503189, **www.ppphealthcare.com**.

Emergencies

The best way of dealing with emergencies is being prepared. Emergency services may be better or worse equipped and faster or slower to respond, depending on where you are. In major cities and tourist areas they tend to be better. One telephone number worth knowing is **t** 112, which serves for the fire brigade (*bombeiros*), the ambulance service (*ambulância*) or the police (*polícia*). Ask for the appropriate service. English is often spoken but you cannot guarantee this, so learn at least those three words and enough Portuguese to describe your location, say your address and explain, however basically, your problem.

It also helps if you learn the words and phrases that relate to any condition you might be suffering from, particularly if this is likely to take a turn for the worse at any given moment. You can learn them off by heart and practise your spiel regularly. The more remote your house, the more important this is. If you have friends and good neighbours that you know you can count on in an emergency, keep their telephone numbers visible, close to your own phone. Most private health schemes also have a number that you can call in emergencies.

Social Services and Welfare Benefits

People can qualify for welfare benefits in one of three ways – by enforced reciprocal EU–EEA rules, under the rules of the country where they pay social security contributions or under the rules of the country where they are living.

The General EU Rules

The basic idea behind the EU–EEA rules is that persons exercising their right to move from one EU–EEA state to another should not lose out on their welfare benefit rights by doing so. The people covered by the EU–EEA rules are:

- **Employed and self-employed nationals of EU–EEA states.**
- **Pensioners who are nationals of EU–EEA states.**
- **Subject to certain restrictions, members of the families of the above, whatever their nationality.**
- **Civil servants of EU–EEA states and members of their families, provided they are not covered by an enhanced scheme for civil servants in their own country. This is generally not a problem for UK civil servants.**

Note that the EU–EEA rules do not cover the economically inactive (people retired early, students, etc.). The rules cover:

- **Sickness and maternity benefits.**
- **Accidents at work.**
- **Occupational diseases.**
- **Invalidity benefits.**
- **Old-age pensions.**
- **Widows and other survivors benefits.**
- **Death grants.**
- **Unemployment benefits.**
- **Family benefits.**

The rules do not replace national benefits that you might qualify for, but co-ordinate the national schemes. They decide in which country you should make a claim and which country's social security system should foot the bill.

The other main principle at work here is that normally you should be subject to the individual rules of one country at any one time. That is, the law of one country cannot take away or reduce your entitlement to any benefit just because you reside in another member state. If you are still entitled, say, to a UK benefit while living in Portugal, you can still be paid, either by the benefit authorities where you live, on behalf of your own country's authority, or directly by your own country's benefit authority.

If you are living and working in Portugal and making **social security payments**, either as an employee or a self-employed worker, you become entitled to a series of benefits that Portuguese workers themselves enjoy, with no discrimination. The system covers health care (including sickness and maternity leave), workplace accidents, unemployment, old age, invalidity and death (survivor's pensions). But be aware that, as wages are low in Portugal, benefits are correspondingly not especially generous. Entitlement to the full range of benefits is not immediate as you must have accumulated 180 days of paid work over the 12 months before being made unemployed in order to qualify for unemployment benefit (*subsídio social de desemprego*), which pays a paltry amount, between 80 per cent and 100 per cent of the minimum wage. You must have worked 540 days of paid work in the 24 months before unemployment to be entitled to income-related unemployment benefit at around 65 per cent of your previous salary.

These benefits, as well as sick leave and maternity leave, are covered more fully in **Working in Portugal**. Information, in English, on a whole series of welfare questions in Portugal is available in English on the EURES website. Go to **http://europa.eu.int/eures/main.jsp**. Click first on 'living & working', then 'select a country' (Portugal) and click on 'living and working conditions'. There are extensive notes on all aspects of the social security system. You need to double check with the social security office in Portugal if this information is still valid.

Previous contributions made into any other EU country's system (and that of other countries with which Portugal has reciprocal agreements) usually count towards benefit entitlement in Portugal, but this is complicated since it involves liaison between the social security systems of two (or more) countries. The general, underlying, principle is that if there is a single market with free movement of labour, then benefits accumulated as a result of that labour and the entitlement thereto must be transferable within the common European space. In practice, it is not so simple and the bureaucracy involved can be slow.

However, there are many cases of EU citizens who, having worked for many years in their own country, and then in Portugal, have become eligible for Portuguese unemployment benefit for the maximum duration permitted and others who have finished their working life in Portugal and become entitled to a full pension based partially on their previous contributions. The system does work, if slowly.

For information on your contributions record from work performed in the UK, contact the **Inland Revenue**, National Insurance Contributions Office, Benton Park View, Newcastle upon Tyne NE98 1ZZ.

Retirement and Pensions

Many expatriates living in Portugal are retired, having never worked in Portugal, and receive their pensions from their home countries. There are many reasons why retired people are attracted to Portugal, especially the (until now) relatively low living costs, the (also until now) affordable properties and the weather. Portugal's climate allows for a healthier, more relaxed lifestyle including the possibility of doing something active in the open air (golf, swimming, gardening, walking) almost year-round. The relatively lower cost of living, though, is something to be considered carefully, as Portugal is no longer *that* cheap.

Pensions

In Portugal the retirement age is generally 65 for men and 60 for women, and workers are usually entitled to a pension if, on reaching that age, they have completed at least 15 years of work, either continuously or over separate periods. Nowadays there are schemes to encourage early retirement, meaning, for example, that workers who reach the age of 55 and have 30 calendar years of registered employment completed can opt to retire on a reduced pension. The long-term unemployed may also be eligible as may those belonging to certain other groups of workers. As far as EU workers goes, the same rules apply. If you meet the requirements after working in Portugal you should qualify for a pension. If you reach retirement age while working in Portugal, having worked in the UK or other EU countries previously, contributions made there should in theory count towards your pension rights in Portugal. Be aware that in Portugal, as elsewhere, the model on which the pension system is based is currently in crisis and its future is uncertain.

UK (and other EU) state pensions can be paid directly into a Portuguese bank account. The same applies to most company pensions unless there are any stipulations to the contrary. In these cases you can in any case make arrangements for the money to be transferred from the receiving bank at home. Even non-EU citizens can receive their pension in Portugal, something that opens the door to obtaining residency. With sufficient means you can live – and spend your money in the local economy – but do not compete with locals in the job market, so you are welcome.

If you receive a pension from abroad, look carefully into payment arrangements. Banks sometimes charge for transferring money abroad, and the receiving bank may also apply a commission – this is against EU regulations – so shop around. Monthly payments may be subject to proportionally higher transfer charges than quarterly ones, making the latter option more attractive. You might even consider making an annual arrangement with a currency dealer whereby the dealer sends you the money at an exchange rate that will apply for the whole year. This provides assured income, but exchange rate fluctuations could mean you lose out.

Anybody residing for more than 183 days per year in Portugal is liable to taxation on their worldwide income. A UK state pension is not taxable in the UK but may be considered income in Portugal, and therefore taxed. Seek advice about your position. UK government pensions are always taxed in the UK, no matter where you are resident, so in order not to pay tax again in Portugal, or to get it reimbursed if you do, contact the **Inland Revenue**, Inspector of Funds, Lynwood Road, Thames Ditton, Surrey KT7 ODP. You can obtain forms from this office, in English and Portuguese, to claim exemption from UK tax. Take both forms to the *Finanças* (Portuguese Inland Revenue); one will be stamped for return to Inland Revenue in the UK, showing that tax has been paid in Portugal.

As not everyone receives income solely from pensions, the problem of double taxation arises, especially during your first year's residency in Portugal. This is because to be exempt from paying tax in the UK you have to be absent for a full year and there is an overlap period between the UK tax year (6 April to 5 April) and Portuguese tax year (the calendar year). Your income may be taxable – and taxed – in both countries. Arrangements can be made to avoid this: for all enquiries concerning double taxation contact **HM Inspector of Taxes**, Public Department 2, Management Unit 2, Ty Glas Road, Llanishen, Cardiff CF14 5XS, **t** (029) 2032 5000, **f** (029) 2032 6342.

If you have not yet retired and move to Portugal, whether you intend to work or not, your UK pension entitlement is frozen. Depending on the number of years' contributions made, you may or may not become eligible to a UK pension on reaching retirement age. To make sure that you are entitled for a UK pension you can make additional payments from Portugal. The decision of whether to continue to make UK payments is an important one – seek advice from the **Inland Revenue**, National Insurance Contributions Office, Benton Park View, Newcastle upon Tyne NE98 1ZZ.

Other useful sources of information are the following websites: **www.dwp. gov.uk** and **www.thepensionservice.gov.uk**.

Inheritance and Wills

Inheritance tax is paid in Portugal on the value of any assets in Portugal as at the date of your death. This includes real estate, cars and boats registered in Portugal and shares registered in Portugal.

The tax is an inheritance tax rather than, as in the UK, an estate tax. That means the tax is calculated by reference to each individual's inheritance rather than on the basis of the estate as a whole. Thus, two people each inheriting part of the estate will each pay their own tax. Even if they each inherit the same amount, the tax they pay may be different, depending on their personal circumstances.

All of the assets will have to be declared for the purposes of UK taxation. Again, double taxation relief will apply so you will not pay the same tax twice. UK tax is not further considered in this book.

The overall value of the part of the estate you inherit is calculated in accordance with guidelines laid down by the tax authorities. Assets are generally valued as at the date of the death. This valuation is declared by the person who inherits but can be challenged by the tax authorities. The death must be declared to the tax office within 30 days if the deceased lived in the area; 60 days if the person lived elsewhere in Portugal; and 180 days if the person lived overseas – e.g. in the UK. The deceased's assets must be listed and declared within 60 days of notification. The amount due can be paid at once or by instalments – but in that case interest is then charged on the amount due. Any debts (including mortgage or overdraft) are deducted from the assets' value as are

medical bills and funeral costs. The tax payable depends, in part, on the amount you inherit and in part on your relationship to the deceased.

Think seriously and take expert advice before making a will, as there are numerous factors related to inheritance. It is far too complex an issue to deal with fully here. Portuguese people cannot dispose of their property as they please when they die. Certain groups of people, family members and so on, have an almost automatic claim on their share of the inheritance. However, expatriates in Portugal can dispose of their wills more or less in accordance with their own country's law. It is much more expensive to implement a UK will than a Portuguese will, so it is worth making a Portuguese will. Disposing of estates by means of UK wills is often a tax disaster in Portugal.

You are strongly recommended to seek the advice of a Portuguese lawyer before making any will, as well as a lawyer in whatever country where you may also have assets. Whatever you do, do not fail to make a will, as dying intestate will bring much confusion and many costs for your heirs.

Shopping

As Portugal's purchasing power increased after the country's entry into the European Union, so did the range of opportunities available for spending that hard-earned cash. Only a couple of decades or so ago, shopping was a very low-key affair in this country, as indeed it still is outside the main urban centres. There were few supermarkets and even fewer chains, boutiques were a rarity, fashion chains were almost non-existent and delis were practically an unknown concept. Portugal was certainly not a place to look for trendy clothes, wacky designer household objects or gourmet food products.

Much has changed, though, in the last 15 years. Many Portuguese people, and foreign residents too, have adopted 'shopping' as a leisure activity as opposed to the necessary action of buying something that one needs. Retail therapy has reached Portugal, and the changes are not only evident in the amounts people spend, or what they buy, but also in the places they go to do it. Large, gleaming shopping malls have sprouted like mushrooms in Lisbon and in other main cities. The, mainly young and newly affluent consumer class proudly see them as signs of Portugal's progress. In Lisbon, many shops that are now household names in neighbouring Spain, such as Zara, the boutique chain, and the Corte Inglés department store, are now well established, and international chains such as FNAC, the French book, video, DVD and music giant, have arrived too, as have Blockbuster video-rental stores. Predictably, high street names that are familiar in Britain and the rest of Europe will most likely be dotted all over Lisbon and other large cities within a few years.

As well as this, some of the larger food retail chains that are commonplace in the rest of Europe have penetrated into the Portuguese market – Lidl, Auchan,

Na Loja – In the Shop

Although it is possible to buy practically anything and everything you could need in the shopping malls found in the larger cities, there are still many traditional, single-product establishments where service may be irritatingly slow and no change available for notes larger than €50 but where you will get a feel of shopping the way it used to be... Use these places if you don't like the shopping malls.

antiguidades antique shop	*manteigaria* grocery store or dairy
barbearia barber's	*mercearia* grocer's
charcutaria pork seller	*padaria* bakery or bread shop
confeitaria sweet shop	*papelaria* stationer's
ervanária herbalist	*pastelaria* cake shop
farmâcia chemist	*sapataria* shoe shop
livraria bookshop	*talho* butcher
loja shop (in general)	

Carrefour and Continente are among them – and competing with them are the Brazilian chain Pão de Açucar and the local Pingo Doce group. As more people own and use cars, these chains have set up out-of-town hypermarkets. This phenomenon has changed many people's shopping habits but has also caused damage to town centres, where smaller traders have suffered from the new competition. It is much more common nowadays for middle-class families to do a big weekly or fortnightly shop and bring it all home in the car than to use the local smaller shops.

In addition, wherever large expatriate communities are to be found there is an increasing number of shops either run by foreigners or enterprising locals that cater to their needs and tastes. It is much less difficult these days to find Marmite, proper teabags, books in English and good jam. For foreign residents, large chains, super and hypermarkets and malls all make for relatively trouble-free shopping, as most of the time no communication is necessary, so language skills are not put to the test.

Small Shops

All these changes, however, only make up part of the story. Shopping in Portugal tends to fit into two extremes, which are worlds apart. Despite the arrival of big names and chains, well over half of all retail trading in Portugal is still in the hands of small, family-run businesses. As a result, in any town or city of a certain size, shoppers will usually find a fascinating, hugely varied range of quirky little shops that sell the same specialised goods and services that they have for generations. Owing to lease laws that allow many small shopkeepers to continue paying laughably low rents, traditional shops have been able to survive in what would otherwise be an impossibly competitive environment.

Thus, those with a sense of adventure or curiosity will find any number of establishments where shopping can be a fun experience, if at times a taxing one. Customer care is a concept that has yet to take root in Portugal and when shopping in smaller establishments you may have to wait while the shopkeeper holds a conversation with a regular customer or finishes reading the newspaper. You can normally attract their attention by politely saying '*faz favor*' but do not expect them to jump to attention or greet you with the forced smile that UK and American shop assistants are trained to put on. Once you get used to this, you learn to accept it as part of the way of life.

Among the many traditional establishments you will find cobblers, salt-cod vendors, haberdashers, herbalists, bespoke tailors, *charcuteries*, *pâtisseries*, numismatists, ceramics and tile dealers, specialised liquor shops and a whole more besides, making for a rich shopping experience. As well as these, in Lisbon and Oporto you are likely to find plenty of small boutiques, jewellery and accessories shops and others catering to the clubbing fraternity which have a funky vibe all of their own. Many even have DJs on the premises.

When shopping in small establishments your language skills will be tested but traditional shopkeepers are usually patient with daft foreigners and appreciative of even the most fumbled attempts at speaking their language. You are more likely to come across English-speaking assistants in trendy boutiques, but do not assume this will be the case. The fun of shopping away from the big stores is that you will find items that are simply unobtainable elsewhere and get a glimpse of the real Portugal.

The Market

Aside from shopping in stores, either big or small, another way of getting a feel of the 'real' Portugal is to go to the market (*o mercado*). Markets are a fundamental part of Portuguese life and are usually colourful, boisterous and fun and definitely worth visiting whether you end up buying anything or not. There are covered, permanent markets in most towns and cities, open on all shopping days and selling fresh produce that is often better-priced and more appetising than the polystyrene- and plastic-wrapped goods on offer in supermarkets, even though much of Portugal's best fruit and vegetables are exported.

Apart from food you will find a range of other products including clothing, footwear, kitchenware, textiles, ceramics, music on CD or tape, fresh flowers and house plants and pottery. New and second-hand books, antiques (and plenty of junk!), old postcards, furniture, live animals and fake designer-label clothes may also be found in markets.

In some regions there are markets on only one or two days of the week, though you are likely to find the same traders and goods in the next town on another day, as they move around a lot. Local tourist offices usually provide information about market days in the different towns and villages in the region.

Opening Hours and Ways of Paying

Shopping hours vary depending on the place and on the type of establishment. Traditional shops and supermarkets in urban areas tend to be open 9–1 and 3–7, but exact times vary. Small, family-run businesses often do not open on Saturday afternoons. Larger shops, hypermarkets and shopping malls often stay open throughout the lunch hour and until much later in the evening, perhaps until 10pm. Many also open on Sundays. Designer boutiques and club-wear shops, on the other hand, often do not open in the morning at all, preferring an afternoon start and trading until as late as midnight. Markets are usually a morning affair, particularly the one-day travelling village markets, but some also open in the afternoons much like normal shops.

Credit and debit cards are widely accepted in larger stores, hypermarkets and shops that do a lot of tourist trade. In smaller shops and markets expect to pay in cash and try to have the right amount of change or at least only small denomination notes. Anything bigger than €50 might be beyond the capacity of the little trader's till.

Shopping across the Border

Portugal is not considered to be one of Europe's better countries for shopping, though that may not matter to you unless you are an inveterate consumer. If you live in the south or in a rural area and find the shopping experience parochial or limited, you can always go to Lisbon, or to Sevilla across the border in Spain, where there is a variety of shops and goods to suit most needs.

Consumer goods such as cameras, TVs, videos, DVDs, stereos and electrical appliances are cheaper than they were but are still more expensive than in many other EU countries. Although the purchasing power of the Portuguese has risen in recent years, it is still not high enough to attract the range of goods at prices expatriates might expect in their own countries. But it is still possible to get the electrical goods and gadgets necessary for the average home locally, especially since they are guaranteed not to be incompatible. Another option is to go to Gibraltar. Many do, to stock up on products that they miss from home and are hard to find in Portugal or Spain, like certain brands of tea, bacon or marmalade.

Traditional Portuguese Products

Probably the best buys in Portugal are locally made craft products – every region, town and village has something unique. Ceramics, tiles, porcelain, wickerwork, embroidery, glasswork, wrought-iron, hand-woven fabrics, leather goods and an almost infinite array of artisan-made products are available just about anywhere. They are ideal as gifts and for giving a local touch to your home décor.

Food and Drink

Eating out in Portugal is delightful, both for the taste buds and the pocket. Food is generally good and inexpensive. Mealtimes are later than in northern Europe: lunch is served from 1 to 3pm and dinner between 8pm and midnight, though 10pm is more to be expected outside of major cities or tourist areas. Quick snacks are available throughout the day in bars and cafeterias.

Eating Out

Restaurants vary in quality. At the most modest end of the range are *tascas*, small, family-run taverns where, despite paper tablecloths and chipped crockery, service is invariably friendly and the food simple but wholesome. Then there are designer restaurants that would hold their own in any major capital. Most come somewhere between these extremes.

International cuisine is increasingly offered in major cities and tourist areas, so pasta, pizza, curry, hamburgers, Tex-Mex and junk food are always available for those not prepared to dine on Portuguese cuisine.

On arrival in a typically Portuguese restaurant, several unordered snacks await you – usually bread rolls (*pão*), a pat of butter (*manteiga*), some little cheeses (*queijinhos*), slices of spicy sausage (*chouriço*) or olives (*azeitonas*). You pay for these starters whether you wanted them or not, but they do make a welcome entrée, especially with a glass of wine. Main courses are served in generous portions, accompanied by rice or potatoes, greens and a salad. In cheaper restaurants this may be meat, rice *and* potatoes! Traditional restaurants still offer a starter, a fish course and then a meat dish plus sweet – great if you can manage it. *Nouvelle cuisine* does not work well in Portugal, as portions are rarely minimalist. If you find portions too large, ask for a half portion, *uma meia dose*, a legitimate request that is usually respected.

Service is not generally charged in simpler cafés and restaurants, though by paying for the starters you effectively pay a form of cover charge. **Tipping** is at the discretion of the diner; 10 per cent is generally accepted to be about right.

Fish and seafood, predictably, figure largely in Portuguese cuisine (*cozinha portuguesa*). Probably the most typical of all fish served is cod (*bacalhau*), for which, they say, 365 different recipes exist. This is certainly an exaggeration but there are many. One of the most common ways of preparing fish – especially cod but also sardines (*sardinhas*) and a type of bream (*dourada*) – is to salt it and grill it. Also found frequently on the menu, battered, fried or baked as appropriate, are red mullet (*salmonetes*), tuna steaks (*atum*), swordfish (*espadarte*), sole (*linguado*), grouper (*garoupa*), which is like bream but better, and scabbard (*peixe de espada*). Seafood-lovers are spoilt for choice, especially when close to the coast. Look out for crabs (*caranguejos*), shrimps (*camarões*), cuttlefish (*chocos*), clams (*ameijoas*), barnacles (*perceves*), squid (*lulas*), prawns (*gambas*) and, of course, lobsters (*lagostas*).

Carnivores also fare well and there is never a lack of choice, though **meat** is prepared with less flair than fish. Steaks – veal, beef or pork – often come simply grilled or done on a hot plate with little or no condiments. They can be livened up with some *piri-piri*, a chilli sauce originally from the former colony of Timor. It goes especially well with chicken (*frango*), which figures on menus almost everywhere. Chicken is best barbecued (*no churrasco*) or grilled (*na grelha*); some restaurants specialise in this and very little else. Beef can be tough and not overly tasty, but pork is usually good. Recommended is pork with clams (*porco à alentejana*), from the Alentejo region. Another scrumptious regional variety is roast suckling pig (*leitão assado*), from the Bairrada area but found everywhere. Lamb is generally very good indeed and plain, grilled ribs, *costoletas*, are the most common way of serving it up, but look out for it in the hearty *ensopado* stew. Roasted kid (*cabrito*) is a great delicacy, but the animal must be slaughtered very young to be savoured at its best.

Soups (*sopas*) and **stews** (*ensopados*) in Portugal are cheap, tasty, wholesome and filling. *Caldo verde* is a standard, a broth made from cabbage and potato, sometimes with chunks of ham. A classic found on many menus is *sopa à alentejana*, a garlic and bread soup served with a poached egg. *Cozido à portuguesa* is a stew with various meats, sausages and cabbage and *feijoada* is a bean stew that comes with either meat, seafood or snails.

Portuguese **desserts** (*sobremesas*) are very good, and the range of sticky, gooey, high-calorie puddings and cakes is bewildering. Typically you find rice pudding (*arroz doce*), custard (*leite creme*), caramel pudding (*pudim*) and chocolate mousse (*mousse de chocolate*), which can be excellent. There are also the exotically named 'nun's belly' (*barriga de freira*), a dessert of breadcrumbs, sugar, eggs and nuts, 'camel drool' (*baba de camelo*), made of egg yolks and sugar and 'pork fat from heaven' (*toucinho do céu*), made of almonds, eggs and sugar. Otherwise try **cheese** (*queijo*), of which there are many varieties like *queijo de ovelha*, ewe's cheese (*queijo fresco*), cottage cheese or *requeijão*, similar to ricotta. If none of this appeals, ask for fresh fruit; most restaurants have a fruit of the day or two.

Vegetarians may fare less well in Portugal, except in tourist areas where restaurants now realise that not *everybody* eats meat or fish. In traditional restaurants you may have to make do with a salad and some cheese, or possibly eggs in some form. Vegetarians usually do better in an Indian, Chinese or Italian restaurant if there is no specifically veggie establishment to be found. Vegans, needless to say, have an even rougher time.

Breakfast – *O Pequeno Almoço*

The Portuguese name for breakfast (*pequeño almoço*), means, as in French, 'little lunch'. For many Portuguese people breakfast is the time for a caffeine hit before work. If you want to take breakfast outside of your home, make for a café

Tasty All Over

Wherever you go in Portugal, the food is good. The country's tremendous geographic and cultural diversity is expressed through its cuisine; every region has something unique.

Alentejo cooking is famous throughout Portugal – many *Lisboetas* drive there at weekends just to eat lunch. Popular local dishes are pork cooked with clams (*porco à alentejana*) and garlic soup (*sopa à alentejana*). Excellent too are kid stew (*ensopado de cabrito*) and rabbit fried in olive oil (*coelho frito*). Bread and cheese provide a simple but satisfying meal – try goat's cheese from Alandroal or ewe's cheese from Serpa, Nisa or Évora. Cakes and pastries here take some beating, especially those from the convents in Portalegre and Beja.

Junk food and bland 'international cuisine' are readily available in the **Algarve**, but the region's specialities are well worth trying for anyone who would like to explore something new. Among them are seafood soups (*sopas de marisco*), Lagos-style octopus on the grill (*polvo na grelha*) and grilled squid or cuttlefish (*lulas grelhadas* or *chocos grelhados*). There are also lots of fig and marzipan pastries, shaped like little animals or fruits.

Lisbon has food from all over Portugal but its own, simple, honest cuisine is worth paying attention to, especially grilled sardines and mackerel. The region produces many cheeses, the best is from Azeitão, a particularly tangy cheese – eat it when still runny. For the sweet-toothed, the custard tarts (*pasteis de nata*) from Belém are a taste of heaven.

Costa de Prata cooking is enriched by fresh fish and seafood, like the popular fish stew (*caldeirada*) and eel (*caldeirada de enguias*) from Aveiro. Meat dishes are good too – grilled pork kebab (*espetada de porco*) made in Barraida and kid

or pastry shop (*pastelaria*). There you will find a basic continental-style breakfast on offer: coffee with a croissant or similar type of pastry. Custard tarts (*pasteis de nata*) are delicious and found everywhere, but are only for the sweet-toothed. Coffee comes in many sizes and forms but at breakfast time a *galão*, a large, milky coffee, is often preferred or, failing that, a simple *café com leite*, white coffee. For an early-morning kick-start, try a *bica*, small, strong and best drunk sweet. For a solid, English-style breakfast, many cafeterias in tourist areas do the full fried works and these days many places cater to foreign breakfasting habits, providing cereals, fruit juice and toast with marmalade or jam.

Lunch – O Almoço

Many Portuguese people lunch out rather than at home, and in all towns and cities many establishments offer *almoços* or *comidas*. Many are not restaurants *per se* but taverns (*tascas*), *cafetarias*, beer houses (*cervejarias*), or specialised fish and seafood establishments known as *marisquerias*. *Casas de pasto*, a dying breed, are cheap dining rooms offering a set three-course menu only at casserole (*chanfana*) from Coimbra. Nearly every town has its own pastries and cakes, generally sweet, though an interesting savoury option is the bean-paste cake (*pastéis de feijão*) from Torres Vedras.

The further north, the heartier the cuisine. In the **Costa Verde** there is a classic cabbage and potato broth (*caldo verde*), cod prepared in many different ways, pork fillets (*rojões*), duck (*pato*) with rice, and octopus (*à margarida da praça*). Also try roasted kid (*cabrito assado*) and the famous Oporto-style tripe (*tripas à moda do Porto*).

Inland, in **Montanhas**, stout food accompanies the harsh climate. Try *alheirãs*, veal and bread sausages from Bragança, particularly popular in the winter, and *feijoada à transmontana*, a bean stew from Vila Real. The meat loaf (*bola de carne*) from Lamego is the region's best-known dish. Excellent too is smoked ham (*presunto*) and young partridges (*perdizes*) from Pinhel. Offal-lovers should try *maranhos*, lamb and chicken giblets with rice, and *morcelas*, blood sausages. Don't forget to try the famous ewe's cheese, *Queijo da Serra*, from the demarcated cheese region of Serra da Estrela.

Offshore Portugal offers many specialities, too. In Madeira there are veal kebabs (*espetadas*), tuna fish steaks (*atum*) and excellent swordfish (*espada*). Honeycake (*bolo de mel*) is a Madeira classic and local tropical fruits are excellent. There are also Madeira wines to try. Azorean cuisine consists largely of grilled fish but there are also original dishes like the 'Holy Ghost' soup, made of beef and vegetables, bass (*robalo*), octopus stew with wine sauce, yam with pork sausages (*linguiças*) and the famous stew (*cozido das furnas*) from São Miguel, which simmers in a pot for 5 or 6hrs in the hot lava of the Furnas Valley. A good, tangy, Cheddar-like cheese is São Jorge, from the island of the same name.

lunchtime. Always worth looking at for a budget option is the *ementa turística*, which does not mean 'tourist menu' but the set meal of the day, usually consisting of two courses with a couple of choices for each plus beer or wine. Going *à la carte* (*à lista*) can be much pricier, especially as everything consumed, requested or not, is charged.

Dinner – *O Jantar*

Served from about 7.30 or 8pm, dinner may be as small and snacky or as Pantagruelian as your system can take. Generally speaking, the *ementa turística* is not served for dinner, and it is more common to go *à lista*.

Snacks between Meals

Bars, cafés, cafeterias and *pastelarias* present a wide range of options for snacking either between or as an alternative to meals especially if you are not feeling up to a blow-out. The classic Portuguese snack is the *prego no pão*, a steak sandwich, which may also come with a fried egg. If a simple steak between bread seems a little bland, ask for some *piri-piri* sauce to liven it up. In Madeira the steak is marinated in this sauce and garlic too.

There are many deep-fried snacks too, such as *rissóis*, a kind of meat patty or rissole, *pastéis de bacalhau*, cod fish cakes and you may see some familiar-looking triangular things which are called *somousas*, fruit of Portugal's historical colonial links with the Indian sub-continent. Sandwiches (*sandes*) of every type are available on demand, commonly filled with cheese (*queijo*), often the bland, processed variety, ham (*fiambre*) or cured ham (*presunto*), which is much tastier. A *sande mista* is a toasted sandwich with ham and cheese.

Drinks

Wine

Portugal produces a great deal of wine but exports relatively little. Everybody has heard of the fortified port and madeira wines, the light *vinho verde* (green wine) and Mateus rosé. Portuguese wine, though, remains a subject for those in the know or who live there.

Except at the very cheapest end of the range it is difficult to find noticeably poor wines, though cheap reds are usually better than similarly priced whites. There is generally something to suit all budgets. Table wines as served in most medium-priced restaurants are mostly drinkable and sometimes very good. In cheaper restaurants, red wine may come chilled, which may be a way of disguising its mediocrity or just disrespect for a decent wine. As everywhere else, most meat dishes are accompanied by red wine (*vinho tinto*), while white wine (*vinho branco*) goes with fish. However, the Portuguese recommend drinking red with cod as the strong flavour of the fish may overpower the taste of a delicate white. Rosé wine (*vinho rosado*) has its defenders and its detractors, but if quite dry can make for a very refreshing accompaniment for either meat or fish.

Portugal has over 20 recognised wine-producing regions, and taste and quality is wide-ranging. One region that enjoys a certain fame in international circles, thanks to the efforts of a handful of top producers, is Dão. This small area in central Portugal produces deeply coloured, full-bodied reds that have been likened to Burgundy wines. Whites from here are also notably aromatic and fruity. Nearby is Bairrada, another leading wine-producing region. Bairrada reds are smooth, deep-coloured and full-bodied; the whites are also quite robust but fruity, holding their own when accompanying strong-tasting food, and the rosés are fresh and fruity. Sparkling wines from here range from medium-dry to *brut*. Further north, inland from Oporto, is the Douro region, famed for port (*see* below) but nowadays in the business of producing table reds with personality and some lovely, fresh, fruity whites.

South of Oporto, in the Minho region, *vinho verde* is made. '*Verde*' refers not to the colour but to the age. These wines are very young and there are actually *vinhos verdes tintos, brancos* and *rosados*. Lower in alcohol content, *vinhos verdes* are light and refreshing, especially the slightly sparkling whites, which can slip down just a little too easily!

The Estremadura region, inland between Leiria and Lisbon, produces light, easy-to-drink lower-priced wines plus some top quality ones. Further inland from Estremadura, northeast of Lisbon and touching on the Alentejo is the Ribatejo region, which produces some excellent reds that are tannic while still young but become full-bodied and slightly spicy after five years. The Alentejo itself, almost a third of all of Portugal's wine-producing area, has had some tough years owing to drought, but there are many small producers who are currently making some of the country's most palatable reds. The Algarve makes more reds than whites and they tend to be robust, richly fruity and high in alcohol content.

Port

Port wine became popular in England in the late 17th century when imports of French wines were banned (1679–85 and 1702–14). The 1703 Methuen Treaty reduced duty on Portuguese wine in return for reductions on those payable on British wool exports. A hugely profitable business thus began. It had been discovered that adding small amounts of brandy helped the wine travel better, though another century would pass before it became the refined, fortified wine product so well known today.

For a while in the mid-18th century port had a bad reputation as unscrupulous exporters passed off adulterated, ersatz port as the genuine thing. The Marquês de Pombal stopped this by founding the *Companhia Geral de Agricultura dos Vinhos do Alto Douro* in 1756, thus establishing the world's first demarcated wine region. Quality was guaranteed by regulating the amount produced, fixing minimum and maximum prices, and passing exclusive and final judgement on all disputes concerning quality.

The demarcated region stretches almost 100km along the upper Douro valley and its tributaries. Vineyards (*quintas*) are on terraced slopes, some up to 500m above sea level. More than 40 varieties of grapes, harvested in September, are used for making port. The semi-fermented *must* is mixed with a controlled quantity of brandy, which prevents fermentation from continuing, leaving the wine free from the natural grape sugar. The wine is then kept in casks until the following March, when it is shipped down the Douro to Vila Nova de Gaia. There it is left to mature, still in the cask (except for vintage ports) inside the lodges (*armazéns*) before bottling. The lodges are mostly owned by multinational companies nowadays.

There are four basic types of port: white (*branco*), red (*tinto*), ruby (*tinto aloirado*) and tawny (*aloirado*). Vintage ports are not made annually but when the wine from a particular *quinta* is judged to be of sufficient quality. These wines are left for a couple of years in the cask and are then bottled and left to mature there. Vintage ports need to spend between 10 and 15 years in the bottle and must be decanted to separate out the sediment. As they are highly expensive, an alternative is to buy late-bottled vintage ports (LBV), usually transferred to the bottle after five or six years; these are almost as good and much cheaper.

Madeira

Offshore Portugal also produces some good wine. One of the best known is fortified madeira wine. Vines were first introduced to the island in the 15th century when the island was still almost completely forested. Land was cleared for cultivation by burning, a process that apparently took seven years, and the resulting mixture of volcanic soil and potash proved highly favourable to vine cultivation. Madeira wine, as it is known today, is made by subjecting it to temperatures of 40–50°C, either before or after fermentation. There are basically four types, each named after the grape used. **Sercial**, aged for eight years, is the driest and is served as an apéritif or with fish. **Verdelho** is medium-dry and is served with cake. **Bual** is medium-sweet and often replaces port. **Malmsey**, the sweetest and heaviest of the four, is best as a digestive after a heavy meal.

Beer

Beer (*cerveja*) is drunk widely in Portugal these days, and while Sagres and Super Bock are found just about everywhere there are also quite a few local brews. The town of Silves, in the Algarve, puts on a week-long beer festival every summer, and a good many lesser-known labels can be tried. If you want a draught beer, ask for '*um imperial*'; if you prefer it in the bottle ask for '*uma garrafa*'. In tourist areas there are many English-style 'pubs' serving household names like Guinness, Bass, Newcastle Brown, Bud, Coronita and more.

Cafés and Bars

In Portugal, quite what constitutes a 'bar', a 'café' or a 'restaurant', and what differentiates one from another, is often illogical. There are cafés on the nightlife circuit, others that by day host a clientele of venerable old men and by night become gay hang-outs. There are bars that offer full-blown meals, beer halls that serve snacks and are pre-clubbing stop-off points, restaurants with live entertainment and in some areas 'pubs', either 'Irish' or 'English' which may be more or less authentic in their décor.

Cafés

It does not take a genius to figure out why Portuguese people, particularly Lisboetas, drink so much coffee and spend so much time in cafés. First, all you need do is take a look at a map of Portugal's colonies during the heyday of its overseas empire and you will notice a sizeable country that occupies a large chunk of the Latin American sub-continent – Brazil. The coffee-bean-bearing plant, *rubiacea*, was by all accounts introduced into Brazil in the early 18th century. It was soon growing abundantly throughout Rio de Janeiro state, and coffee production rose steeply; Brazil was the largest producer in the world by the mid-19th century. Portugal, as the colonial ruler, therefore had a ready supply of the best coffee in the world, and the Portuguese have since then become serious consumers of the stimulating beverage.

At around the same time an emerging bourgeoisie, especially in the Chiado neighbourhood of Lisbon, would spend their time arguing endlessly about politics, philosophy and art in beautifully appointed cafés such as the long-since disappeared Café Marrare, and the A Brasileira, which still survives today. This café's heyday was the 1920s and 1930s, when the likes of the poet Fernando Pessoa would spend hours there, sipping on his absinthe and numerous *bicas*, highly charged black coffees served in a tiny cup. Grand café society is long gone but all over Portugal, from Lisbon to Oporto, Coimbra to Aveiro and from Évora to Faro, there are still a vast number of places in which to drink coffee, which is invariably good.

Nowadays it is not so much intellectuals who are most found slurping coffee, but overworked office staff; Portugal still has a 40-hour working week, and they need the caffeine to get them through the day. Most cafés not only serve coffee but also a range of soft and alcoholic drinks.

What anyone visiting Portugal for the first time will notice is the seemingly endless selection of *cafetarias*, *pastelarias* or *confeitarias*, cafés that also sell a vast range of sticky, sweet cakes to accompany the coffee. This is possibly one of the reasons why so many Portuguese people of a certain generation have bad teeth, though poverty is another explanation. It also, partly, explains why the same age group, men especially, tend to be rotund.

An additional attraction of café life is that the benign climate allows one to sit at outside tables, which on the *esplanada* on a sunny day is especially pleasant. Cafés are an essential part of Portuguese life, one that it is not difficult to slip into if you have some time on your hands. Join in, make your coffee last for hours, read the newspaper and watch the world go by.

Bars

Bars are maybe less ubiquitous than cafés and as places to go solely to drink are losing out to other establishments that offer food, perhaps some music, a DJ or the possibility of dancing. But there are still bars around, particularly in the older areas of bigger cities. The Alfama district of Lisbon has a good selection of little places that have not changed for decades, grubby establishments patronised by rough and ready – but friendly – old men, where the wine is strong and dyes your lips red. It is often served with a couple of mini-cheeses (*queijinhos*) and bread to soak up the wine.

Going a little more upscale, you find beer houses (*cervejarias*) where they serve not only beer but also wine and snacks and sometimes full meals. This is the case of the famous, and not-to-be-missed, Cervejaria da Trinidade in Lisbon, or the Adega do Olho in Oporto. Both are very traditional in their décor but popular with locals of all ages, foreign residents and tourists. It is in places like these where the distinction between bar and eatery becomes a little blurred. Not totally different from the traditional *cervejaria* is the *marisqueria*, a bar-restaurant that specialises in fish and seafood.

The bars suit all tastes for those who visit them at night, ranging from the loud and louche to the quiet and cosy. It depends what you want but in the bigger cities and more frequented tourist areas you will find the whole gamut. Again, distinctions start to become blurred. Some have music blaring out of the loudspeakers, others have live music. If you look in any good tourist guide you will find, in the 'nightlife' section, all manner of establishments going by the name of 'Bar this' or 'Café that' which are not classified as clubs but in some cases have bouncers on the door, have a cover charge, and offer customers the chance to dance to the latest DJ creations. And then there are clubs of the type that Londoners or Mancunians think of when they go out clubbing. In fact Lisbon has a nightlife scene that compares well with anywhere in Europe.

Transport

One of Portugal's virtues, from the point of view of getting around, is its compact size. This means that, apart from journeys from the far north to the south coast, travelling from A to B for business or pleasure is usually quite manageable. Public transport infrastructures have improved considerably in recent years and between the main cities and the most developed tourist areas connections are fairly frequent, reasonably quick and not too expensive. As well as this, EU funding has helped to improve the main road and motorway network immensely and there are now more motorways under construction. There are, however, parts of the country that the government seems to have overlooked in terms of public transport. Unfortunately, these also tend to be the areas where road improvements have been least in evidence. Moreover, not all newly built roads are up to scratch.

Public Transport

Trains

Rail travel is cheap, reasonably fast, comfortable and safe. The network operated by the national rail company, Caminhos de Ferro Portugueses (CP), reaches most major towns and cities but leaves many rural areas in the interior with no service. Stations are sometimes inconveniently located outside the centre of small towns.

CP has invested in rolling stock in recent years and the Lisbon–Oporto route takes just 3hrs 25mins by sleek, streamlined *Alfa Pendular* (*AP*). One can travel first class (*conforto*) or second class (*turística*) on this service, known as the *rápido*. Other major cities off the Lisbon–Oporto line are served by the intercity *Intercidade* (*IC*) trains (*comboios*), which are only slightly inferior to the *Alfa Pendular*. *Interregional* (*IR*) services are slower than *Intercidade*, with more stops, but cover much of the network. These trains keep the old denominations of first and second class. Finally, *Suburbano*, otherwise known as *Regional* (*R*) services, stop at every town, village and halt and make no class distinctions.

Travel is comparatively cheap: a tourist-class **ticket** from Lisbon to Oporto costs €22.50 or you can go *conforto* for €33. Buy your ticket before departure, as you will be fined for travelling without one, though you may pay the conductor on regional services. Tickets are sold at stations, travel agents and by telephone or online from CP: **t** 808 208 208 (7am–11pm), **www.cp.pt**. *Alfa Pendular* and *Intercidade* tickets can be bought up to 30 days in advance from any train station or from ATM machines up to 21 days in advance, and as late as 15mins before departure.

Discount schemes apply to children under the age of 4 who travel free if not occupying a seat and 4–11 year olds who pay half price. Young persons between ages 12 and 26 benefit from the *Cartão Jovem* (Youth Card), which brings a 30 per cent discount on full prices for certain journeys on certain lines, though not on the *Alfa Pendular*. There is also a *Bilhete Turístico* (Tourist ticket), valid for 7, 14 or 21 days at a price of €110, €187 and €275, respectively, half price for concession groups. There is a *Cheque Trem* (train cheque) by which you buy prepaid travel up to a certain price for a 10 per cent discount. All discounts are subject to restrictions on certain days and times.

The network centres on Lisbon, which has four mainline stations. Rossio station serves Sintra and other points west of the capital. Santa Apolónia serves the north and east and handles international services. Cais do Sodré serves the Estoril and Cascais line. Barreiro, on the southern bank of the Tagus, reached by ferry, serves all points south. In addition the new Gare de Oriente, built for Expo '98, with good metro connections, is a convenient halt on north- and east-bound lines as well as international trains. It is, in fact, easier to get to than Santa Apolónia, which has no metro.

Coaches

Inter-city coaches (*autocarros*) are the fastest and most popular form of travel in Portugal. The network reaches just about everywhere, though services to remote rural areas are sometimes infrequent.

The main operator is the publicly owned Rede Nacional de Expressos (National Express Network), which has fast services to a great number of destinations. It is inexpensive; Lisbon to Faro, for example, is €14.50 one way. Tickets are sold at coach stations, travel agencies and via the (Portuguese-language) website, **www.rede-expressos.pt**.

Otherwise, private companies operate many regional routes. Eva Bus, for example, covers the Algarve and connects this region to Lisbon and other points with luxury coaches (*alta qualidade*). Fares are reasonable and comparable with those of Rede Expressos. Most towns and cities have a centrally located bus station, something that the trains do not.

Internal Air Travel

Given Portugal's size, the need for domestic flights, which can be quite expensive, is not great, but the privately owned **Portugália** (**t** +351 218 425 500 or 087 075 500 25 (within the UK), **f** 218 425 623, **www.pga.pt**) flies between Lisbon, Oporto and Faro, and sometimes operates charters to and from Madeira. Between the Azores and mainland Portugal, as well as Frankfurt, flights are operated by **SATA** (**www.sata.pt**).

Urban Transport

The quality of urban transport systems varies, depending on where you are. Lisbon and Oporto have good transport systems. The capital has an extensive **tram** network, including the famous yellow trams, which are over a hundred years old, plus ultra-rapid models on some lines. In addition, there is a good underground, the metro, which has four lines and is being expanded. Otherwise, Lisboetas move around on buses, funicular trains that negotiate some of the steeper hills, local trains and ferry services to the far bank of the Tagus. Oporto also has a metro, though this is more an overland light railway. Portuenses also travel by bus and tram, though the old network, the first in the country, is now a pale shadow of its former glory. Smaller cities make do with local buses.

Coming from Britain or Ireland you will find urban transport to be inexpensive. In most places there are discount schemes of one-, two- or three-day unlimited travel cards, weekly or monthly travel cards and reduced prices for children and the elderly.

Taxis

Taxis are easily spotted, being either the traditional black with a green roof or the more fashionable cream or buff colour. As anywhere, you have to be careful of unscrupulous taxi drivers for whom newly arrived tourists and residents are easy prey. City taxis are fitted with a **meter** which has a standing charge and then clocks up the distance. Expect to pay a **night supplement** after 10pm and an extra charge for placing luggage in the boot. When arriving by air, the information points at the airports usually provide a list of sample fares.

It is easier to find a taxi at a rank rather than hailing one in the street though on major thoroughfares in larger cities this not a problem. **Tipping** is discretionary, maybe 10 per cent of the fare.

Driving

For a number of reasons, accident and fatality rates in Portugal are among the highest in Europe. Poor illumination, bad signposting, potholed roads and reckless driving are usually cited as causes. The latter may be explained by the meteoric rise in car ownership over recent years as there is a new generation of young drivers, many of whom have not inherited 'driving culture' from their parents, who have often never driven themselves. Not all expats are entirely free from blame, either; many take advantage of lax policing to drink and drive. The poor policing and inadequately enforced regulations contributes to the situation.

Anyone who plans to live in Portugal should be aware of these dangers, but the Portuguese authorities, under pressure from civil action groups, have recently made a concerted effort to improve matters. Tougher laws are being enforced and the grim statistics are slowly dropping.

You may download a complete English text of the Portuguese Highway Code (or 'Road Code' as they call it) from the website of the *Direcção-Geral de Viação*

Roads and Speed Limits

Speed limits on Portuguese roads are:

- Urban areas: the speed limit is 50kph.

- *Estradas Municipais*, main roads between towns and villages in country areas: speed limit is 90kph. These roads are usually narrow and often have no painted lines or guard-rails but are fairly safe.

- *Estradas Nacionais* (national highways): speed limit is 100kph, reduced to 80kph when pulling a trailer. These roads often have only two lanes. Similar, but slightly higher in grade than these roads, are the *Itinerários Complementares* (principal routes), which often become four-lane roads and pass directly through towns and villages, and *Itinerários Principais* (which you would think should translate as main roads but which are actually 'highways' of near-motorway status), usually having three lanes. These are subject to the same speed limits as the *Estradas Nacionais* and in many cases are ENs which have been upgraded and widened recently.

- *Autoestradas* (motorways): speed limit is 120kph, reduced to 100kph if you are pulling a trailer.

Staying Alive

When driving, there are certain precautions you can take to avoid engrossing the accident statistics. Above all, concentrate and be on the defensive. Note the following points:

- All traffic coming from the right has priority – always give way if you are not sure who has this in any particular circumstance.

- On roundabouts, traffic approaching from the left has priority.

- Stay out of bus and taxi lanes, which are anyway often obstructed by illegally parked cars so you gain nothing by using them.

- Do not use your horn at night except in an emergency.

- Use your headlamps, dipped, at night and in foggy conditions.

- If drivers flash their headlights at you, it could be warning of a speed trap ahead.

- Solid single or two solid lines indicate that no overtaking is permitted.

- If there is a single broken line overtaking is permitted. A double line, broken on your side of the road, also shows that you may overtake. Be extra-careful if you are driving a right-hand-drive car.

- The international sign depicting a black car and a red one side by side also means no overtaking.

- Traffic lights follow a red, green, amber, red sequence. Many Portuguese drivers go through on amber – if you stop you may get hit by the car behind you.

- Flashing amber means proceed but with caution.

- Be especially cautious at railway crossings, particularly those with no barrier.

- Be careful of youths on mopeds; many ride without lights at night. Take extra care when overtaking them.

- In rural areas, watch out for domestic and farm animals on the roads.

- Park only where legally permitted. Illegally parked cars may be clamped or towed away.

- Wear a crash helmet if you ride a bicycle or a motorbike.

- If you are caught speeding or otherwise committing an infraction you usually have to pay the fine on the spot. Residents have up to 15 days to pay.

- Do not drink and drive. Penalties can be stiff, see below.

- If possible, buy a left-hand-drive car as a right-hand-drive model leaves you more exposed to danger.

(**www.dgv.pt**; click on 'English', then 'Road Code'). The 72-page file occupies 1.3 megabytes and the English translation is at times a little confusing but it is a valuable document nevertheless.

The road system is constantly being expanded and improved, so try to buy as recent a road map as possible.

Tolls are paid on many motorways. The private motorway management company has an automatic payment scheme known as the *Via Verde*, the 'Green Way', by which subscribers can avoid long queues at toll gates. They are issued with a special vehicle ID device, then on approaching the toll they go to the *Linha Verde* gate, swipe their Multibanco card through the machine and the amount is automatically deducted from their account. In addition to tolls on the main stretches of *autoestradas*, it is worth remembering that there is a toll on southbound vehicles crossing the 25 de Abril Bridge which links Lisbon with the south bank of the Tagus River at the end of the Vila Franca de Xira expressway.

Penalties for Drinking and Driving

Amount in blood	Fine	Additional Sanction
0.5–0.8 g/l	€240–1,200	Minimum: 1-month ban Maximum: 1-year ban
0.8 g/l–1.19 g/l	€360–1,800	Minimum: 2-month ban Maximum: 2-year ban
1.2 g/l or above	Imprisonment up to 1 year or fine + imprisonment up to 120 days	Minimum: 3-month ban Maximum: 3-year ban

Regulations

Carry the following items at all times:

- the vehicle registration document (*livrete*).
- your ownership registration document (*título de registo de propriedade*).
- an insurance certificate and, if insured outside Portugal, the green card valid in Portugal; the insurance stamp is displayed in the bottom right-hand corner of the windscreen.
- your road tax disk, purchased annually in June from the local tax office or selected newsagents and displayed in the top right-hand corner of the windscreen.
- proof that your vehicle has passed an MOT-equivalent test (*see* below).
- your ID, passport or residency card.
- a valid driving licence.
- written permission to drive if you are not the owner (car hire contract or owner's declaration).

- a red warning triangle and a first-aid kit (applies to hired cars, also).
- a spare wheel and a tool-kit for changing the wheel.

Children under 12 years may not sit in the front, and car seat belts must be worn in the front and the rear seats; failure to do so may earn you a fine.

MOT

The MOT (*Inspecção Periódica Obrigatória* or *IPO*) is compulsory for all vehicles over four years old, is biannual for vehicles between four and seven years, annual from then on and must be carried out at an authorised garage. You must produce proof of ownership, the log book and your tax card before the inspection is done. Once the test is passed, garage staff will give you a stamp, which should be placed below the insurance stamp in the bottom right-hand corner of the windscreen.

Accidents and Breakdowns

The **AA** (**www.theaa.com**) and the **RAC** (**www.rac.co.uk**) offer their members European breakdown coverage. The Automóvel Clube de Portugal (ACP, **www. acp.pt**) has reciprocal agreements with most foreign automobile organisations though if you become a resident you are better off joining it directly.

The ACP's emergency breakdown number is **t** 707 509 510. Orange emergency phones are placed at regular intervals on motorways and other main roads. Otherwise you can usually phone from a bar or café, though keep a phone card handy for using call boxes, or carry a mobile. Non-members of automobile associations have to look for a garage (*oficina de reparagem*) by themselves.

For inconsequential bumps you do not have to call the police if you and the other driver agree who was to blame. Having both moved your vehicles out of the way of other traffic, complete the European Accident Statement (*Declaração Amigável de Acidente Automóvel*) to send to your respective insurance companies. In more serious accidents, or if you disagree about who was to blame, call the police. Do not remove your vehicle until they come; just display the red warning triangle. When the police arrive, both parties and any witnesses must make a statement. Copies of police reports are sent to both parties' insurance companies who argue it out between them. If you are incorrectly insured you could be in serious trouble. If you were not at fault and the other driver was uninsured there is a compensation board for claims. The police and your insurance company will tell you how to proceed. *See also* 'Insuring Your Car', pp.166–7.

Petrol Stations

The larger petrol stations (*postos de gasolina*) on motorways and in urban areas are mainly operated by GALP and BP, and are usually open 24hrs a day. Smaller, independent stations are open from 7 or 8am until 7pm midweek and

9am until about 1pm on Saturdays. Petrol types are *normal* (equivalent to 2-star), *super* (equivalent to 4-star) and *sem chumbo* (unleaded). Some cars run on *gasóleo* (diesel). Petrol have recently risen to around €1.40 per litre. *Credit cards are not universally accepted, so always have some cash on you when filling up.*

Driving Licences

When settling in Portugal, it is not obligatory to exchange community model driving licences, which may be used until their expiry date, but there are several good reasons for exchanging them for a Portuguese licence.

As in the UK, the address on the licence must be correct and up to date. If the licence is lost or damaged, it may only be renewed or reissued by the issuing authority. Some authorities, including the DVLA, will not renew or replace a licence to an overseas address. When the licence eventually expires, the Portuguese licensing authority (Direcção Geral de Viação) will only renew it if the driver passes a driving test in Portugal.

National driver's licences, the old green model, must anyway be exchanged for a Portuguese licence. Contact the nearest local office of the Direcção Geral de Viação where you will be required to hand in the original licence for a locally issued one.

Importing a Vehicle

You may temporarily import any EU-registered vehicle for a continuous period of up to 180 days within a given calendar year. It must be:

- **registered in the name of a person not resident in Portugal.**
- **brought into the country by its registered owner or the person looking after it (the 'keeper' – written authorisation is needed).**
- **only for private use and only driven by its registered owner(s), or keeper(s), who themselves may not reside or work in Portugal.**

The owner or keeper must carry all relevant documents at all times.

If you intend to become resident, you may import a vehicle tax free provided that you meet the following conditions:

- **The vehicle is only for your private use.**
- **You are in the process of transferring your residency from another EU country in which you have resided legally for at least 185 days.**
- **You bought the vehicle and paid full tax on the transaction in your former country of residence.**
- **You, as the registered owner, have used it in that former country of residence for at least six months before importing it.**

For further details about importing a vehicle, consult the nearest Direcção Geral de Viação.

Buying a Car in Portugal

Given the complications of bringing your car from home, you may choose to buy, new or second-hand, when you arrive in Portugal. This is anyway a good idea as driving a right-hand-drive cars exposes you to more danger on the already-perilous roads, and foreign-registered cars are more easily targeted by thieves and vandals. However, Portugal is one of the more expensive EU countries in terms of car prices, owing mainly to taxes – the third-highest in western Europe. An average of 55.6 per cent is added on to the import price and annual road taxes are based on the age of the car and its engine capacity. Thus you see many old, small cars on Portuguese roads. There is a flourishing market for second-hand cars, given that many second-hand upmarket cars retail at the same price as a small new car, so Portuguese buyers often prefer to acquire a second-hand BMW. Imported used cars are popular, particularly expensive German models, which work out to be competitively priced.

For day-to-day purposes, and according to your needs, a medium-sized second-hand car should not cost you too much. There are dealerships for all major manufacturers if you want to buy new.

The documents that are needed, by both seller and buyer, are:

- A vehicle registration document (*livrete*).
- The ownership registration document (*título de registo de propriedade*).
- A declaration of sale, signed by the buyer and the seller.
- A photocopy of the buyer's and seller's ID.
- A photocopy of the tax cards (*cartões de contribuinte*) of buyer and seller.

If possible, get someone to help you with the paperwork for registering the vehicle with the Direcção-Geral de Viação.

Insuring your Car

Most aspects of car insurance are now standardised within EU regulations, which require that all vehicles within the Union be fully insured for third-party damage. This means that you can insure your vehicle with a company in the UK or Portugal and are covered for accidents that occur in any EU country. The following stipulations are made concerning insurance companies:

- **The company must be a member of the national motor vehicle insurers' bureau and the guarantee fund of the member state in which your vehicle is registered.**
- **If the company does not have an establishment in the member state in which your vehicle is registered, it must have designated a representative authorised to settle claims in that member state.**

If you cause a road accident, your green card or your insurance certificate is proof that you have compulsory third party insurance, which means the victims can claim compensation. Notify your insurance company of the accident and supply any necessary documents (such as the police report of the accident). The injured party will contact his own insurer, who will in turn contact the National Motor Vehicle Insurance Bureau. This bureau will look after the formalities between the two insurance companies and the injured party.

In the event of an accident for which you are not liable, you are entitled to compensation in accordance with the rules in force either in that member state where the accident occurred or in your country of residence (if the level of compensation is higher there). These rules still differ from one member state to another but you have minimum cover of €350,000 for any personal injuries sustained and €100,000 for material damage. If the accident is caused by an uninsured or unidentifiable car, you are entitled under EU law to compensation from the motor vehicle guarantee fund of the member state in which the accident occurred, in accordance with the rules in force in that member state.

Be sure to take out the correct type of insurance, as uninsured drivers who have an accident and damage another vehicle (or worse) can face stiff penalties and may have to pay victims a lot in compensation. Cover for eventualities such as fire or theft is optional, but comprehensive insurance is recommended.

For more information, consult: **http://europa.eu.int/scadplus/citizens/en/pt/01080002.htm**.

Car Hire

Car hire is cheap in Portugal and, apart from the large international companies such as Avis, Europcar, Hertz and Budget, there are many small, local rental companies. The big names all have offices at international airports. To look for companies on the Internet, do a Google search with 'portugal + car + rentals' and literally hundreds will pop up on your screen. Choosing the right model is important, especially if you are travelling with a family and lots of luggage.

To hire a car you must show proof of identity (resident's card or passport for EU citizens, passport for other nationals) and a valid driving licence. A green card is essential and it is wise to take out insurance coverage and collision insurance. Cars are not usually hired out to anyone under the age of 21; some companies may set the lower age limit at 23. Rental companies often ask for proof that you have held your licence for at least 12 months.

Mopeds and Motorbikes

In Portugal, as elsewhere, a moped is defined as a motorised two-wheel vehicle of up to 49cc engine capacity. Anything larger than that is classed as a motorbike. A Class A licence is needed in order to ride a motorbike, though it is not technically necessary if you only want to ride a moped. Persons over age 16 may ride mopeds; the age limit for larger machines is 18.

You may not ride a moped on motorways and are restricted to 40kph in urban areas and 45kph on other roads. If you ride a motorbike of 50cc or over you may drive at 50kph in urban areas, 120kph on motorways, 100kph on main roads (IPs) and 90kph on 'other public ways'. The latter three limits are each reduced by 20kph if you have a sidecar. When riding a moped or motorbike you are particularly vulnerable and exposed, so take extra care, and do wear a helmet (many people do not). The law prohibits riding with your hands off the handlebars, or your feet off the pedals or supports, and you may not legally do a 'wheelie' when moving off.

Bicycles

Bicycles are used more for leisure than as a means of transport in Portugal but there is nothing to stop you from cycling to and from work. Residents of Lisbon, Oporto and other hilly cities such as Coimbra may find the steep slopes and cobbled surfaces daunting. In addition, Portuguese drivers have little respect for cyclists and there are few cycle lanes anywhere. Therefore, for safety, wear a helmet and when cycling at night a fluorescent yellow or orange jacket. A back light or a reflector are also recommended. Portugal has many lovely spots for recreational cycling and mountain biking.

Crime and the Police

Though law and order is perceived to be deteriorating, Portugal remains a safe place when compared with other European countries. Violent crime is not unknown, but rarely affects foreign residents, being mainly restricted to drug-related incidents in the slum areas outside Lisbon and other larger cities. That said, an English football supporter was stabbed to death by his mugger, whom he chased after being robbed, in Lisbon during the Euro 2004 tournament. This is the exception rather than the rule: a UN survey in 2000 on violent crime worldwide ranked Portugal as one of the safest countries in which to live.

Burglaries are a problem in areas with large numbers of foreign residents, and again they are often drug-related. Second and holiday homeowners are easier prey than full-time residents as their properties are left empty for long periods. Burglars tend not to be sophisticated – they go for anything that is easy to sell such as cameras, jewellery and, of course, cash. Residents in villa developments in places such as the Algarve should follow the recommendations of their insurance company, which will not let them take out a policy without first having made their home minimally secure (see p.122).

Street crime is more common in cities such as Lisbon or Oporto. While mugging statistics are still relatively low, pickpockets and bag-snatchers who operate in shopping areas and on public transport are the main problem. You

Avoid Pickpockets and Bag Snatchers

Avoiding street crime is really a question of being practical, alert and showing common sense.

• When travelling, especially on arrival in major cities, always keep your luggage in full view. Spread money, credit cards and important documents around as many different pockets, handbags and money belts as possible. This reduces the risk of losing everything in one go.

• If you are sitting outside at a café, do not drape coats, bags or jackets over the back of a chair, or leave them out of view under the table. Keep them on your lap or in an empty chair next to you.

• Carry shoulder bags, handbags or small rucksacks across your chest. If you are walking along a narrow street keep them on the pavement side, away from the road. Keep a hand placed over your bag, which should be zipped up or fastened.

• Do not carry large amounts of cash; just take enough for your needs. Use a money belt; if it is not too hot, wear a jacket with an inside pocket that can be fastened or zipped.

• When changing money or withdrawing from a bank, ask for small denomination notes (€5, €10, €20 or, maximum, €50). If you have larger denominations, do not wave them around; try to get to a bank or shop where you can change them for smaller notes.

• Do not wear expensive jewellery or watches when out in unknown areas.

• Body language can make you a target or dissuade thieves; even if you do not know your way around, try not to look lost, but walk in a confident manner, looking straight ahead. Be careful of standing on a street corner looking at a map; this is asking for trouble. Plan where you are going before setting off and try to memorise the route.

• Watch out for thieves who work in pairs or teams, one at either end of a street; they often use mobile telephones to communicate the presence of their next victim. Be careful of strangers who ask for directions or who 'politely' let you get on to the bus or tram in front of them.

• If you turn into a street where there is obviously drug-pushing (and consuming) going on, turn around and walk away briskly.

• If you are held up at knife or gunpoint, hand over the goods; do not argue or try to be the hero. You may lose some money, but this is minor compared to what might happen.

can take certain common sense steps to reduce to a minimum the chances of being robbed (*see* box, above).

Car crime is also fairly common, particularly in areas with large communities of foreign residents and tourists. Foreign-registered cars are frequently singled out for break-ins and robberies. Nothing valuable should ever be left in a car, either in full view or even hidden. In smaller towns and cities, street crime is rarely encountered.

Police Forces

As elsewhere in Europe, Portugal has more than one police force, and the police are often armed. Each has certain areas of responsibility, though these may overlap. It has taken a long time for Portuguese people to overcome their mistrust of law enforcement bodies after their role in the Salazar dictatorship. They have worked hard to improve their image but old, authoritarian attitudes sometimes surface.

Public Security Police (*Policia de Segurança Pública*)

The grey-uniformed PSP are the city police. Foreign residents have dealings with them as they are responsible for residency cards, traffic offences in cities, directing the traffic and patrolling the streets. They are the force to which most crime is reported.

Traffic Police (*Brigada de Trânsito*)

The traffic police, or highway patrol, are to be seen on the main roads and are responsible for controlling speeding, dangerous driving, non-use of seat belts – for which they may fine you on the spot – and other traffic offences. They normally deal with accidents.

Coastguard (*Guarda Fiscal*)

As Portugal is now on the drug importation route from South America, the 'Fiscal Guard' have plenty of work. Their operative area extends to towns and villages a little way inland.

National Republican Guard (*Guarda Nacional Repúblicana*)

Not to be messed with, the GNR is a paramilitary organisation that is generally called in when there is a threat to public order.

Taking Your Pet

If you have a pet and wish to take it with you on trips home, or if you are taking it to Portugal, you should be aware of current regulations. Portugal (including Madeira and the Azores) and the UK both belong to the PETS 'animal passports' scheme, by which animals may be moved freely between those EU (and other) signatory countries. The Republic of Ireland is not currently a signatory to the scheme and quarantine laws thus apply. However, if you take your animal into the Republic via the UK you will have no problem as there is free movement between the two countries. The Republic of Ireland will soon also become a signatory to the scheme.

The animal passports scheme applies only to dogs and cats (including guide and hearing dogs) resident in PETS signatory countries. Animals that meet the scheme's rules can enter (or re-enter) the UK without having to spend six months in quarantine; the same applies in reverse. Animals that don't meet requirements must go into quarantine, though you might be able to obtain early release.

To travel between PETS countries you must do the following, *in this order*:

- Have your pet fitted with a microchip for identification purposes, which can be done in any country. Microchips should be of ISO Standard 11784 or Annexe A to ISO Standard 11785.

- Get your pet vaccinated against rabies. This may only be done in a signatory country and animals must be at least three months old.

- Once vaccinated, the animal must be blood-tested to make sure the vaccine has given it sufficient protection against rabies. The test must also be done in a participating country.

- Once the animal is declared rabies-free, you will be given the PETS certificate. This is effectively the animal's 'passport'.

- If you have this done outside the UK and intend to take the animal back, you will have to wait for six months before the PETS certificate becomes valid, as an animal that was infected before vaccination would not be protected against rabies. An infected animal would show symptoms of rabies within six months, equivalent to the quarantine period.

- If you wish to keep your pet ready to travel under the PETS scheme, give it an anti-rabies booster jab on, or before, the 'Valid until' date on the PETS certificate. You should then apply to your government-approved vet (a local veterinary inspector in the UK) for a new PETS certificate.

- If you lose the certificate you will need to obtain a new one from a government-authorised vet in a qualifying country. The vet will need to be satisfied that your pet had been through the necessary steps already.

- When taking your pet back to the UK, treat it against ticks and tapeworm between 24 and 48hrs before it is checked in for the journey. Any qualified vet can do this and must issue an official certificate to show the treatment is complete. You will have to sign a declaration (PETS 3) that your animal has not been outside any of the PETS qualifying countries in the six months before it enters the UK. Your animal must enter from a PETS country, travelling on approved route with an approved transport company.

Animal Authorities

For full information about travelling with animals, vaccination, quarantine and related questions, contact the following bodies in England, Scotland, Wales, Northern Ireland, the Republic of Ireland and Portugal:

- **Department for Environment, Food and Rural Affairs (DEFRA)**, PETS helpline t 0870 241 1710 (*open Mon–Fri 8.30–5*), f (020) 7904 6206, **pets. helpline@defra.gsi.gov.uk**, **www.defra.gov.uk** (enclose your address and daytime telephone number). From the website you may download fact sheets in PDF format with full information about the PETS scheme.
- **Scottish Executive Environment and Rural Affairs Department (SEERAD)**, t (0131) 244 6182/1, f (0131) 244 6616, **animal.health@scotland.gsi.gov.uk**.
- **National Assembly of Wales Agriculture Department (NAWAD)**, t (01286) 662070 (English/Welsh), **AnimalByProductsCaernarfon@wales.gsi.gov.uk**.
- **Department of Agriculture and Rural Development**, Northern Ireland (DARD), t (02890) 524622.
- **Department of Agriculture, Food and Fisheries**, Kildaire Street, Dublin 2, Eire, t (01) 607 2000, **www.irlgov.ie/daff**.
- **Direcção-Geral de Veterinária**, Largo da Academia Nacional das Belas Artes, 2, 1200-005 Lisbon, t 213 239 5 00, **veterinaria@mail.telepac.pt**.

Living with Children

It is generally agreed that Portugal is a good country where children are concerned. Those who have children feel happy about bringing them up in Portugal, which is, by and large, a safe country with a relaxed, easygoing culture.

There are good reasons for this. First, the attitude that most Portuguese people display towards children is welcoming and warm, as is typical in Mediterranean countries. The Portuguese appreciate the presence of children: babies are cooed over by strangers, children are seen *and* heard in restaurants and all public places, and nobody seems to mind. Waiters are quite likely to spend time chatting to or playing with children rather than getting on with the job of serving other customers. Many foreigners, in fact, comment that the family-centred Portuguese are, if anything, overindulgent with their own children. Portuguese kids, despite the benign climate, are often seen bundled up in several layers of clothes. You might find that older women seem overly concerned about children who are let out in a flimsy T-shirt and shorts, insisting that they are going to catch their death of cold, even on perfectly clement days.

Despite this, there are some apparent contradictions. One is that the Portuguese, who place such importance on the family, are now having ever fewer children. Despite the Church's prohibition on artificial methods of birth control, most married women, especially those who work, use contraception.

Case Study: Simon Mount, Schoolteacher

Q What brought you to Portugal originally and how is it working here?

SM I got a summer job coaching tennis on the Algarve, met a girl, fell in love and moved to the Lisbon area to teach geography at a British school nearby. I applied on spec for a job at St Julian's School and got lucky. The pay is lower than in an equivalent job at home, but the working day is shorter and more relaxed, and holidays are longer.

Q What do you like and dislike about living and working in Portugal?

SM The climate – it's not England! People are reasonable generally and there is excellent environmental, sporting and cultural variety within a stone's throw of the capital. The worse thing is petty bureaucracy, though you just learn to live with it. I don't think it's improved, really; the most annoying thing is the attitude that the punter is always wrong and/or criminally minded, and the total inflexibility of it. Also, I don't like the appalling attitudes towards the environment, nor do I like the Portuguese *nouveau riche*, who desperately ape anyone else's aristocracy and are hugely arrogant and lacking in charm. There is also lots of third world poverty in the African migrant communities etc. and no apparent action or activism. Racism is not overt but there is pandemic *laissez faire* attitude.

Q Do you live mainly in the expat community or have you integrated?

SM Half and half. I actually can't stand the British expat community, especially along the *Linha de Cascais*. As I work at a British school most of my colleagues fall into that category, although the students are mainly Portuguese or international. The Lisbon Players [an expat, English-language theatre group] crowd from Lisbon are far more progressive and interesting, it should be said. I always had Portuguese girlfriends and recently married a Portuguese woman. Most of my friends are Portuguese or 'mixtures'. I have been here for 12 years and speak the language fairly well and find most Portuguese very friendly and easy to integrate with, though it was not so easy before I learnt the language.

Q How do you find bringing up children bilingually?

SM Our son is not one yet, so it's too early to say. If we stay here, he will go to St Julian's; it's a good school and free for me. He goes to a good crèche; it costs €200 a month. My wife and I speak Portuguese, but I will try to speak with him in English. I feel very positive about bringing him up here.

The average family nowadays consists of two parents and approximately 1.5 children. In the case of middle-class families, the single child is becoming the norm. This is for economic reasons, namely that women's participation in the labour market has grown rapidly since the revolution, thanks to greater opportunities and the fact that few families can survive on one salary so both husband and wife need to work. The family, in a sense, is strengthened by this as parents tend to rely on their own parents to help bring up the children. Many Portuguese children are dropped of and picked up from school by their grandmothers. Nowadays it is immigrants from Africa, Brazil and Eastern Europe who are helping to keep Portugal's population young.

Another contradiction is the apparent lack of facilities, particularly indoor ones, specifically for children. This of course depends entirely on where you decide to live. Central areas of cities such as Lisbon and Oporto have play areas but these are frequently the reserve of domino-playing old men and dog owners; take care when letting your child play in the sandpit. Attractions and museum exhibits are the exception rather than the rule. Restaurants, though happy to serve entire families, do not usually have high chairs, and the children's menu is something of an alien concept. You can get around this by asking for a half portion (*uma meia dose*). Few restaurants have playing facilities, though as many are close to beaches and green areas there is often no problem if children want to run off and play while their parents finish their meal. In addition, as Portugal becomes more global, there is now a good range of establishments serving hamburgers and pizzas. English-speaking children interested in films and TV are spoilt, as films are rarely dubbed and most expats have access to English-language TV with cartoons and other children's programmes.

On the other hand, as most expatriates live in either the Greater Lisbon area, the Algarve or Oporto, they have the advantage of being close to the sea. This presents numerous advantages. Children in general love the beach, which is of course free, and all three regions offer numerous possibilities for outdoor pursuits of many types. Owing to the growth of tourist infrastructures there are facilities for horse riding and a great range of water sports. Older Portuguese towns and cities invariably have castles where smaller children can have fun playing on the battlements, and nowadays there are more adventure and soft playgrounds in shopping malls and tourist resorts. Overall, your children are likely to be able to enjoy themselves just as much as they would at home, only with more opportunities to do so outdoors.

Moving to Portugal with children raises many issues and will influence decisions and choices, especially about where you eventually live. See 'Education', below, for a description of the Portuguese educational system. You may decide to put your children through the free Portuguese system, or be able to send them to a fee-paying English-speaking school, should you wish. Your choice may be determined by your income and by the accessibility of English-speaking schools in the area that you live.

Although children generally adapt fairly quickly and pick up foreign languages more easily than adults, not all do, and dropping them into a Portuguese-only school may be more traumatic for them than you had expected. If you choose to live away from the expatriate community it is worth making an effort to learn the language so that you can integrate with local people as quickly as possible. Your children may well serve as a bridge, as they are likely to make friends before you.

Education

The State System

Infant Education

Education is compulsory in Portugal, though pre-school is optional. But it is worth sending your children to a state-run *jardim de infância*, which is free, as this will give them a head start in Portuguese and help them mix with other children. Places may be limited depending on demand in the area where you live. As an alternative, there are many privately run pre-school facilities, which may have better facilities. Expect to pay in the region of €200 per month.

Primary Education

Compulsory basic education, *ensino básico*, starting at age six, consists of three stages and lasts until age 15. Children aged six on or before 15 September must be enrolled for their first year at school during that calendar year. Those reaching age six between 16 September and 31 December may also be admitted if parents request this during the enrolment period.

During the first stage, pupils are taught by the same teacher; in the second and third stages they are taught by different teachers for each subject. In the first stage, core subjects include the environment, Portuguese language, mathematics, and personal and social development or religious education. These same areas are continued in the second stage in wider multidisciplinary areas that embrace languages, social studies, science, art and technology, physical education and extra-curricular activities. In addition to the same core subjects, in the third stage students may opt to do courses in a second foreign language, music or technology.

Children are tested through continuous assessment and written exams, which are regulated nationally. During the second cycle, students who perform badly in more than three subjects, particularly if two of them are Portuguese and mathematics, may have to repeat the entire year. On finishing the third stage, students must pass tests on all third-stage curricular subjects (*provas escritas globais*). At the end of the third stage, satisfactory attendance and passing the exams earns a basic education certificate (*diploma de ensino básico*).

Upper Secondary and Post-secondary Education

Education at this level is really the second stage of secondary education, and can take the form of general education (*ensino secundário/cursos gerais*), technological courses (*cursos tecnológicos*), practical studies in vocational schools (*escolas profissionais*), or art courses. Entry is determined by successful completion of the nine years of compulsory education. Students wishing to enter vocational schools (*escolas profissionais*) must have completed compulsory education or obtained an equivalent qualification. The national curriculum core subjects in general and technological education are Portuguese, a foreign language, introductory philosophy, PE and personal and social education or religion. Courses are organised into four branches of study: science and natural science, arts, economic and social sciences, and humanities. Within each of these groups, there are separate courses for general and technological students.

Assessment is carried out by teachers according to ministerial guidelines. Progress is determined by students' performance in end-of-year exams and national final examinations are taken at the end of the three years of general education. Successful students receive a *diploma de estudos secundários*; students completing the technological courses receive a vocational certificate. In vocational schools, successful students receive a *diploma de estudos secundários* and a vocational certificate.

The state system has many deficiencies. Drop-out and failure rates are high. Facilities for music, technology, physical education and extra-curricular activities are often woefully lacking, as are many basic educational materials. The system seems to work well enough for those who are self-confident, but less assured pupils can find it difficult to make progress.

Private Schools

Many foreign residents send their children to private, English-speaking schools. This is not only because of the perceived deficiencies of the state system but because they prefer their children to get an education that is more in tune with their cultural background. As many expatriates move to Portugal when their children have already become accustomed to the English or American system, they feel it would be unfair to disrupt their child's education by changing systems. As not all residents are in Portugal permanently, some being on a two- or three-year posting with an international company, the education on offer may also be found elsewhere, when they move on, providing continuity. Private English-language schools are concentrated in areas favoured by expats, such as Greater Lisbon, Oporto, the Algarve and Madeira. If you choose to move to the Alentejo or Trás-os-Montes, the local system, or a boarding school, will be your only choices.

Some foreign schools provide education that goes from pre-school through to pre-university levels. Some even have nursery facilities. Other exclusively nursery schools act as feeders to a nearby infants' school. Some are excellent, and most are quite good, but others are not up to standard. Watch out for schools that are obviously run on a shoestring budget, the educational equivalent of the 'bucket-shop'. None is free. If you are planning to send your child to a private school it is essential to visit first or at least ask other parents for advice.

British schools in Portugal teach the national curriculum syllabus leading to GCSE and A-levels. American schools prepare students for equivalent high school qualifications. Many also prepare students for the International Bacca-laureate (IB), which is especially useful for those who plan to go on to university, as the title is recognised in many countries other than the UK, Ireland or the USA. While most claim to achieve academic excellence, emphasis is also placed on other aspects of the child's overall development and the result is often a well-rounded education that gives the student a broad outlook and a well-trained, flexible mind. This is further enhanced by the presence of children from a variety of backgrounds, since foreign businesspeople and diplomats from many countries also tend to send their children to such schools. In addition, facilities can be excellent – many schools have sports halls, auditoriums, horse-riding facilities and swimming pools. A very high percentage of students from the better private schools in Portugal – some schools claim rates as high as 90 per cent – go on to university studies in many other countries.

Fees are not cheap. Pre-school could cost more than €2,000 per annum, infants' school between €4,000–5,000, junior school €5,000–8,000 and the final years more than €8,000. Add on the cost of uniforms (sometimes compul-sory), extra-curricular activities, the bus to and from school, lunch, trips and a few extras – and get out your calculator.

English-speaking Schools in Portugal

This list is for reference purposes only and should in no way be considered an endorsement of the schools, either as potential employers or as educational centres. It is not definitive: contact the British consulate for a full list.

Lisbon Area

- **Boa Ventura Montessori School**, Rua Nunes dos Santos, 5, 2765, São Pedro do Estoril, **t** 214 688 023. Non-selective, coeducational nursery and infant school for children aged 2–5 years.

- **The Carlucci American International School of Lisbon (CAISL)**, Rua António dos Reis 95, 2710-301, Sintra, **t** 219 239 800, **f** 219 239 899, **www.ecis.org/aislisbon/index.html**.

- **The Cascais International School**, Rua das Faias, Lote 7, Torre, 2750-688, Cascais, **t** 214 846 260. Non-selective, co-educational nursery and infant school for children aged 1–6 years.

- **International Preparatory School**, Rua do Boror, 12, 2775, Carcavelos, **t** 214 570 149, **f** 214 573 501. Non-selective, coeducational infant/primary school for children aged 1–13.

- **Queen Elizabeth's School**, Rua Filipe Magalhães, 1, Alvalade, 1700 Lisbon, **t** 218 486 928, **f** 218 472 513. Non-selective, coeducational infant/primary school, mainly for Portuguese children aged from 3–11 years, but with an emphasis on the British educational system.

- **St Dominic's College**, Rua Maria Brown, Outeiro da Polima, 2789-506, and São Domingos de Rana, 2777-506, Parede, t 214 440 434/214 480 550, f 214 443 072, **adm@dominic.mailpac.pt**, **www.dominics.org**. Non-selective, coeducational school for children aged 3–18 years. IB Primary Years, IB Middle Years and IB Diploma programmes.

- **St George's School**, Avenida do Lidador, 322, São João do Estoril, 2765-333, Estoril, t 214 661 774. Non-selective, co-educational infant/primary school for children aged from 3–13 years. Portuguese and British curriculum.

- **St Julian's School**, Quinta Nova, 2776-601, Carcavelos, t 214 570 140, f 214 583 729, **mail@stjulians.com**, **www.stjulians.com**. Non-selective, co-educational school for children aged 3–18 years. Portuguese and British curriculum. GCSE and International Baccalaureate courses available.

Oporto area

- **CLIP, The Oporto International School**, Rua de Vila Nova, 1071, 4100-506, Oporto, t 226 199 160, f 226 199 167, **clip.porto@clip.pt**, **www.clip.pt**.

- **The Oporto British School**, Rua da Cerca, 326, Foz do Douro, 4150-201 Oporto, t 226 166 660, f 226 166 668. Non-selective, co-educational, primary/secondary school.

Algarve area

- **The International School of the Algarve**, Barros Brancos Porches, 8400-400, Lagoa, t 282 342 547/8, f 282 353 787, **www.internationalschool ofthealgarve.com**. Non-selective, coeducational day school with limited boarding facilities for children aged 5–16 years.

- **Escola Internacional São Lourenço**, Cx 445N, Sítio da Rabona, 8135, Almancil, t 289 398 328, f 289 398 298, **eisl@mail.telepac.pt**, **www. eisl-pt.org**. For children from nursery to university entrance.

- **The Vilamoura International School**, Quintinhas, Apt 856, 8125-911, Vilamoura, t 289 303 280, f 289 303 288, **info@cl-int-vilamoura.rcts.pt**, **www.cl-int-vilamoura.rcts.pt**. A co-educational private day school with Portuguese and English studies.

Madeira

- **The British School**, Rua dos Ilheus, 85, 9000-176 Funchal, t 291 773 218, f 291 232 077. Non-selective, co-educational infant/primary school for children up to 10 years.

- **The International School of Madeira**, Calçada do Pico n° 5, 9000-206 Funchal, t/f 291 225 870, **escola.int.madeira@mail.telepac.pt**, **www.madeira-international-school.com**. Fully bilingual (English and Portuguese), non-selective, fully licensed, co-educational, nursery, pre- and primary school for children aged from 3 to 10 years.

Studying in Portugal

Just as anyone from any EU member state may take up residence, work, practise a profession or operate a business in any other member state, so also may you study, provided you meet the entry requirements. This is a relatively recent development as it used to be hard to get on to a university course without already holding an undergraduate or sometimes a postgraduate degree. It is somewhat easier nowadays, though do not expect to be admitted on to a course if your Portuguese is not up to the level required.

University education goes back a long way in Portugal, dating from the establishment of the Universidade de Coimbra in 1290, one of the oldest universities in the world. Long considered the most prestigious university in Portugal, this title is now hotly disputed by the Universidade de Lisboa, itself an ancient institution. As recently as 1970, Portugal had only five universities. Four were public, two of them in Lisbon and one each in Coimbra and Oporto, and there was one private, Catholic-run university, Universidade Católica, also in Lisbon. Since then there has been great expansion and there are now 14 universities dotted around the country and offshore Portugal. Cities and provinces such as the Algarve, Alto Douro, Aveiro, Beira, Évora, Minho and Trás-os-Montes all have universities. In Lisbon itself there are five. Apart from the two already mentioned there are the Universidade Técnica de Lisboa, the Universidade Nova de Lisboa and the Universidade Lusíada. In addition there are other higher education institutes, often offering vocational and practical courses rather than academic degrees.

Higher education in Portugal is divided into two subsystems: university education and non-university higher (polytechnic) education. It is provided in autonomously administered public universities, private universities, polytechnic institutions and private higher education institutions of other types. In addition, there is a university institution that offers vocational and academic courses. The Portuguese Catholic University was instituted by decree of the Holy See and is recognised by the Portuguese government. Private higher education institutions cannot operate without Ministry of Education approval and recognition. Access is regulated by the same procedures as those for state higher education institutions. The two systems of higher education (university and polytechnic) are linked, and it is possible to transfer from one to the other. It is also possible to transfer from a public institution to a private one and vice-versa.

Diplomas and Degrees

University Level First Stage: *Bacharel/Licenciado*

In universities, the first stage leads to the award of the *Bacharel* after three years. This is not the equivalent of a bachelor's degree, having more the value of a diploma. The *Licenciado*, really a BA or BSc, is awarded after completing a course usually lasting for four years, but possibly five or even six. Most *Licenciatura* courses are organised in credit units, but some are still organised per term or academic year.

University Level Second Stage: *Mestre*

The *Mestre* (Master) is an advanced degree in a specific scientific field, indicating that the student is ready to conduct practical research. Courses usually last for four semesters and include lectures and preparing and discussing an original dissertation. It is usually restricted to those who have obtained 14 or more out of 20 in the *Licenciatura* course.

University Level Third Stage: *Doutor*

The *Doutor* is awarded by universities to those who have passed the doctorate examinations and have defended a thesis. There is no fixed period to prepare for the doctorate examinations. Candidates must hold the degree of *Mestre* or the *Licenciado* degree (or an equivalent qualification) with a final mark of at least 16 out of 20 and have a level of competence and merit recognised by the university.

University Level Fourth Stage: *Agregação*

This is the highest qualification, reserved for holders of the *Doutor* degree. Students must have the capacity to undertake high-level research and special pedagogical competence in a specific field. It is awarded after passing specific examinations.

Admissions Procedures

Admission to Higher Education

To enter higher education, both to study non-university or university level courses, candidates must have passed the *Diploma de Ensino Secundário* or equivalent. A levels are usually accepted, but contact NARIC, *see* 'Contacts' below, to make sure. Alternatively, students aged 25 or over who lack this qualification may sit a special ad-hoc examination to gain admission.

The entrance exam is called the *Concurso Nacional* (for public institutions) or the *Concurso Local* (for private institutions). The principle of *numerus clausus* applies: that is, the institution in question, whether public or private, establishes the number of places available for each course; this must be ratified by the Ministry of Education. In addition to passing entrance and access tests, students must fulfil particular prerequisites for the chosen course.

Universities make their entrance requirements known in a booklet distributed to applicants by the regional office of the Direcção de Serviços de Accesão ao Ensino Superior (Admissions Body) that is responsible for placing applicants on courses according to preference. Vacancies allocated by public institutions are filled by a national competition organised by the Direcção-Geral do Ensino

Superior. Each private institute fills its places through a local competitive examination which they organise themselves.

Admission of Foreign Students

Foreign students must have a certified copy of their country's equivalent of
secondary school leaving certificate, which in the case of British students may
be A-levels. In order to enter university they must also pass an entrance examination. In some cases they have to be able to prove that they have a scholarship
(if necessary), or at least be able to show that they have the means to live while
studying. For those already working in Portugal this should not be a problem.
Students must have a good knowledge of Portuguese, though some universities organise immersion language courses. Applications are handled by the
National Admissions Body (*see* 'Educational Institutions' overleaf).

Socrates Erasmus Programmes

Many EU students are able to study for semesters or full academic years in
other member states under the aegis of the Socrates Erasmus Programme. This
programme was set up as Erasmus in 1987 by the European Commission's
Educational Programme for Higher Education Students, Teachers and
Institutions, with the aim of increasing student mobility within the then
European Community, subsequently the European Economic Area countries,
and now also the Associated Countries of Central and Eastern Europe, Cyprus
and Malta. In 1995 it was reorganised into the new Socrates Programme, which
covers education from school to university to lifelong learning.

Paying for Your Studies

In order to obtain financial aid for first degree studies students must address
themselves directly to the welfare services of the institutions they wish to
attend. Students must be Portuguese nationals or citizens of the European
Union, political refugees, or citizens from a country with bilateral agreements
with Portugal to which this type of support may be granted. Your chances of
getting full funding are slim, however, so you may have to find work to support
your studies, which is not easy. Probably the best bet is to look for English-
teaching and/or translation work, or any other type of employment that fits
around your study schedule.

The Open University

If you cannot, or do not want to enrol in a Portuguese university, there is
always the possibility of distance studying with the UK Open University. For
information about their worldwide programmes, contact the **Open University**

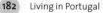

in Europe, Eldon House, Regent Centre, Gosforth, Newcastle upon Tyne NE3 3PW, t (0191) 213 1380, f (0191) 284 6592, **europe@open.ac.uk, www.open.ac.uk**. In Portugal, the OU is represented by the British Council, Rua Luís Fernandes, 1–3, 1249-062 Lisbon, t 213 214 554, f 213 476 151, **c.trewinnard@open.ac.uk**.

Educational Institutions

• **Ministry of Science and Higher Education** (Ministério da Ciência e Ensino Superior), Palácio das Larangeiras, Estrada das Larangerais n°197-205, 1649-018 Lisbon, t 217 231 092, f 217 271 457.

• **Directorate General of Higher Education** (Direcção Geral do Ensino Superior), Avenida Duque d'Avila 137, 169-016 Lisbon, t 213 126 060, f 213 126 061, **www.desup.min-edu.pt**.

• **National Council for Education** (Conselho Nacional de Educação), Rua Florbela Espanca, 1700-195 Lisbon, t 217 935 245, f 217 939 093, **cneme@mail.telepac.pt, www.cnedu.pt**.

• **Coordinating Council for Polytechnic Institutes** (Conselho Coordenador dos Institutos Politécnicos, CCISP), Avenida 5 de Outubro 89-3°, 1050-050 Lisbon, t 217 928 350, f 217 928 369, **ccisp@mail.telepac.pt, www.ccisp.pt**.

• **Council for Higher Education-Business Co-operation** (Conselho para a Cooperação Ensino Superior-Empresa), Rua Pinheiro Chagas 17-3, 1050 Lisbon, t 213 575 501, f 213 579 111.

• **Co-ordinating Council for Private and Co-operative Higher Education** (Conselho Coordenador do Ensino Superior Particular e Cooperativo), Avenida 5 de Outubro 89-2°, 1050-050 Lisbon, t 217 972 910, f 217 956 793.

• **National Admissions Body** (Direcção-Geral do Ensino Superior, Direcção de Serviços de Acesso ao Ensino Superior), Avenida Infante Santo no 2, 1350-178 Lisbon, t 213 912 200, f 213 912 241.

• **NARIC**, General Directorate for Higher Education, Ministry of Education (Direcção Geral do Ensino Superior), Avenida Duque d'Avila, 137-4° Andar, 1069-016 Lisbon, t 213 126 098, f 213 126 041, **www.min-edu.pt**. For questions relating to recognition of studies and qualifications.

• **Socrates Erasmus Programme (UK)**, Socrates-Erasmus Council, R&D Building, The University, Canterbury, Kent CT2 7PD, t (0122) 776 2712, f (0122) 776 2711, **erasmus@ukc.ac.uk, www.erasmus.ac.uk**.

• **Socrates Erasmus Programme (Republic of Ireland)**, Erasmus National Agency, Higher Education Authority, 3rd Floor, Marine House, Clanwilliam Court, Dublin 2, t (01) 661 2748, f (01) 661 0492, **mkerr@hea.ie, www.hea.ie**.

• **Socrates Leonardo da Vinci Programme (Portugal)**, National Agency for the Socrates and Leonardo da Vinci Programmes (Agência Nacional para os Programas Sócrates e Leonardo da Vinci), Avenida Dom. João II. Lote 1.07.2.1, Ed. Administrativo do Parque Expo, Piso 1 Ala B, 1990-096 Lisbon.

- **http://europa.eu.int/comm/education/programmes/socrates/ erasmus/what_en.html.**
- **www.ploteus.net/ploteus/portal/searchcustom.jsp.**
- *Study Abroad*, published annually by UNESCO, is useful. The 2004–2005 edition costs €18.50 and may be bought from the UNESCO website at **http://publishing.unesco.org/details.aspx?Code_Livre=4039**. In the UK contact the Stationery Office Books, Publications Centre, 51 Nine Elms Lane, London SW8 5DR, **t** 0870 240 3701, **f** 0870 600 5533(orders), **book.enquiries@tso.co.uk, www.tso.co.uk/bookshop**. In Ireland contact the Educational Company of Ireland Ltd, PO Box 43A, Ballymount Road, Walkinstown, Dublin 12, **t** (01) 450 0611, **f** (01) 450 0993.

Sports

Football

Without doubt, when it comes to spectator sport in Portugal, *o futebol* is king. Apart from generating the most-read press in the country, football is also one of the most frequent topics of impassioned conversation. The Euro 2004 tournament, said by UEFA to be the 'best organised ever', put Portugal on hundreds of millions of TV screens in the summer of 2004, but glory was snatched away from the national team in the final by the disciplined, defensive Greeks. The tournament has provided the country with eight new and two totally revamped stadia, but the deep-seated problems of the domestic game, low attendances, the critical financial situation of many clubs, the exodus of talented players to more powerful leagues and allegations of corruption remain.

Football is practically the only sport in which Portuguese players, clubs and the national team have ever shone on the international stage. In the early 1960s the marvellous Benfica team looked set to overtake Real Madrid as the continent's leading side. They won the European Cup twice, in 1961 and 1962, the second time led by the legendary Eusebio, in a memorable 5:3 victory over Real Madrid. Benfica's local rivals, Sporting, carried off the 1964 Cup-Winners Cup but from then on Portuguese football began a long, slow decline. Benfica lost the 1968 European Cup final at Wembley, another classic, against the Manchester United team of Charlton, Best and company. Since then the only Portuguese team to achieve anything in Europe has been FC Porto, which has now been proclaimed European Champions twice: in 1987 beating mighty Bayern Munich and in 2004 defeating surprise finalists Monaco. The 'Dragons', as they are known, also won the UEFA Cup in 2003, beating Celtic in an exciting match.

The domestic game, however, has for years been a rather stale three-way affair involving the two big Lisbon clubs and Porto. Even then Porto have been overly dominant, winning league after league, much to the chagrin of Sporting and Benfica fans, who, it is claimed, have five million supporters, half the population! Benfica recently sealed a return to the Champions' League, as runners-up, and carried off the domestic cup against – guess who – Porto. But these achievements are just two bright spots in an otherwise gloomy panorama. One of the case study interviewees in this book said the following of the Portuguese League, 'It is pathetic, it makes the Scottish league look impressive. The Porto manager last season said they played harder in training than they do for league matches. The referees are also beyond words. If I were in Spain I'd have gone local over football. Here, it's too bad to watch.'

Portuguese football certainly has many deep-seated problems, and until 2004 was in a state of crisis. Years of mismanagement put the big clubs into a precarious financial state, attendances were poor and talented young players were invariably snapped up by clubs in Europe's bigger, wealthier leagues. To top it all there was more than a whiff of suspicion that corruption had spread its tentacles to the world of football. In April 2004 a major corruption investigation which had lasted for a year resulted in 'Operation Golden Whistle', a police swoop involving the arrest of 16 referees and football executives, among them the Portuguese League chairman. Those arrested were questioned about suspected match-fixing, bribes, forgery and irregular payments to players. This could not have come at a worse time, as Portugal was gearing up for Euro 2004, the tournament that, it was hoped, would not only bring in masses of revenue but also serve to inject some life back into the domestic game. There was optimism that the tournament would, for three weeks at least, focus attention on to the more savoury aspects of the game. *See* also **Portugal Today**, p.64.

Bullfighting (*A Tourada*)

As in Spain, bullfighting is not considered a sport but rather an art form, an expression of aesthetics. Unlike in Spain, the bull is not usually put to the sword in the arena but slaughtered later, out of sight. In Spain the chief figure is called the *matador*; in Portugal it is the *cavaleiro*, who is decked out in splendid 18th-century attire and mounted on a magnificent Lusitano horse. He goads the bull by pricking it with small spears. The horsemanship of the *cavaleiro* is greatly appreciated by the crowd and an important part of the spectacle. Another difference between the *tourada* and the Spanish *corrida* is that this phase is not the prelude to the entrance of the *matador* but is followed by the dramatic struggle between the half-dozen *forcados* and the bull. The lead *forcado* awaits the charge of the bull and then hangs on for dear life, often to the horns, which are usually capped. Then, with the aid of the remaining *forcados* the objective is to wrestle the bull to a standstill.

The *tourada* does not have a mass following any more but nor is there much of an anti-bullfighting lobby. Recently, the law banning the killing of bulls in the ring has been challenged. In Barranco, close to the Spanish border in the Alentejo, bulls have in fact been killed in the arena for years and no action was taken against the *matadores*, who were usually touring Spanish or Mexican bullfighters. Animal rights campaigners went to court to see the law applied; parliament responded by maintaining the ban but reducing the sentence from a lengthy jail sentence to a small fine in those places where there was actually a tradition of lethal bullfights. Barrancos thus enjoys special status, which may serve as a precedent, allowing more towns to adopt the Spanish-type fights.

Other Spectator Sports

There are other spectator sports in Portugal. At the Fernanda Pires da Silva racing circuit, near Estoril, **motor-racing** enthusiasts can see car and bike racing. Management is currently trying to upgrade the facilities to bring Formula One back to Portugal. **Tennis** fans can take in the Estoril Open tournament, held around Easter time, which often attracts several top names. Portugal also has a long tradition of **dressage**, and the Hipódromo do Campo Grande in Lisbon hosts the Internacional Concurso Oficial de Saltos. **Golf** fans should look out for the Algarve Open, held every year in April at the prestigious Vale do Lobo course, with many top names participating.

Recreational Sports

Owing to its climate and lengthy coastline, Portugal offers a great many possibilities for taking part in active sports and other recreational activities. Joining a sports club is an excellent way of meeting new people, whether expats or locals. Outdoor sports are hugely popular, but in the larger cities it is also possible to find gyms for squash, badminton and martial arts.

Golf

Golf is a minority sport in Portugal and is played mainly by tourists and well-off foreign residents. There is no shortage of courses in Portugal. In the Algarve alone there almost 20 and there are a further dozen or so in the Lisbon area, more along the Costa de Prata, another half dozen or so around Oporto and a few scattered around in inland areas such as Montanhas and the Alentejo. In addition, you may play in Madeira and the Azores. Part of the attraction of golf in Portugal, apart from the game itself, is the fact that many courses are in stunningly beautiful locations and are themselves superbly landscaped. Fees vary widely, depending on the course and the time of year, with discounts for low season; spring and autumn tend to be more expensive than winter and the height of summer.

For information about courses throughout Portugal, look at **www.golfeurope. com** or, for courses in the Algarve, see **www.algarvegolf.net**. Otherwise, contact the Portuguese Golf Federation (*see* 'Sports Federations', below).

Water Sports

Water sports fans also fare well in Portugal, in particular surfers, windsurfers and kitesurfers. Portugal has over 600km of west-facing Atlantic coast with dozens of practically undiscovered small bays as well as well-known surf beaches. The south-facing Algarve also has many good surfing and windsurfing spots. The best season for surfing is late winter and early spring, and serious surfers say that Nazaré, on the Costa de Prata, has the best swell on the coast. There are international surfing and bodyboarding events throughout the year. For more information, look at **www.offitsface.com** and **www.wannasurf.com**, or the Portuguese Surf Federation's website (*see* below) which lists some 44 recognised clubs. If you prefer scuba-diving and snorkelling, there are many spots where you can do this, especially in the Algarve. It is easy to rent equipment.

Sailing

Portugal is also a magnet for sailors; there are no fewer than 19 marinas listed at **www.marina-info.com** and several more ports with anchorage facilities. Some of them are very swish, such as the one at Vilamoura, others brand new, such as in Lagos, and there are sailing or yacht clubs in main coastal towns.

Tennis

Tennis is also popular with foreign residents and the Portuguese alike, and is probably the third most-played sport in the country. There are clubs in all major cities and most towns and the playing surfaces range from all-weather and artificial grass to American clay.

Other Recreational Sports

As well as this, there are expatriate **cricket clubs** and a great many other facilities for sports, mainly where the tourist industry has responded to demand and sports include **archery, horse-riding, lawn bowls, hill-walking, sailing** and **water-skiing**. In the Montanhas region of the Serra da Estrela there are **winter sports**, though many skiers go to Spain where there is a greater range of *pistes*.

Sports Federations

- **Federação Portuguesa de Atletismo** (Portuguese Athletics Federation), Largo da Lagoa, 15B, 795-116 Linda-a-Velha, **t** 214 146 020, **f** 214 146 021, **fpa@fpatletismo.pt, www.fpatletismo.pt**.

- **Federação Portuguesa de Ciclismo** (Portuguese Cycling Federation), Rua Camões, 57, 2500-174 Caldas da Rainha, **t** 262 840 970/262 840 971, **f** 262 834 434, **geral@uvp-fpc.pt**, **www.uvp-fpc.pt**.
- **Federação Portuguesa de Cricket** (Portuguese Cricket Federation), PO Box 76, 2766-901, Estoril, **t** 214 446 466, **f** 219 243 004, **mail@portugal cricket.org**.
- **Federação Portuguesa de Futebol** (Portuguese Football Federation), Praça da Alegria, 25, 1250-004 Lisbon, **t** 213 252 700, **f** 213 252 780, **www.fpf.pt**.
- **Federação Portuguesa de Golfe** (Portuguese Golf Federation), Avenida das Túlipas, 6, Edifício Miraflores, 17°, Miraflores, 1495-161 Algés, **t** 214 123 780, **f** 214 107 972, **fpg@fpg.pt**, **www.fpg.pt**.
- **Federação Portuguesa de Surf** (Portuguese Surfing Federation), Complexo Desportivo de Ouressa, 2725-320 Mem-Martins, Sintra, **t** 219 228 914, **f** 219 228 915, **fps@surfingportugal.com**, **www.surfingportugal.com**.
- **Federação Portuguesa de Ténis** (Portuguese Tennis Federation), Rua Actor Chaby Pinheiro, 7ª, 2795-060, Linda-a-Velha, **t** 214 151 356/94, **f** 214 141 520, **fptenis@mail.telepac.pt**, **www.fptenis.pt**.
- **Federação Portuguesa de Vela** (Portuguese Sailing Federation), Doca de Belém, 1300-038 Lisbon, **t** 213 658 500, **f** 213 620 215, **fpvela@fpvela.pt**, **www.fpvela.pt**.

Hobbies and Recreational Activities

Hobbies and recreational activities are not very high on the agenda of many Portuguese people, since work (which in many cases involves very long hours) and family are far more important. This leaves little time for basket-weaving, pottery or yoga. In rural areas some people make their living through craftwork and they don't consider it to be a recreational activity.

However, things are changing, and for the better. If you want to pursue a hobby or recreational course you can, though you might have to look around quite a lot before finding one that suits you. There is a paucity of institutionally run activities, unlike in some other countries where local and borough councils provide all manner of courses in FE colleges, cultural centres and adult educa-tion centres. This is unlikely to change in the current climate of government cutbacks and budget austerity. You are more likely to find courses that are organised by private institutions and individuals than council-backed ones.

Much depends on what you want you want to do. In the section above we have given many pointers to sporting activities, for which there are an increasing number of facilities, especially in the more developed coastal areas and those with a large expatriate population. In larger towns and cities there are nowadays an increasing number of franchised gyms where you can do fitness, yoga, martial arts and more besides. The best place to find these is by looking in the *Yellow Pages* or simply asking your colleagues or neighbours.

If your aim is to do something more 'arty' or creative, you may have to delve a little further. One place to go is to your nearest university (*see* 'Studying in Portugal', pp.179–83). Most have an arts faculty where students do full-time degrees in *belas artes*. There may be courses in photography or drawing that are organised for non-faculty people, but these are uncommon as courses are, in general, serious rather than recreational. Alternatively, you may find adverts for courses on noticeboards in bookshops, bars and cafés. A good source, by all accounts, is 'Irish pubs', of which there are several in Lisbon, Oporto and the Algarve – an advert for Irish dancing was spotted in one! Course content may cover tile-making, painting, photography, pottery or other crafts and these courses would probably be run privately.

Expat sources may be useful and should not be looked down upon. English language news papers such as *The News* typically have this type of information, though it is mostly aimed at Algarve residents. The online version may be especially helpful as there are downloadable classifieds and lifestyle sections, in PDF format. Go to **www.the-news.net** and follow the links for the most recent sections. In addition, Lisbon residents can pick up a free publication called *Follow me Lisboa*, which is available in many bars and hotels. It mainly contains listings information, but there are sometimes adverts for courses and other recreational activities. Similarly, on the Lisboa Tourism site, **www.atlturismolisboa.pt**, there may be some useful pointers.

Thespians and theatre-lovers who do not dare to tread the boards in Portuguese are catered for in Lisbon and the Algarve, where there are English-language amateur theatre groups that always welcome new members, whether to act in plays or help backstage or with production. On the Algarve there is 'The Algarveans', an experimental theatre group that is constantly looking for new members. As well as experimental work, the Algarveans also do a pantomime during the Christmas period which is fun to be involved in. They advertise regularly in *The News* – check in the 'Entertainment and Leisure' section or look on their unofficial website, **www.valegrifo.com/algarveans**. To contact them, e-mail the chairman, Sue Bickerdike, on **susi-b@clix.pt**.

In Lisbon, the Lisbon Players regularly put on performances that in recent years have included plays by Shakespeare, Tennessee Williams, Beckett, Fernando Pessoa, David Mamet, Oscar Wilde and Steven Berkoff as well as musical productions of *The Beggar's Opera* and *Oh What a Lovely War!*. They can be contacted at Rua da Estrela, 10, 1200 Lisbon, **t** 213 961 946, **lisbon players@lisbonplayers.com.pt**, **www.lisbonplayers.com.pt/EN/english.html**.

Working in Portugal

08

Nobody should be under any illusions that finding a job or freelance work, or setting up and running a successful business in Portugal, is easy. Stable and well remunerated jobs are especially hard to find and are likely to become more so as legislation tends to liberalise the labour market. The government says that this will create more jobs, but predictably they will be more short-term and precarious in nature. Curiously, it is also difficult to enter at the bottom end of the job ladder as competition is fierce, especially from other non-Portuguese workers who come from the former colonies and Eastern Europe.

English-speakers may find that the only real opportunities arise in those sectors where their language puts them at an advantage – language instruction and (private) school teaching, the tourist industry and its spin-off activities, and UK and international firms where there is a need for English-speakers in secretarial and middle management posts. Enterprising and determined people may also do well as freelancers in a number of fields; success really comes down to the qualities of the individual concerned and the standard of work offered. The same applies to running a small business where, despite myriad obstacles, anyone who finds a niche can do well. What nobody should take as given is that they are going to become rich quickly, or at all.

Business Etiquette

The Portuguese professional and business environment is comparatively formal. Differences in business and working culture are reflected in clothing, body language, procedures for making appointments, forms of address, negotiating and topics of conversation, when not discussing business *per se*.

People in the working world are usually well dressed. Except maybe in banking and the legal professions, a sports jacket, trousers and a tie is acceptable enough for men, though a suit is always a safe option. Younger Portuguese business people have a penchant for designer labels but power-dressing is not overly common. Women should err on the conservative side when dressing for work or meetings, but trousers are perfectly acceptable as part of a smart suit or outfit. If you are hot in a meeting, you may take off your jacket, though it is a good policy to ask if anyone minds before you do. Only in less formal business sectors, such as computing, the media or graphic design, do people dress down. Even then, a scruffy or grungy look situates you outside of dress code parameters. If invited to social occasions, casual clothes are acceptable, but even there avoid too informal a look.

Portuguese people stand closer to one another and maintain eye contact for longer than is customary in Anglo Saxon culture. Physical contact is also more common; gentle gripping of the arm or placing a hand on the shoulder when walking down a street indicates warmth and trust, not anything untoward. Always shake hands when meeting with a contact. Whether you are being introduced for the first time or have met them many times before, the handshake should not be too firm. Women tend to kiss each other, and male colleagues, once on each cheek, when meeting. Knowing exactly when to do this instead of shaking hands is difficult. Extend your hand and only kiss if the woman offers her cheek. The Portuguese are fairly relaxed about public behaviour and are not easily upset by 'rules' being broken, as long as it is clear that your intentions are polite. Otherwise, avoid the following: stretching in public, eating with your fingers (or licking them), writing in red, turning your back on people at a table, smoking without asking first, slovenly postures. Always attempt to be polite, and say 'please' when handing something to somebody. Beware that sexist comments and conduct may arise, thankfully less so than in the past, but do not be surprised by them.

Office hours vary but are roughly 9–1 and 2–6. Lunch is sacred – many meetings in fact take place around a table and deals are often closed there. Avoid fixing appointments for before 10am or immediately after lunch. Probably the best times are around 11am, when things are moving, or 4pm, when lunch has gone down. Do not be surprised if a meeting is fixed for 6 or 7pm. Be punctual (or even a little early) for meetings but don't be surprised if this is not reciprocated. If you are kept waiting for a few minutes, possibly as many as 20, do not be offended or assume there are any power games going on. If you are kept waiting more than half an hour, expressing your irritation will be understood. If you are likely to be late for an appointment, phone ahead with your apologies and excuses.

Many Portuguese professionals and business people speak English to a good level, quite possibly French and maybe Spanish. Even so, if you can hold your own in Portuguese you will make great headway from the start. If English is the language used, avoid using slang and speak slowly and clearly. Be careful with Spanish as Portuguese people almost always understand it but may not speak it, and for historical reasons are sometimes loath to be spoken to in their neighbours' tongue. Besides, however good your Spanish is, you may not understand a quick-fire reply in Portuguese.

Conversations at social gatherings or as a preamble to a meeting tend to be a little more formal than in the UK or the USA, though people are generally prepared to engage in idle chit-chat provided the topics are not controversial or directly taboo. Football, the climate, the economy, food and wine (especially if you extol the virtues of Portuguese cuisine and wine), the family, films and books are all safe topics. Avoid subjects such as religion, politics (interestingly, many business people in Portugal are left-leaning, so do not assume that their professional background implies centre or centre-right views), sex, people's positions, careers or salaries. However, the Portuguese, as a trading nation, have plenty of experience of working with foreigners and cultural differences do not

The Right Form of Address

In English, the person we are speaking to is always 'you', be it our friend in the pub or the manager of the bank to which we are applying for a mortgage: 'Here, get us a pint while you're at it, will you?' and 'Could you see your way to loaning me £200,000?' are, linguistically, essentially the same: the first person (speaker) is asking the second person (listener) for a favour. The difference lies in the terms in which each request is couched: in the first our tone is familiar, in the second we are deferential. But in each case we address our listener as 'you'.

Other languages have forms to distinguish addressees. The French *tu* and Spanish *tú* mean 'you' the friend, family member, co-worker, subordinate, person of same age and social status, child. *Vous* (French) and *usted* (Spanish) are for 'you' the bank manager, police officer, boss, venerable elderly person, newly introduced business contact and so on. In each language the third-person singular of the verb accompanies the polite form of address.

Portuguese is much more complex and expressing the correct level of deference can take foreigners a long time to master.

To begin with, *tu*, the informal second-person singular form of address, should be avoided except when speaking to your family, intimate friends, children, pets or God. Don't use *tu* to business acquaintances, bosses, civil servants or any unknown adult person, whatever their rank. Also, be careful of using first names unless you have been told that you may do so.

What form to use, then? It depends. Historically, the limited access to higher education has meant that a university degree confers prestige on the holder. It is still common to refer to a graduate in any discipline as *Senhor/a Doutor/a*, even if s/he does not practise medicine or hold a PhD. Architects and engineers are addressed as *Senhor/a Arquitecto/a* and *Senhor/a Engenheiro/a*, respectively. The title is usually preceded by the addressee's surname. Thus, if your business contact is a graduate, but not an architect or engineer, and has the surname Gomes, you would address him as *Senhor Doutor Gomes*; if your female boss is an architect surnamed Ferreira you would call her *Senhora Arquitecta Ferreira*. If you know nothing specific about your interlocutor, you are usually safe using the third-person form of address *O senhor* or *A senhora*.

This might all seem antiquated, and it is, and it actually gets a whole lot more Byzantine than this brief outline has room to explain. But be aware that these forms of address are not restricted to awards ceremonies or formal correspondence, they are part of everyday speech.

faze them; you would have to be quite clumsy to commit a serious *faux pas*. Possibly the most difficult area is choosing which form of address to use, some indications are given in the box above.

It is common practice to present gifts to established or prospective partners or clients. Never reject a gift when it is offered to you as it is a personal gesture, a mark of respect, not an intended bribe. Appreciated, and appropriate, gifts may be something from your own country or region or relatively expensive items such as a fountain pen, a porcelain ornament or a coffee table book. Personal items of dress – a tie or a scarf – are also safe bets. A bottle of spirits is usually well received, though wine is best avoided as the Portuguese are rightly proud of their own. Your company's own branded gifts may go down well, or not, depending what they are. A bunch of cheap biros will not get you very far. While business contacts are rarely invited home, if you do receive an invitation take flowers or chocolates and something for the children, whom you will almost certainly meet. Take care to make these gifts age-appropriate.

The Labour Market

The Portuguese labour market, like that of any other EU country, is open to all EU citizens, whichever member state they come from. One of the most important principles involved is that, in theory, there is no discrimination against any person on the grounds of their nationality. Provided you are qualified for any job you apply for, you should be able to compete on an equal footing with other, similarly qualified, contenders and the job should be given to the best candidate.

The job market, though, is a tough, cut-throat place. The state of the market at any given time is inseparable from the state of the economy. In 2004 Portugal's economy was not buoyant. Unemployment, having dropped during the 'boom' years following Portugal's entry into the EU and throughout the late 1990s until 2002, has since been climbing again and is currently around 7 per cent. Despite a slight economic upturn in the last quarter of 2003, the Bank of Portugal was forced early in 2004 to reduce its GDP growth forecasts both for 2004 and 2005 in the face of an expected downturn in domestic demand. There was a sharp rise in companies filing for bankruptcy in the early months of 2004.

Foreign investment in Portugal plummeted from around €6.6 billion in 2001 to slightly less than €1 billion in 2003, and business leaders are concerned that the 10 new member states will lure investors eastwards. There, monthly wages average €500, compared with Portugal's €845, and workforces are well qualified. Portugal also stands to lose many of the EU subsidies that have been so crucial in helping the country overhaul its infrastructures. All of this affects everyone's chances of finding employment, and although the new Labour Code (*Código do Trabalho*), effective from 1 December 2003 may make for a more agile labour market, with more short-term work available, stable, long-term employment will most likely to be harder than ever to find.

Therefore the prospects do not look too bright – and even in the good years Portugal has never offered foreigners a great many work opportunities. Despite the theoretical equality enjoyed by EU citizens in the labour market, Portuguese enterprises do not tend to employ foreign workers. Again, if you want work in Portugal, keep in mind that your chances of finding it are vastly increased if you can speak the language fluently. You can hardly expect to compete on equal terms with native-speaking Portuguese workers, who are prepared to work for much less than you might expect yourself, if you cannot even cope with an interview in the language.

Despite this, English-speakers do find openings, sometimes using their English language skills; a small expatriate labour market exists parallel to and independently of the global one, as will be seen in the next section. The interviewees who have contributed case studies to this book all have work and are at least getting by, if not doing very well. There is no reason why you cannot do so too.

Job Ideas

While many areas of the working world are effectively closed off to foreigners, there are areas where English-speakers stand a much greater chance of finding employment or being able to work as freelancers. English-language teaching, tourism and providing services to the burgeoning expat community in areas such as the Algarve are all areas where you will stand a chance. Teaching will be considered in a section of its own (*see* pp.210–13), as will the ins and outs of freelancing (*see* pp.213–15). At the higher end of the job market, management and secretarial posts are to be found in British and multinational companies that operate in Portugal. Whatever area you wish to work in, it is better to start looking before you leave for Portugal or, at the very least, make a reconnaissance trip first.

UK and International Companies

There are any number of British and international enterprises with a presence in Portugal, many of them household names in Britain, Ireland and worldwide. They operate in the fields of accountancy, consulting, banking, import–export, insurance, information technology, the law, manufacturing, marketing, property, shipping and freight, telecommunications, translation, travel and tourism and the wine industry. As a rule, such companies tend to be established either in Lisbon and Oporto, and possibly in the Algarve or Madeira, but anyone looking for a job in these fields should expect to end up living and working in either of the major cities. It is not uncommon to find English speakers in the middle and higher levels of management of these companies, though many of them are in the Portuguese arm of their company as a result of having been seconded there by the head office.

A good source of information about foreign companies is the British–Portuguese **Chamber of Commerce**, based in Lisbon, which produces a members' directory annually. This lists Portuguese companies that deal with

Case Study: Martin O'Donnell

Martin O'Donnell is from Dublin, where he worked in the electronic security business after leaving school, initially as a technician, then in sales and marketing and eventually in management. When he moved to Portugal three years ago this mixed background proved very useful for finding employment, as such a range of experiences is unusual in Portugal.

Q What brought you to Portugal originally?

MO I came to watch Ireland play Portugal, met a girl and after several weekends in Ireland and Portugal we decided one of us should relocate. My girlfriend had already been teaching English for 10 years in Portugal, and I had previously only lived abroad for short periods so decided that a longer-term experience of living abroad would make an interesting change.

Q How did you find your job?

MO Before leaving Ireland I researched on the Internet and applied to several international companies in my business field. I also applied to some bigger local companies. Lack of Portuguese was a barrier both with the local companies and branches of international companies. Eventually, through the European HQ of an international company, I heard there was a vacancy for a product manager in Lisbon. Much of the job involves liaising with external suppliers in Switzerland, Germany, Britain, Italy, etc. so fluent English was a bonus. Internally, however, communication is in Portuguese so it was essential to learn it. I did an intensive one-to-one course to get the basics and picked up more by being in a Portuguese-speaking environment. It's still not 100 per cent and probably never will be, but it works!

Q How do you find working here compares with working at home?

MO Very different. I find there is a lot more red tape within companies. Workers do not have the same autonomy; modern human resource concepts have not yet arrived. In general people are more relaxed; possibly because of the low salary levels, workers do not feel that they should stress themselves too much. Becoming a full-time employee is a long process which will probably get longer in the future. It is not unusual to have an initial six- or twelve-month contract which may be renewed. When (if) it is renewed for the third time you become '*efectivo*' (permanent) in your job, which brings more security. The norm is for people get a job and stay there; most of my colleagues of a similar age have been with the same company for 10–15 years! Almost unheard of in Irish private industry.

Q Any tips for would-be residents?

MO Get a job at home that will relocate you to Portugal and pay you a UK or Irish salary! That way you'll get the best of both worlds: plenty of money and excellent weather.

British and other international clients, or British and international companies that operate in Portugal. With slightly more than 230 pages, at a couple of entries per page, this directory is an invaluable source of information for the job-seeker or anyone looking for companies to trade with. Full addresses, contact information and the names of the directors or managers are provided. A good many have names that are distinctly not Portuguese, which illustrates the extent to which foreign management experts have established themselves in the Portuguese business world. However, although a name and logo might be well known, you may find that an apparently 'British' company is actually run and staffed by a majority of Portuguese nationals whose needs for anglophone staff might be minimal, and limited precisely to English language liaison functions, though you would be expected to speak Portuguese daily.

Among the Chamber's aims, as can be seen from its mission statement, is to 'advise on recruitment of...English-speaking personnel'. The Chamber does not act as a recruiting agency but is a good point of contact between job seekers and potential employers. The **Câmara de Comércio Luso-Británica** is at Rua da Estrela, 8, 1200-699 Lisbon, **t** 213 942 020, **f** 213 942 029, **info@bpcc.pt**, **www. bilateral.biz**.

Tourism

Tourism is one of Portugal's most important industries and provides work, either directly or indirectly, for many people, local and foreign. The nature of tourism is slowly changing. Portugal is looking to move away from the mass, sun-and-sand package deal type of tourism and more towards other alternatives such as cultural, rural and eco-tourism. It is felt that the resort-based tourism such as exists already may have reached saturation point or, were it to continue, would wreak further environmental damage. But packages of a week or fortnight are still a vital part of the industry and will be for some time to come. Newer forms of tourism will not necessarily reduce job prospects but will require personnel with a different outlook, skills and qualifications.

There are approximately 250 tour operators worldwide with Portugal on their list of destinations. Jobs generated include resort administration, tour representatives and looking after children and elderly tourists. For jobs directly in the tourist industry, approach major tour operators, such as Thomas Cook. Indirectly, resorts throw up many job opportunities, usually short-term, for activities such as sports coaching, scuba-diving, horse-riding, tennis or golf. The catering sector is clearly linked to the tourist industry and in popular destinations there are often jobs for bar staff, waiters and cooks. Similarly, there is a demand for bar staff, bouncers and DJs in the nightlife and tourist entertainment industry.

Most tourist areas have large expatriate communities, bringing opportunities for people with a wide range of skills. Many second- and holiday-home owners do not speak Portuguese and feel more comfortable contracting services from an English-speaker. If you have a skill or a trade to offer, there may be chances of plying it. Nannies, hairdressers, plumbers, gardeners, electricians, maids, tilers and various other tradespeople can and do find work, especially in the Algarve. In addition, anyone with a background in property-sales or management may find opportunities in that area. Do be aware, though, that your chances of finding a stable job or continuous employment are slim, unless you are lucky or have enough money to live on and can stay the course while looking.

Translating and Interpreting

Portugal has many economic ties with the rest of the world, so many business documents and correspondence need translating, and companies sometimes require staff to interpret at conferences. As well as this, proofreading work is sometimes available. Most translators work freelance, as there are few full-time posts available. You need to build up a lot of contacts before you can be assured of reasonable and regular earnings but you can get jobs that are farmed out by translation agencies to self-employed translators. Find them in the *Yellow Pages* or contact either of the following, which are well-established and reputable:

- **Traducta Serviços de Tradução e Interpretação**, Rua Rodrigo da Fonseca, 127, 1º Dto, 1070-240 Lisbon, **t** 213 883 384, **f** 213 857 886, **info@traducta.pt**, **www.traducta.pt**

- **AIP-Assistentes Intérpretes de Portugal**, Avenida da República, 41–43, 1050-187 Lisbon, **t** 217 994 360, **f** 217 994 369.

While many residents find translating just by virtue of the fact that they live in Portugal, speak the language and have a few contacts, some form of qualification is useful. The London-based **Institute of Linguists** (Saxon House, 48 Southwark Street, London SE1 1UN, **t** (020) 7940 3100, **f** (020) 7940 3101, **info@iol.org.uk**, **www.iol.org.uk**) offers a qualification in translating that helps when seeking work.

Journalism

Apart from correspondents working for British and international newspapers or agencies such as Reuters, most work in journalism is likely to be freelance. See 'Freelancing or Part-time Work', pp.213–15.

The Public Sector

In theory you should be able to compete for jobs within the public sector, along with Portuguese nationals. Entry to the Civil Service is normally by competitive exam. Currently some 700,000 people form the state bureaucracy, 15 per cent of the overall workforce. As Portugal is aiming to downsize its

Jobs for the Boys

Certain stories sometimes come to light in the press, on websites and in chat rooms, about how people in Portugal find their ways into employment for which they are not necessarily qualified or even where there is apparently no vacancy.

Take the following case, found on a website that specialises in blowing the whistle on administrative graft: 'Now, it seems that there was this teacher, who was sent to a school in Viseu, without that school even asking [the Education Ministry] for a teacher. Why? I don't know, but it seems that schoolmistress was candidate number 157 for that school, and she got the job over all the other candidates. Might it be because she was the cousin of a deputy elect [MP] for the Viseu constituency? Any suggestion of a *'cunha'* was rejected immediately until...today...the Regional Director of Education for the Centre of Portugal admitted that he had always pushed to help the good lady be given a job.'

Whether or not this is true, the most important word in the above paragraph is *'cunha'*, pronounced *'KOO-nyah'*, which translates as 'wedge' but means knowing someone who is in a position to pull strings on your behalf. If you have *'uma boa cunha'* your chances of getting a civil service job are much enhanced. Technically speaking, admission to public posts is by competitive exam and examinees are admitted according to the points they obtain and other merits. But having *'uma cunha'* on the *júri*, the panel that awards the marks, will certainly help you to climb closer to the top of the pile.

This is nothing new. In 1870, the great writer Eça de Queiroz sat an exam for the vacant post of consul in Brazil. He got top marks but not the post. That went to the second-placed Manuel Saldanha da Gama, who had a *'cunha'*. During Salazar's regime, it became absolutely indispensable to have *'cunha'*, even to get a job as doorman at the local council. It was hoped that the 1974 revolution would put paid to the practice. Some hope. One columnist claims that the *'cunha'* has become a national institution and that no government since then, of whatever political leaning, can claim to have clean hands, whatever they may have said they would do to combat it while in opposition. The English phrase, 'jobs for the boys' has come into common parlance now and, as the writer of the article above says, 'It's worse than before, now we've got "jobs for the boys' cousins and even "jobs for the boys' daughters",'– in reference to a recent, widely reported case involving a minister's daughter getting a place in medical school, for which she had not obtained sufficient grades.

administration the whole question of public sector employment is up for review, so few opportunities are likely to come up. Here, more than anywhere, you will also not be competing on equal terms unless you have lived in the country for a long time and know its language and culture extremely well. You also need *'uma boa cunha'*, see box, above.

Looking for Work

Before looking at the ins and outs of being employed, some pointers about finding employment in the first place might be useful. Ideally you should aim to arrive in Portugal with a job already set up, rather than turning up and starting your search there. If you plan to do this, though, make sure to have a good cushion of funds to tide you over while you search.

Trawling the Net

In any job centre in the EU you can look at the database of the **EURES** scheme, on which job vacancies are posted Europe-wide. Alternatively look at the website **http://europa.eu.int/jobs/eures**, where jobs are advertised in all EU countries. This may be a a long shot, though, as very few jobs are posted there for Portugal.

There are many websites on which you can search for jobs. Most display vacancies by sector, location or salary range and also allow you to place your CV online for perusal by prospective employers. There are international sites with links to the country you want to work in and there are also some Portugal-specific sites. Some suggested sites are:

- **www.anyworkanywhere.com**: Clearly aimed at young people, specialises in jobs in the tourist industry and related fields.
- **www.eurojobs.com**: Has a reasonable selection of jobs.
- **www.hays.pt**: The Portuguese site of Hays, a very serious, professional recruitment and human resources specialist; it may be viewed in English.
- **www.manpower.pt**: Portuguese page of the international agency.
- **http://jobsearch.netscape.monster.co.uk/european**: Monster does not have a specifically Portuguese site but jobs in Portugal may be viewed from here.
- **http://jobs.escapeartist.com/Openings/Portugal**: Worldwide expatriate site with a few openings in Portugal.
- **www.infojobs.net**: A Spanish-language site though by clicking on 'international' and choosing 'Portugal' you can view Portuguese vacancies.
- **www.net-empregos.com**: Portuguese-language site where you can file a CV and view and apply for job offers online.
- **www.stepstone.pt/home_fs.htm**: Portuguese page of the international www.stepstone.com
- **http://superemprego.sapo.pt/pt/index_emprego.htm**: Portuguese-language site with a similar structure to **www.net-empregos.com**.

Targeting Companies

Another way of making yourself known is to target companies in which you would like to work or where you think you might find a job. The Chamber of Commerce directory and the Internet will help you here. It may seem speculative, but a good, well-presented CV that arrives unsolicited on a personnel manager's desk may attract more attention than one sent in reply to an advertised post (where it will be just one among many). In addition, as practically all multinational companies have their own web pages nowadays, usually with a 'work with us' button, you can easily find out if any of them have vacancies at their Portugal offices.

Newspapers

Few jobs in Portugal are advertised in the main daily British and international newspapers. Those that are will most probably be at the higher end of the market, executive posts and so on, or in the field of education. Sector-specific trade journals do carry job adverts, so if you are already working in, for example, chemicals, electronics or textiles, consult its specialist magazine.

If you read Portuguese, you can look in any of the major Portuguese-language newspapers (*see* **Portugal Today**, 'Newspapers', pp.56–7). There you will find many jobs in the classifieds under '*emprego*' (employment). As these papers are not sold widely abroad, you may find it easier to consult their online editions:

- *Correio da Manhã*: **www.correiomanha.pt**.
- *Diário de Notícias*: **www.dn.pt**.
- *Diário Económico*: **www.diarioeconomico.com**.
- *Expresso*: **http://online.expresso.pt**.
- *Jornal de Notícias*: **www.jnoticias.pt**.
- *Público*: **www.publico.pt**.

The English-language newspapers *The News* (**www.the-news.net**) and the *Anglo-Portuguese News* can be useful.

Recruitment and Temporary Agencies

There are many temporary work agencies, the majority based in Lisbon and Oporto and a few smaller ones in the Algarve. They are worth contacting, as they may help you to get a temporary placement and a foot in the door. Look in the *Yellow Pages* under *Pessoal Temporário* or *Recrutamento e Selecção*. A well-known agency is **Manpower**, Rua Jose Fontana, 9C, 1050 Lisbon, **t** 213 129 830, **f** 213 129 849, **www.manpower.pt**.

Case Study: Kevin the All-rounder

Kevin Rose, 34, a graduate in international relations with a Masters degree in European affairs, has been in Portugal since 1992. He works as a university lecturer and freelance translator, interpreter and journalist. He has a Portuguese wife and three young children.

Q How do you find working here compares with working at home?

KR Wages are much lower but so are expectations as to productivity or standards. Generally, private sector employees work long hours or require two sources of income to remain 'middle class'. Foreigners are 'accepted' only where required to supply a particular service. Companies are hierarchical, promotion is less on merit and more on a complex cocktail of contacts, length of service, favouritism, etc.

Q Do you live mainly in the expat community or have you integrated?

KR My social life is mixed. With other expats it is mainly because of a common background and sense of humour, interest in beer and Premier League football, better 'friends' and networking for jobs. With Portuguese people it is easy to make superficial relationships but concepts of friendship are different, and women tend to want serious commitment. Relationships are always difficult, owing, I feel, to lingering social influences of Salazar dictatorship, lack of trust in the authorities, the hierarchical nature of society's structures and the high level of competition for benefits brought by the development of the 1990s.

Q How do you find bringing up your children bilingually?

KR I have three small children. I speak to them in English, and to my wife in Portuguese. English-language schools are out of the price range of all but senior expat management so we have used a local private school through to primary age and my eldest is due to start at the state school in September. Portugal is very child-friendly in terms of restaurants, public transport and in general. Academic standards are good for the small percentage who cope easily, but the rest struggle. Many of the locals use the extended family to get round the reality of long working hours – many a granny picks up kids from school.

Q What changes have you observed since you have been here?

KR There has been a certain loss of character, and prices have risen, Lisbon remains a beautiful and rather unusual place. Much more could have been done but what has been done has been done relatively well, e.g. public utilities work, the vastly improved metro/transport system, Expo '98. Law and order is perceived to be deteriorating but I think it remains a 'safe' place by European standards. Wages and social security remain low, with little progress in more complicated or less high priority areas, such as health, justice, cycle lanes, parking regulations.

For 'real' jobs, generally at the higher end of the spectrum, contact a recruitment agency. One of the best, in many countries and Portugal, is **Hays Specialist Recruitment**, Avenida da República, n° 90-1° Fracção 2 1600-206 Lisbon, **t** 217 826 560, **f** 217 826 566, **Lisbon@hays.pt, www.hays.pt**. The **Luso-British Chamber of Commerce** website, **www.bilateral.biz**, also lists several more Portuguese recruitment and employment agencies.

Portuguese Job Centres (*Centros de Emprego*)

On arriving in Portugal, if you do not yet have a job you may register as a jobseeker with a local job centre, or *centro de emprego*. They are run by the Ministério do Emprego e Segurança Social (Employment and Social Security Ministry) and have offices in most towns and cities. Do not expect job centres to be especially helpful if you do not speak Portuguese, but they may have jobs posted on the noticeboard and should you need to get specialist training you can ask about possible courses. To find the address of your nearest office, look in the telephone book or ask at the town hall. The main regional delegations are:

- **Delegação Regional de Lisbon e Vale do Tejo**, Rua das Picoas, 14, 1069-003 Lisbon, **t** 213 307 400.

- **Delegação Regional do Centro**, Avenida Fernão de Magalhães, 660, 3001-174 Coimbra, **t** 239 860 800.

- **Delegação Regional do Alentejo**, Rua do Menino Jesus, 47–51, 7000-601 Évora, **t** 266 760 500.

- **Delegação Regional do Norte**, Rua Eng° Ezequiel Campos, 488, 4149-004 Porto, **t** 226 159 200.

- **Delegação Regional do Alagarve**, Rua Dr Cândido Guerreiro, 45-1°, Edifício Nascente, 8000-318 Faro, **t** 289 890 100.

Advertising Yourself

Whether you are seeking a job or freelance work, it helps if you take the initiative and advertise yourself. The Algarve-based weekly *The News* accepts adverts from individuals. Place an advert by calling **t** 282 341 100 or send it by e-mail to **ClassAds@The-News.net**. The *Anglo-Portuguese News* (APN, Apartado 113, 2766-902, Estoril, **t** 214 661 423, **f** 214 660 358, **apn@mail.telepac.pt**) also accepts adverts by mail, fax or e-mail. When you contact them state whether you want a box or normal classified advert. The Luso-British Chamber of Commerce also allows you to place your CV on the website **www.bilateral.biz**. As a last resort you can place adverts in local bookshops, bars, universities or even telephone kiosks. You might be pleasantly surprised at the results.

Applications and Job Interviews

Cover Letters, Application Forms and CVs

When applying for a job, your covering letter may be hand-written or typed (printed). Some employers prefer a well laid-out letter created on a computer but 'topped and tailed' by hand. Keep the letter short and to the point, try not to use more than one A4 page, and enclose your CV. Educational certificates and other qualifications will not be needed until the interview stage.

Portuguese companies frequently use application forms as a way of evaluating a potential worker's profile. Some are standardised; others are less structured, with spaces for open questions. Standard questions cover personal details, education and training, work experience, and knowledge of languages. Discrimination on any grounds is not allowed. CVs are usually arranged in chronological order and should not go beyond two or at most three pages. You may be asked to attach a photograph. *See* the sample CV, overleaf.

Interviews

Personal interviews are the main selection technique used in Portugal. For high-powered jobs you may be asked back a second or even a third time. Certain aspects of interview technique, such as punctuality, dressing smartly and politeness, are universal, and basic common sense. Make sure you have done your homework and know something about the company. Take copies of your CV, qualifications, diplomas and any other relevant documents. On entering, you may find you are facing a panel; if so, shake hands with everybody and wait to be invited to sit. In the Portuguese context, showing some background knowledge of the country and its culture will stand you in good stead, as will employing the correct modes of address. Be attentive, show interest in the job, ask pertinent questions and avoid monosyllabic 'yes' and 'no' answers. Body language is important; reinforce your verbal messages with physical actions, and give the impression that you are determined to get the job. Avoid asking about salaries at this stage; you will probably have a chance to ask about this later in the process.

Aptitude and Psychometric Tests

If you successfully pass the interview stage, be prepared for aptitude and psychometric technical tests, which are widespread practice in Portugal when selecting middle management personnel. Companies frequently use recruitment consultants who offer testing as a specific service to an employer or as part of a complete recruitment process. Sometimes consultants use graphology for senior appointments.

CURRICULUM VITAE

Harold Davies
Tel: +351 213 063 948
Mobile: 918 452 286
E-mail: davies_harold@yahoo.co.uk
Rua de São Domingos, 10, 1° Andar, 1269-083 LISBOA
Resident's Card n°: 7852349
Tax Card n°: 909236741
DOB: 04/06/78

EDUCATIONAL BACKGROUND
1999   BSc in Information Technology (IT).
University of North West London.

FURTHER TRAINING
2001   MBA in Internet and e-business.
London Business School, Holborn.

WORK EXPERIENCE
Sept 1999 – Jan 2000   **Systems and Networks Administrator**.
Datasystems and Applications PLC
Functions: In charge of installing and maintaining internal systems and networks for customers.

Jan 2000 – Jun 2001   **IT Consultant (freelance)**.
Haringey Borough Council, London
Functions: Employed on a freelance basis to design and maintain Haringey Borough Council's official web-site as well as installing the internal Intranet system used by different council departments.

Sept 2001 – Aug 2004   **IT and English Language Teacher**.
ENFP – Escola de Negócios y Formação Profissional, Lisboa (Business & Professional Training Academy)
Functions: Teaching MBA students to use computer applications and English language.

LANGUAGES
English: native-speaker level, reading, writing and verbal.
Portuguese: Reading, advanced; Writing, advanced; Verbal, advanced.
German: Reading, intermediate; Writing, low intermediate; Verbal, advanced.

ADDITIONAL INFORMATION
Available to work immediately in any company specialising in Internet and e-business.

CURRICULUM VITAE

Nome: **Harold Davies**
Morada: Rua de São Domingos, 10, 1º Andar - 1269-083 LISBOA
Tel: 213 063 948
Telemóvel: 918 452 286
E-mail: davies_harold@yahoo.co.uk
Cartão de Residência: 7852349
Contribuinte nº: 909236741

HABILITAÇÕES LITERÁRIAS

1999   Licenciatura em Tecnologias de Informação (TI).
        Universidade de North West London.

FURTHER TRAINING

2002   MBA em Internet e Comércio Electrónico.
        London Business School, Holborn.

EXPERIÊNCIA PROFISSIONAL

Set 1999 – Jan 2000   **Administrador de Sistemas e de Redes.**
                           Datasystems and Applications PLC
Funções: Responsável pela instalação e operacionalidade do sistema interno
e redes de vários clientes.

Jan 2000 – Jun 2001   **Consultor de TI (freelancer).**
                           Haringey Borough Council, London
Funções: Empregado numa base de freelancer para conceber e manter o site
oficial do Haringey Borough Council, bem como para instalar o sistema
interno de intranet usado pelos diferentes departamentos do concelho.

Set 2001 – Ag 2004   **Professor de TI e de Inglês.**
                           ENFP – Escola de Negócios e Formação Profissional,
                           Lisboa.
Funções: Ensinar os estudantes do MBA a usarem aplicações informáticas em
língua inglesa

LINGUAS ESTRANGEIRAS

INGLÊS: falante nativo, leitura, escrita e oralidade.
Português: leitura, avançado; escrita, nível avançado; oralidade, nível
avançado.
Alemão: leitura, nível intermédio; escrita, nível intermédio baixo; oralidade,
nível avançado.

OUTRAS INFORMAÇÕES

Disponível para trabalhar imediatamente em qualquer empresa especial-
izada em comércio electrónico.

Employment Contracts

Employment contracts in Portugal are agreements whereby the contracted person agrees to provide intellectual or manual activity (work) in exchange for remuneration under the authority and direction of the contractor. For a long time, and until recently, indefinite contracts were the norm and fixed-term, or temporary, contracts were somewhat rarer. These are likely to become more common as a result of the new Labour Code (*Código do Trabalho*), which widens the scope for short-term contracts being made. The new law stipulates that the terms of the contract must fully explain and justify *why* it is fixed-term and not permanent, as well as stating its duration. The contract must be signed by both parties. As a rule, short contracts are for a minimum of six months and may only be for a shorter period in very special circumstances, which must also be justified by the employer. Employers may automatically renew temporary contracts, two times within a period of three years. The new law, however, allows employers the possibility, at the end of the three-year period, of renewing the contract one more time for a minimum of one and a maximum of three years. So, the maximum time limit for temporary contracts is now six years with three renewals allowed. After that the worker's contract may not be renewed or must be made indefinite.

What Do Your Wages Consist Of?

A facetious answer to that question might be 'not much'. As has been seen, average monthly earnings in Portugal in 2003 were around €845, which with two extra payments per annum (at Christmas and in summer) is an annual total of €11,830, somewhat less than £8,000. The cost of living is not so much lower in Portugal than it is in affluent northern Europe that it compensates for this. Portugal, some surveys show, actually ranks as the sixth most expensive EU country. This is especially noticeable in the prices of fuel, utilities, cars, electrical and other imported goods. High-flying foreigners in Portugal tend to work for foreign companies and are paid UK-equivalent salaries. When Martin O'Donnell recommends getting a job with a UK or Irish salary in his case study, he is not joking. Questioned on this after the interview, he commented that salaries in his native Ireland are *three times* those of Portugal while most manufactured goods are cheaper, food prices are similar and only eating and drinking out is markedly more expensive. As a result, far more highly qualified Portuguese professionals work abroad than the other way around. If you cannot find a job of this kind, and work for local rates, you will necessarily have to get used to a much lower standard of living. Many Portuguese are deeply in debt and few manage to save at the end of the month. Be careful not to find yourself in the same situation.

Salaries in Portugal may be low, but they are nonetheless subject to certain conditions. They are usually paid monthly, but wages may be paid daily or weekly and commissions, as everywhere, are common in sales work. Apart from the base salary, the total amount usually includes a meal allowance and possibly length-of-service bonuses. In the private sector these bonuses are negotiated in sectorial collective agreements. For overtime work and work on days of rest, statutory increases are paid.

Wages must be paid between established and equal periods of time, which may be a week, 15 days or a month, the latter being the most common nowadays. Payment should be made on workdays, during working hours or immediately after these. When the wage is variable and the period of time that serves as a basis for the wage calculation exceeds 15 days, the worker may demand to be paid fortnightly.

Annual salaries in Portugal are divided into 14 payments, with an 'extra' salary paid at Christmas and in the summer. This is not actually anything 'extra'; rather part of your overall annual salary is retained and paid to you in two chunks. You might argue that it would be fairer to receive the full amount every month and then have the possibility of banking a percentage and earning interest on it.

Tax and social security deductions eat up about 23 per cent of your salary.

Working Conditions

The Working Week

The standard, full-time working week in Portugal is 40hrs, spread, usually, over five days per week and eight hours per day. By law, Sunday is a compulsory day of rest, and provision is made for an additional full or half-day free. Exceptions to this are the health, catering, leisure and entertainment, transport and communications sectors, where there is no compulsory day of rest. Some activities allow for the possibility of taking a rest day other than on Sunday, namely in services that cannot be interrupted, such as maintenance, cleaning or repairs outside normal hours, domestic work, or work carried out in alternate shifts.

Effective working time is calculated on the hours during which the employee is actually at the disposal of the employer. Breaks must be of a minimum of one hour and a maximum of two hours to ensure that no one ever works more than five consecutive hours, though this does not apply to management. The space between two working periods is, on average, 12hrs, but may be reduced under some labour agreements.

Overtime

Overtime includes any hour worked in excess of the maximum (legal or contractual) duration of work. Women who are pregnant or who have children under 11 months, disabled people and minors are not obliged to work overtime. Overtime is limited to 2hrs per day and 200hrs per year, or to a number of hours that is equivalent to half a normal working day on weekly rest days or public holidays. The first hour of overtime must be paid at time and a half, and further hours at time and three quarters. Overtime worked on a day of rest or a public holiday is paid at a double the normal hourly rate.

Holidays

All full-time employed people are entitled to a statutory 22 weekdays of paid holiday. A provision in the new Labour Code increases this to 25 days if the worker has not been absent or has three or fewer justified absences. This right starts from the moment of signing the contract. The right to take annual leave, however, is only effective from 1 January each calendar year. During the first year of employment, employees are entitled to two days of paid holiday for each month of work (which can only be taken after 6 months' consecutive work), up to a maximum of 20 days. If this leave cannot be taken before the end of the first year it may be taken the following year, though no more than 30 days' holiday can be carried over to the following year. If a worker takes their holiday in split periods, one of the periods must be a minimum of 10 days. There are also 13 statutory national holidays and, in most places, one more local holiday. When they fall on a Friday or a Monday, these holidays make for a welcome long weekend.

All the above information concerning contracts, salaries, working hours and leave is also of interest to entrepreneurs who plan to hire staff; see 'Starting Your Own Business', p.203.

Health Insurance

Technically, if you are employed or self-employed, your social security contributions should cover you for all contingencies. The Portuguese health system offers free essential medicines and visits to the doctor, through the local *centros de saúde*. Non-essential medicines are sometimes partially subsidised and there are charges for items such as glasses or dentures. But the system is in a critical state despite the attempts being made to right this situation, an example being a recent decree by which more than 100 medicines were taken off the 'essential' list and are no longer free. In the meantime, many Portuguese and foreign workers who can afford it opt to take out private health insurance. If you work for a British company or a multinational, the chances are your employers will arrange a scheme on your behalf. Otherwise, *see* p.141 for a list of insurers to try contacting.

Sick Leave and Disability Pay

'Sickies' are a major issue in Portugal, where employees take an average of 18 a year, the highest rate in the EU, which may account for Portugal's productivity levels being among the lowest in Europe. Labour Ministry officials have seen a clear link between these two phenomena, arguing that with anything up to 200,000 workers being absent on any given day, Portugal can never be competitive. The new Labour Code, therefore, aims to crack down on this, allowing companies to sack employees who fail to turn up for work either four days in a row or eight days during a year without valid justification. As an incentive, people who don't take sick leave are awarded three extra days' holiday. Employers ought not to begrudge you this if levels of absenteeism are acceptable. It is certainly more cost-effective for them than having staff who take up to 18 days' sick leave a year.

If you are ill, the system provides for you. The sickness insurance fund does not cover the first three days of illness, except in cases of tuberculosis or hospitalisation, but thereafter the fund pays 65 per cent of the average pay earned over the six-month period preceding the second month immediately before falling ill. Workers who have not been absent in the 365 days before falling ill receive 70 per cent of their salary. Anyone who is off sick for a full three years (1,095 days) then receives a provisional invalidity pension and must undergo a medical examination to determine whether they are permanently incapacitated for work.

Maternity leave is for a total of 120 days and may begin six weeks before the birth. During lactation, the mother may leave work twice a day for an hour in order to breastfeed her child. This right continues until the child's first birthday. Fathers may take the first five days after the child's birth as paternity leave. If they adopt a child under the age of 15, employees may take 100 days 'adoption leave', which must be taken immediately after the arrival of the child in the household. Special unpaid leave of up to two years is granted to parents, either the mother or the father, who wish to stay at home and look after their child until the age of three.

In addition, workers are entitled to leave of differing duration in certain personal circumstances such as marriage, the death of a spouse or other first-degree family members or illness in the family. If employees know in advance that they are going to be absent, they should give their employer five days' warning. As this is not always possible, the employer should be notified as soon as possible.

Leaving Your Job and Signing On

If you have been working in Portugal and lose your job – i.e. you become unemployed involuntarily – you may be entitled to:

- **unemployment benefit** (*subsídio de desemprego*)
- **social unemployment benefit** (*subsídio social de desemprego*)
- **partial unemployment benefit** (*subsídio parcial de desemprego*)

One of these is usually applicable if you are insured under the general scheme for employed persons – that is, if your employer has made contributions to the social security *caixa* on your behalf.

On losing your job you should register at your nearest job centre (*centro de emprego; see* 'Portuguese Job Centres', p.202) within 90 days and make a claim for unemployment benefit at the nearest Regional Social Security Office (CRSS) within the same period.

You are entitled to unemployment benefit (*subsídio de desemprego*) if you have completed a period of 540 days of paid work for an employer in the 24 months immediately preceding the date of unemployment. Usually the amount of benefit is 65 per cent of the average daily wage during the previous 12 months though this may vary depending on how much you earned.

Social unemployment benefit (*subsídio social de desemprego*) is paid if you have done 180 days of paid work in the 12 months before becoming unemployed, and may also be paid in other circumstances. The amount is paltry, between 80 and 100 per cent of the statutory minimum wage (€356.60 per month) depending on family circumstances.

Partial unemployment benefit (*subsídio parcial de desemprego*) may be paid to previously unemployed people who have taken up a part-time job whose salary is not greater than unemployment benefit itself.

All of these benefits are for a limited duration, which depends on your age and contributions made. In no case will you be entitled to more than 30 months' benefit. For full information concerning benefits, contact your nearest job centre and social security office.

Teaching

Expat teachers in Portugal usually find work either in the TEFL/TESOL field teaching English, or as a schoolteacher in one of the many international schools that serve the expat community. Both are reasonable options for anybody looking for work initially, and offer opportunities for career development. Full teaching qualifications are usually required to work in schoolteaching. A qualification of some sort is also recommended for anyone working in TEFL, though some employers are prepared to waive this requirement.

TEFL

There are many good reasons why TEFL is a thriving business, not least Portugal's role as a trading nation and local people's awareness of the need to communicate with other peoples. This is especially in the context of a single European market and a global economy. Demand comes mainly from parents, who wish to see their children learn more than the school system offers, from teenagers and young adults who have a passable level and wish to improve it, and from business people who need to brush up their English for trips and meetings.

Many English-speakers, though originally graduates in some other discipline or trained for something quite different, end up working in TEFL. There are private academies in most towns and cities of any size, though there is a greater concentration in commercial and industrial central and northern Portugal than in the Algarve. Most academies, despite English-sounding names like 'Oxford School' or 'Cambridge Language Centre', are run by Portuguese entrepreneurs though internationally well-known outfits such as **International House** are present in many cities. In addition, the **British Council** has main centres in Lisbon and Oporto as well as smaller centres in many other provincial capitals. Through the British Council it is also possible to get a list of reputable private schools in which you may seek work.

Try to get some training before looking to work. Many centres both in the UK and Portugal run training courses leading to the TEFL or CELTA certificates. Once you have experience you can upgrade your qualifications by doing the full RSA Certificate. A teaching qualification is valid throughout the world, and there is a certain breed of TEFLer who moves from country to country for many years before settling down in any one place. For information on courses, *see* overleaf.

Business English is taught year-round; lessons for children and teenagers usually begin with the school term in September or October. If you can find a job with a full-time contract, so much the better. Otherwise, many people work part-time in an academy, or more than one, and supplement this with a few private classes. This may involve teaching in a company before work at 8am, doing some morning hours in the academy, a free afternoon off, starting again at around 5pm and finishing at 9pm. Once you are established, it will be easier to get a full-time contract at one school, though by then you may have enough experience and contacts to work freelance, which pays more.

While a qualification is not absolutely necessary, it does help you find work, as does a degree and some experience. A driving licence may be an additional requirement. Full-time teaching contracts generally last nine months with three weeks' paid holiday. Salaries may be in the region of €1,200, though some academies pay less. This can be topped up with a couple of private classes. Some contracts may include flights and/or accommodation.

Tax and social security deductions eat up about 23 per cent of your salary.

Getting Qualified and Finding Work

There are scores of organisations that provide TEFL training and help with finding work both in the UK and abroad. A good many have made use of the Internet to advertise their services and there are many resources available online for teachers. A simple search on Google using 'TEFL + courses + jobs' throws up many results. Here, along with some well-known bodies, are some of them:

- **The British Council**, 10 Spring Gardens, London SW1A 2BN, **t** (020) 7389 4004, **f** (020) 7389 4426, **www.britishcouncil.org**. The Council is present in Portugal; apart from its school in central Lisbon there are several centres throughout the metropolitan area and in Coimbra and Oporto.

- **Dave's ESL Café, www.eslcafe.com**. This site bills itself as 'the Internet's meeting place for ESL and EFL teachers and students from all around the world.'

- **The English Language Centre** (admissions office), 1st Floor, 60 St James's Street, London SW1A 1LE, **t/f** (01943) 830818 (*office hours 9.30–4.30, Mon–Fri*), **info@englishlanguagecentre.com**, **www.englishlanguagecentre. com**. Distance courses for prospective teachers of English worldwide.

- **International House**, 106 Piccadilly, London W1J 7NL, **t** (020) 7518 6950, **f** (020) 7518 6951, **www.ihworld.com**. For information about courses. You need not train in London; courses are held at IH centres in many locations and distance courses are also available. Getting qualified with IH may also lead to a job in one of their several centres in Portugal.

- **The London Teacher Training Centre**, Dalton House, 60 Windsor Avenue, London SW19 2RR, **t** (020) 8452 301 062, **f** (020) 8452 301 063, **lttc@ teachenglish.co.uk**, **www.teachenglish.co.uk**. Distance learning and TEFL jobs are also published in the *TES* (*Times Educational Supplement*) on Fridays and in the *Guardian's* EFL pages on Tuesdays. Otherwise, look in the *Yellow Pages* in any Portuguese city, where you will find many private language schools.

- **TEFL, www.tefl.net**. An online resource centre packed with information about jobs and courses worldwide as well as reviews of teaching materials on the market and downloadable lesson plans. The ELT portal **www.tefl.com** claims to have the world's largest database. Whether it is true or not, there is an impressively huge amount of information about all aspects of the TEFL world.

Schoolteaching

The existence of large expat communities supports a good many private schools, with English as the language of instruction. They tend to be in the

Lisbon area, Oporto and the Algarve, where expats are concentrated. These schools offer an education based either on the National Curriculum or the American system; many also prepare their alumni for the International Baccalaureate. Consequently, and owing also to a certain amount of turnover of staff, there is demand for teachers, generally to cover vacancies at the beginning of the year. *See* 'English-speaking Schools in Portugal', pp.177–8, or **http://the-news.net** and click on 'downloads' for addresses of some of the main schools. Jobs at these schools are frequently snapped up by those living locally but if you hold a B Ed or PGCE qualification, send your CV halfway through the academic year for possible September vacancies. The Algarve weekly *The News* has a classified advertising section where jobs may appear and regular special reports on schools and education. The online version (*see* above) has downloadable, PDF format documents with the classifieds and education reports.

Freelancing or Part-time Work

Given the difficulties in finding stable employment, many people turn to freelancing, or self-employment. This is particularly the case for translators, journalists and, in many instances, TEFLers, though many people make a living doing some combination of all three. As well as this, foreign freelancers work as photographers, IT consultants, graphic designers and just about any other line of work where self-employment is common anywhere. In expat areas such as the Algarve, as has been mentioned, there are people who make a living as nannies, plumbers, hairdressers, home helps, gardeners, travel writers and more. Depending on your background, training, skills, determination and luck, you could be successful.

When operating as a **self-employed worker** (*trabalhador por conta própria*) or as a **sole trader** (*empresário em nome individual*) you do not have the security of a work contract, paid holidays or compensation if you lose work. Nor may you claim unemployment benefits if your source of income dries up. Work can come in fits and starts and you may be loath to refuse an unattractive job or commission because you do not know what the next week or month will bring. At times you may be overworked and at others have nothing to do. You can, on the other hand, organise your time to suit yourself, and if the skill you offer is in demand and you build up a good client base, you may find that on average you make more money than you would in a stable job, and with no boss to answer to.

There are certain aspects of bureaucracy that must be considered when setting up as a self-employed person. In Chapter 05, **Red Tape**, the steps necessary for getting a residency permit are outlined; *see* pp.91–3. You must also register with the **tax authorities** and have a **tax or fiscal card** (*cartão de contribuinte*). On registering you will be given a **receipts book** (*caderneta de recibos*) in which you record payments received and show when you make your

Case Study: Rupert Eden, Freelance Journalist and Writer

Rupert Eden, a graduate in Hispanic Studies from Liverpool University, is a free-lance journalist, travel writer and photographer. He grew up between sheep farms on Scotland's west coast and, later, Portugal's Alentejo hills, where his parents farm. Having travelled widely, he now lives in Cascais, on the Lisbon coast.

Q What brought you here originally?

RE My parents have farmed in the Alentejo since the 1960s, except for a six-year spell in Scotland during Portugal's Communist revolution. I choose to live near Lisbon for work reasons.

Q How did you get work? How do you find working?

RE As a journalist I used my established media contacts to pitch for Portugal-related work. Freelancing has its advantages, like choosing your own hours. Drawbacks include cash flow, late payments and no regular income. It is an advantage for me to earn in sterling or dollars at UK wage rates.

Q What are the good points and the bad points of living and working in Portugal and how do you cope with red tape?

RE Things are improving: you no longer queue as long in banks or post offices, except in the provinces. One innovation is the Multibanco system, which lets you pay gas, water, electricity, pay-as-you-go mobile phone bills, etc. through ATMs. Getting resident permits, driving licences and tax-paying status is still slow and the health, pension and social security systems are chaotic.

Q Do you mix with expats or locals?

RE I mix with both as I speak Portuguese and have expat friends through work and family ties. The Portuguese are friendly and very easy to get to know; just be confident and keep an open mind without being arrogant or superior.

Q How do you find it price-wise?

RE It is still very cheap, despite rents creeping up. Food, drink, wine, eating out, nightlife, etc. are very reasonable. Utility and phone costs are the highest in the EU, though, and petrol is expensive.

Q What tips would you give to any would-be residents?

RE Learn the language quickly. Join a gym or a club. Travel around and try to integrate; avoid English pubs.

Q How have things changed in the time that you have been here?

RE Life has definitely improved, especially things like transport, communications, fashion, film, cosmopolitan dining and the party scene. People are slowly accepting things like gays and immigration and there isn't much racism, though the far right is here and football violence is appearing. Also, a lot of Salazar-generation 40-somethings are reluctant to let go and allow new ideas to filter down, especially on issues like abortion or sexual freedoms. There is still a lingering prudish, apathetic and repressed mentality, plus extreme poverty that you see nowhere else in Western Europe.

tax declarations. Many of the expenses incurred in self-employment, such as entertaining clients, travelling, purchasing of equipment and so on, are tax-deductible. In general, the deductible limit may not exceed 32.5 per cent of gross income from self-employment.

As well as this you have to make your own monthly contributions to **social security** (*segurança social*), which are paid into a fund (*caixa*) – the equivalent of making NI payments in the UK. The amount you have to pay in social security contributions is calculated on a base that you yourself may choose. It varies between one and 12 times the monthly minimum national salary. In 2004 the monthly minimum national salary is €356.60. Self-employed individuals may reduce their contribution bases without restriction. However, they may increase their contribution bases by one bracket once a year as long as they are under 55 years of age. Doing either will eventually affect the amount of pension to which you are entitled on retiring. To encourage people to become self-employed, the government has a scheme whereby you may be exempt from making these contributions during the first 12 months of initiating the activity. After that you must register to pay. The minimum amount you can expect to pay monthly is a little over €90.

These are the contribution rates for self-employed persons:

- **25.4 per cent for the compulsory coverage only, which provides for retirement, disability, death and old age**
- **32 per cent for compulsory coverage plus optional coverage for professional sickness and illness and other family benefits.**

Payments must be made at the treasury department of the local social security office. Unfortunately, not all offices have a treasury department and you will be referred to one that has, even though for other questions you must continue to use the one in your catchment area. Another option is to pay electronically, using the Multibanco system. This saves going in person and standing in queues. Payments must be made by the 15th of the month following the month to which the contributions relate. Late payments are penalised by hefty interest rates, which begin from the first day of non-payment (though one freelance journalist consulted on this issue said that she has on occasion paid a few days late via Multibanco and not been charged interest; this is presumably because it is in the government's interest for people to pay this way as it helps to reduce costs, so a few days' grace is given).

Both tax and social security benefits for self-employed people (and for salaried workers and business owners) are very complex matters. If you plan to be self-employed, seek the advice of a good accountant as you could end up paying over the odds or, unwittingly, not enough only to be stung later if the tax authorities carry out an inspection.

See also 'Taxation', pp.135–8.

Starting Your Own Business

If you plan to set up in business in Portugal, approach the question with exactly the same caution as you would at home, if not more. Plan meticulously, carry out market and feasibility surveys, look at various sources of finance, consider what to do in the worst case scenario (failure) and weigh up all manner of other pros and cons. Seek sound legal advice, engage the services of a reliable accountant and maybe a consulting agency. In short, do not sink your capital into any scheme without first assuring yourself that it has at least a fighting chance.

Not everybody who sets up in business in Portugal goes about it so cautiously. Many people are erroneously under the illusion that running a shop, a bar, a restaurant or a B&B guarantees a livelihood in a pleasant, sunny place. It does not. In the Algarve, particularly, according to one long-established resident, 'there are a lot of bars, restaurants and B&Bs for sale; it is not easy for foreigners to do well in catering because it is so competitive. There is over-trading in many businesses and few niche areas are unfilled.' Other areas of the country are maybe not so overexploited but nobody should assume they will be successful wherever they set up business. The Portuguese economy is largely made up of small and medium enterprises. Some 85 per cent of all businesses average 15 or fewer employees, most are family-owned concerns and few make massive amounts of money. This is the context in which you will be operating.

Many people do not do sufficient homework before embarking on a business scheme in Portugal. They may try to establish a business without ever having run one before, or in a line of business in which they have no experience. Too few take into the account the 'Portugal factor' – different operating and market conditions, cumbersome (but slowly improving) bureaucracy and, in most cases, low returns, even from a going concern. Too few look at the overall economic situation, which is not good at the moment. The early months of 2004 have seen a sharp rise in the number of businesses filing for bankruptcy. If many businesses are up for sale in certain areas, there must be a good reason why. In addition, many entrepreneurs forge ahead without a working know-ledge of the Portuguese language. This is a recipe for disaster.

It is not the intention here to put people off. By no means all business ventures fail. Some business-owners make a reasonable living, others do well, and a few get rich. Those who survive and prosper do so because they have chosen a viable line of business, researched the market properly, chosen the right location, listened to sensible advice. They will also have worked hard and, quite possibly, had a little luck too. Do not get into a situation where luck is the crucial factor.

Portugal does need investors, and the government wishes to encourage people to establish themselves there. One recent step to make the country more attractive for investors has been to slash the corporate tax rate from 30 per cent to 25 per cent. There are also incentive schemes for small- and medium-sized companies, especially those that have plans to invest in economically depressed areas. Find out what initiatives are available and take advantage of them if they would further your interests.

If you wish to succeed you should bear in mind the following points:

- **Previous experience of running a business is helpful, especially if it is in the same sector as you are planning to set up in.**

- **You should calculate how much capital you have available and make sure you have enough of a cushion to tide you over in the difficult early years and keep some aside to fall back on in the event of failure.**

- **Research the geographical area in which you plan to set up and be sure that there is a niche for your planned venture. This could mean going to an area that is not so fashionable or well known.**

- **Aside from choosing the region, city or town, make sure you find a locale in a good spot, especially if your business relies on customers walking in off the street. Remember: location, location, location!**

- **Bear in mind that if your business relies on tourist trade, there are seasonal ups and downs and you may have to live on high-season earnings for the rest of the year.**

- **Look exhaustively at all the bureaucratic, tax and legal issues involved, with the help of reputable and specialist lawyers and accountants.**

- **Weigh up the pros and cons of starting a business from scratch versus buying one that already exists.**

- **Consider whether you will need to employ staff in your business and how many.**

- **Speak to other foreign business owners, both the successful ones and those that have not done well.**

- **Expect, initially at least, to work long hours.**

- **New businesses that are likely to create stable employment in depressed areas, or that may encourage the use of new, clean technologies or contribute generally to raising Portugal's productivity, may qualify for grants. Find out about them.**

- **Learn Portuguese to at least a good, functional level and learn about Portugal, its culture and its ways.**

Getting Started

Once you have decided, on the basis of exhaustive research, on your line of business, location, whether to start up a new venture or buy an existing one, and are convinced that you can make a success of it, it is time to get moving.

A Taxing Issue

If you are operating a business in Portugal, you will need to be aware of taxes that are payable. The Portuguese tax system is outdated and incredibly complicated. Though successive governments have slowly been overhauling it over the last few years, the tax system is a still complex and difficult to deal with, as is getting reliable information on tax. The website of the Inland Revenue (*Direcção Geral dos Impostos*, **www.dgci.min-financas.pt/siteinternet/_sgt/ frtaxsystem.htm**) has some pages with information in English, but do not pay too much heed to them as they were at least two years out of date when consulted for this book shortly before publication!

Any of the bodies listed in the section 'Getting Help' should be able to give you some good guidelines on the tax minefield but once you are actually going ahead with your business plan, seek professional help from a specialist tax lawyer.

A few points to bear in mind are as follows:

• The standard rate of corporate tax is 25 per cent plus 2.5 per cent municipal tax, making a total of 27.5 per cent.

• Companies with a turnover that is less than the limit defined in law may elect an alternative method of tax calculation that is based on the profit coefficients defined in the law.

• Companies in the free trade zone of Madeira are eligible for a reduced tax rate of between 2 per cent and 12.5 per cent, depending on the type of company and the year in which the company was set up in the free trade zone.

The first thing to work out is which type of company you are going to set up. The most common forms of company organisation are:

• a private limited liability company (*sociedade por quotas* or *Lda.*).
• a corporation or public company (*sociedade anónima* or *SA*).
• a company with a single shareholder (*sociedade unipessoal*).

Private Limited Company

This is the most common form of company and, as its administrative and supervisory structure is not especially complex, it is the most convenient form for small- and medium-sized businesses. The principal feature of a Lda. is that its partners are liable not only for their own contributions but also, jointly with the others, for all contributions necessary to pay up the total amount of the company's share capital.

Lda. members own 'quotas', rather than shares, which are defined in the articles of association rather than being represented by share certificates. 'Quotas' can only be transferred by public deed. Usually, an Lda. is set up by two members, though it is possible to set one up with just one. Quotaholder(s) may be individuals or legal entities resident or not in Portugal but not another Portuguese private limited liability company with a single quotaholder. The minimum capital is €5,000. An Lda. must maintain a legal reserve, to protect third parties and cover any losses, thus a minimum of 5 per cent of profits must be appropriated to the reserve each year.

Corporation or Public Company

Corporations or public companies are more complex from an administrative and supervisory point of view, so are the more appropriate form of organisation for large and dispersed enterprises, especially if the aim is to have the shares listed on the Stock Exchange. The principal feature of an SA is that its shareholders are liable only for the amount of their own contributions necessary to pay up the shares subscribed by them.

The minimum capital required is €50,000 and it may be incorporated by public or private subscriptions. Shares may be of nominative or bearer form, either of which may be converted to the other. Shares may also be ordinary or preference. Both non-voting preference shares and redeemable preference shares are allowed. Redeemable preference shares may be redeemed with or without reduction of share capital.

Company with a Single Shareholder

The company comprises one single shareholder. Liability is only for the assets of the company and not that of the shareholder personally. An individual may open only one company of this sort in Portugal.

Setting up a Company in Portugal

The process for setting up a company in Portugal is broadly as follows.

Define your company's principal activity and give it a corporate name. You must apply for a certificate of admissibility and a provisional corporate name certificate at the National Registry of Companies (Registo Nacional de Pessoas Colectivas, RNCP, **www.rnpc.mj.pt**). The application must:

- **indicate a proposed name plus two alternatives.**
- **reflect the activities the company intends to carry out.**
- **not be misleading about the proposed business activities.**
- **not be confused with another name already registered.**

Registered names are protected by the exclusivity principle in Portugal and, once the name has been approved, the Registry issues a certificate of registration accompanied by a provisional tax registration card.

You must fix a date for the public registering of the company at the Notary Office and present:

- **the certificate of company admissibility.**
- **the number of the provisional company identification card.**
- **photocopies of the IDs of the entities who are to sign.**
- **an official auditor's report for the different asset participations (quota-holders or shareholders).**

The articles of association or incorporation must be drawn up and executed, then signed and sealed by a notary public. The deed can be replaced by a private document if the company to be incorporated is owned by one person whose share capital is entirely paid up in cash or in assets.

Once the incorporation deed has been executed, you must register the company's activity with the local tax authorities and get the signature of the auditor responsible for the company accounts. Declare the start of the company's activity at the government tax office (Direcção Geral dos Impostos, DGCI). Information is available on the website **www.dgci.min-financas.pt**.

You must register the company with:

- **the Commercial Registry (Registo Comercial); registration is published in the Portuguese *Official Journal* (*Diario da Republica*).**
- **the National Register of Companies (Registo Nacional de Pessoas Colectivas, RNCP).**
- **the regional social security office (see information in Portuguese on www.seg-social.pt) within 30 days of start-up.**
- **the Department for Trade and Competition (Cadastro Comercial ou Industrial) or the corresponding Regional Directorate of the Ministry of Economy.**

In all, you should expect the whole process of setting up and registering a company to take around two months.

Employing Staff

The recently revised Labour Code (*Código do Trabalho*), which became law in December 2003, is aimed at making the labour market more agile and giving employers more room to manoeuvre. Among other things, it facilitates relocation, eases restrictions on short-term hiring, reduces the number of hours that may be considered night work and makes collective bargaining more flexible.

For information on your obligations to your hired staff, *see* 'Employment Contracts', p.206–207, and 'Working Conditions', pp.207–209. The information there is pertinent to both employers and employees.

Apart from the information, you should be aware that social security contributions are payable on all salaries, wages, regular bonuses and other regular income, excluding lunch subsidies. No ceiling applies to the amount of wages subject to social security contributions for employers or employees. The contribution rates, which are applied to monthly salaries, are 23.75 per cent for employers and 11 per cent for employees. You must deduct an employee's contribution from the salary and pay the total amount to the *caixa* of the social security by the 15th of the following month.

In addition to the modalities of contract dealt with above, you may also contract workers via a temporary employment agency. All forms of contract provide for a trial period, which varies in length but during which it is possible to dismiss the worker at fairly short notice if their work is poor. This get-out clause is sometimes abused by employers. You must know what you can and cannot do legally and what your obligations are *vis-à-vis* your workers. Overall, employing people is a thorny issue and you are advised to seek legal advice.

Getting Help

Setting up a business is a challenge, not least from the bureaucratic point of view, but the administration has tried to make life easier for would-be entrepreneurs and there are now bodies to provide help and advice.

One is ICEP, the Portuguese Investment, Trade and Tourism Institute, which is the nearest thing possible to a one-stop shop for people wanting to do business. The ICEP has offices throughout Portugal and abroad and its role is to promote Portuguese businesses abroad and provide information for potential investors in Portugal. English-speaking help is usually available in any of their offices.

Also of great use are the *centros de formalidades das empresas* or CFEs (business formalities centres), which are also one-stop shops for the setting up of a company (*sociedade*). Staff will explain the setting-up process from A to Z, tell you what documents are needed and where to get them, provide advice on the most appropriate type of corporate structure, inform you about legal and financial aspects and put you in contact with relevant government bodies. This can be particularly useful, as there are government agencies that may give help to certain types of business, especially those that encourage the use of new technologies, raise product quality, help to bring production methods into line with EU requirements and encourage the improvement of productivity, hygiene and environmentally friendly practices. Help may also be available to enterprises that are likely to bring employment in depressed areas.

The body that channels incentives, in close collaboration with the CFEs, is the **Instituto de Apoio às Pequenas e Médias e ao Investimento** (**IAPMEI**; Institute for Small- and Medium-Sized Enterprises and Investment). The **Agência**

Portuguesa para o Investimento (API; Foreign Investment Agency), has recently been created and may also be useful.

Useful Contacts

- **ICEP**, head office, Avenida 5º de Outubro, 101, 1050-051 Lisbon, t 217 950 500, f 217 937 521, **www.icep.pt**. In the UK the ICEP shares premises with the Portuguese–UK Chamber of Commerce at 22–25ª Sackville Street, London W1X 1DE, t (020) 7494 1844, f (020) 7494 1822, **www.portuguese-chamber.org.uk**. In the Irish Republic the ICEP's address is 54 Dawson Street, Dublin 2, t (01) 670 9133/4, f (01) 670 9141, **info@icep.ie**.

- **Centros de Formalidades das Empresas**, head office, Avenida Columbano Bordalo Pinheiro, 86, 1070-065 Lisbon, t 217 232 300, f 217 232 323, **www.cfe.iapmei.pt**.

- **IAPMEI**, Rua Rodrigo Fonseca, 73/73ª, 1269-158 Lisbon, t 213 836 000, f 213 836 283, **www.iapmei.pt**.

- **Agência Portuguesa para o Investimento, E.P.E, (API)**, Edifício Península Praça do Bom Sucesso 126–131, Sala 702, 4150-146 Porto Portugal, t 226 055 300, f 226 055 399, **api@investinportugal.pt**, **www.investinportugal.pt**.

- **Ministry for the Economy**, **www.min-economia.pt/port/guia_inv/port/mostra_faq_ing-php_qual-122.html**. This website has useful information on incentives for investors in English.

Volunteering

Portugal has a relatively small voluntary sector and a large proportion of voluntary work is carried out by the Church, which has traditionally played a dominant role in society. One of the interviewees featured in this book commented, off the record and rather scathingly, that many of the 'good works' carried out are really 'Victorian-style lording it over the plebs'. This may or may not be true, but the recipients of charity probably do not mind. It should not be forgotten that one in five people in Portugal live below the EU's official poverty line and an estimated 200,000 people cannot feed themselves, so there is clearly a need for relief work, whoever takes responsibility for it.

Apart from Church-run charities, big business is gradually becoming involved and dedicating a small percentage of profits to solidarity programmes. In addition, some internationally known NGOs such as Amnesty International have delegations in Portugal. In general, if you have time and energy to give to voluntary projects you will be welcome, provided you have reasonable spoken Portuguese. If you have some particular skill to offer you may also be able to provide more valuable collaboration.

Before going to Portugal, if you are in the UK contact the **British Council's** Information Centre (Bridgewater House, 58 Whitworth Street Manchester M1 6BB, **education.enquiries@britishcouncil.org**, **www.britishcouncil.org**), which handles education and training enquiries. The London offices of the British Council are at 10 Spring Gardens London SW1A 2B, **t** (020) 7389 4004, **f** (020) 7389 4426. The British Council publishes *Working Holidays* and *Volunteer Work*, which are not specific to Portugal but provide addresses of useful organisations. Also, before leaving for Portugal you could look at **http://europa.eu.int/ youth/volunteeringexchanges/index_pt_pt.html**, which has the addresses of many charitable and solidarity organisations. Some useful Portuguese voluntary organisations are mentioned below.

Portuguese Voluntary Agencies

- **Associaçao de Turismo Estudentil e Juvenil (ATEJ)**, Apartado 4586, P-4009 Oporto, Portugal, One agency in Portugal that accepts volunteers; it places a small number of volunteers on farms, archaeological digs, and projects aimed at people with disabilities. **Turicoop** is associated with them, and this agency runs nature conservancy and archaeological projects and work camps. Both also deal with au pair work.

- **Aldeias Internacionais de Crianças** (Children's Villages), Rua Anchieta, 29-4°, 1200, Lisbon, **t** 213 477 647. A not-for-profit organisation, part of UNESCO, whose objective is education and peace for children. It offers disadvantaged and abandoned children a home.

- **Rotajovem**, Largo do Mercado, 2750-431 Cascais, **t/f** 214 862 005, **rotaevs@portugalmail.pt**, **www.rotajovem.com**. Carries out youth projects and is also integrated with several other youth organisations in Europe and worldwide.

- **Banco Alimentar Contra o Fome** (the Food Bank Against Hunger), Estação de CP de Alcântara Terra/Armazem 1 Avenida de Ceuta, 1300-125 Lisbon, **t** 213 649 655 (Lisbon), t 229 983 140 (Oporto). An institution created by a priest, Padre Vaz Pinto, with the aim of reducing hunger by preventing food being thrown away and redistributing it among the needy. There are an estimated 200,000 people in Portugal who cannot feed themselves. Donations of unprepared food and electrical equipment such as refrigerators and freezers are welcomed. Food collections are organised several times a year in supermarkets and the organisation is often looking for volunteers.

- **Plataforma Portuguesa das Organizações Não Governamentais para o Desenvolvimento**, Rua da Madalena, 91, 2° Esq., 1100-319 Lisbon, **t** 218 872 239, **f** 218 872 241, **www.plataformaongd.pt**. An umbrella organisation of NGOs for development. On the website, in Portuguese only, if you click on

the '*membros*' button, you access a list of almost 50 different NGOs. Most are based in Lisbon but there are a few in Oporto, Coimbra, Aveiro and Lagos (Algarve). Some are clearly of a religious bent, others are, judging by their names, linked to the new, anti- globalisation left, and there are also well-known groups such as UNICEF.

• **Amnistia Internacional**, 13, 1º Andar, 1070-128 Lisbon, **t** 213 861 664/652, **f** 213 861 782, **aiportugal@amnistia-internacional.pt, www.amnistia-internacional.pt**. Amnesty International may well need volunteers and if you speak Portuguese and English you could be of great use to them.

References

09

Portugal at a Glance

Capital city: Lisbon
Official name of country: República Portuguêsa
Type of government: Republic
Head of government: President of the Republic, Jorge Sampaio
Prime Minister: Pedro Santana Lopes (replaced José Manuel Durão Barroso, who resigned in July 2004 in order to preside over the European Commission)
Area: 92,391 sq km
Length: distance from Viano do Castelo (on northern border with Spain) to Faro (in the southern province of the Algarve) is 703km
Maximum width: 220km
Geographic highlights: Green mountains, fast flowing rivers and deep river valleys in the north; rolling plains in the south; straight coastline with almost continuous beach through north and central area; salt flats in Sado estuary, south of Setúbal; long beaches and intimate coves in the Algarve; islands formed by volcanic action in the Azores
Independent states within Portugal: none, though the country has two autonomous regions, Madeira and the Azores Islands
Languages and dialects: Portuguese
Bordering countries: Spain
Surrounding seas: Atlantic
Population: 10,100,000
Religion: Roman Catholic 94 per cent; other 6 per cent
GDP purchasing power parity: US$195.2 billion (2002 est.); €157.3 billion (2002 est.)
GDP growth rate: 1.4 per cent (2004 est.)
GDP per capita: US$19,400 (2002 est.); €15,636
Unemployment: 7 per cent

Further Reading

General Portugal Tourist Guides

Blue Guide: Portugal, Ian Robertson (A&C Black).
Exploring Rural Portugal, Joe Staines and Lia Duarte (Christopher Helm).
Fodor's Portugal, Eugene Fodor (Fodor's Travel Publications).
Frommer's Portugal, Porter (John Wiley & Sons Inc, 18th ed, 2004).
Insight Guides: Portugal (APA Publications).
Lonely Planet: Portugal (Country and Regional Guides) Julia Wilkinson, John King (Lonely Planet).

Michelin Red Guide: España and Portugal 2003 (Michelin Red Guides).
Michelin Portugal, Martin Symington (Dorling Kindersley Publishing, DK Eyewitness Travel Guides).
The Rough Guide to Portugal, Mark Ellingham et al (Rough Guides).
Top 10 Travel Guide: Algarve (Dorling Kindersley, DK Eyewitness Top 10 Travel Guides).

Guides to the Algarve
Algarve, Jane O'Callaghan (New Holland Publishers, Globetrotter Travel Guide).
Algarve and Southern Portugal, Susie Boulton, *et al* (Thomas Cook Publishing, Thomas Cook Travellers).
Algarve in Your Pocket, Len Port (Vista Ibérica).
Get to Know the Algarve, Len Port (Vista Ibérica).
The Mini Rough Guide to the Algarve, Matthew Hancock (Mini Rough Guides).

Guides to Lisbon and Surrounding Area
Time Out Guide to Lisbon, Time Out (Penguin Books).
DK Eyewitness Travel Guides: Lisbon (Dorling Kindersley, Eyewitness Travel Guides).
Lonely Planet: Lisbon, Julia Wilkinson (Lonely Planet Publications).
Sintra: a Glorious Eden, Malcom Jack (Carcanet Press).
The Mini Rough Guide to Lisbon, Matthew Hancock (Rough Guides).

Madeira and the Azores
Azores: The Bradt Travel Guide, David Sayers (Bradt Travel Guides).
Madeira and Porto Santo, Rodney Bolt (Cadogan Guides).
Madeira and Porto Santo, Andrew Gravette (Cassell Reference, Windrush Island Guides).
Madeira: a Traveller's Guide, Mary Tisdall, Archie Tisdall (Roger Lascelles).
The Mini Rough Guide to Madeira, Matthew Hancock (Rough Guides).
Walking in Madeira, Paddy Dillon (Cicerone Press).

Food and Wine
Cuisines of Portuguese Encounters, Cherie Hamilton (Hippocrene Books, Inc).
Port and the Douro, Richard Mayson (Mitchell Beazley Publications, Classic Wine Library).
Portugal's Wines and Winemakers, Richard Mayson (Mitchell Beazley Publications).
Portuguese Cooking: the Authentic and Robust Cuisine of Portugal, Carol Robertson (North Atlantic Books).
Portuguese Homestyle Cooking, Ana Patuleia Ortins (Roundhouse Publishing).
The Food of Portugal, Jean Anderson, William Morrow (Hearst).
The Taste of Portugal: a Voyage of Gastronomic Discovery Combined with Recipes, History and Folklore, Edite Viera (Grub Street Publishing).
The Wines and Vineyards of Portugal, Richard Mayson (Mitchell Beazley Publications, Classic Wine Library).
Uma Casa Portuguesa: Portuguese Home Cooking, C. Azevedo (Summerhill Press).

Phrase Books, Portuguese Courses and Dictionaries

The Rough Guide to Portuguese (Rough Guides). A dictionary phrasebook.

Portuguese Made Nice and Easy! (Research and Education Association).

Teach Yourself Portuguese Language, Life and Culture, Sue Tyson-Ward, (Hodder & Stoughton).

Portuguese Verbs and Essentials of Grammar, Sue Tyson-Ward (NTC).

Teach Yourself Beginner's Portuguese, Sue Tyson-Ward (Hodder & Stoughton).

An Essential Course in Modern Portuguese, Clive Willis (Harrap).

Collins Pocket Portuguese Dictionary (Collins).

Discovering Portuguese, Book and Cassettes (BBC).

Get By in Portuguese, Book and Cassettes (BBC).

Traveller's Portuguese (Collins).

History and Contemporary Politics

The Discoverers, Daniel J. Boorstin (Penguin).

Portugal in Africa: The Last Hundred Years, Malyn Newitt (C. Hurst & Co).

The Developing Place of Portugal in the European Union, Jose M. Magone (Transaction Publishers).

The Last Empire: Thirty Years of Portuguese Decolonisation, Steward Lloyd-Jones (ed.), Antonio Costa Pinto (ed.) (Intellect Books).

Portuguese Seaborne Empire, CR Boxer (Carcanet Press).

Muslim Spain and Portugal: a Political History of Al-Andalus, Hugh Kennedy (Longman).

The Portuguese Empire, 1415-1808: A World on the Move, AJR Russell-Wood (The Johns Hopkins University Press).

Journey to Portugal: A Pursuit of Portugal's History and Culture, Jose Saramago, et al. (The Harvill Press)

Prince Henry 'the Navigator': A Life, Peter Russell (Yale University Press).

A Concise History of Portugal, David Birmingham (Cambridge University Press).

Portugal, The Land and Its People, M. Kaplan (Penguin).

Special Interest: Sports, Architecture

Birdwatching Guide to the Algarve, Kevin Carlson, Arlequin Publications.

Globetrotter Golfer's Guide: Portugal, Michael Gedye (New Holland Publishers, Globetrotter Golfer's Guides). Over 50 courses and facilities.

Oceansurf Guidebooks: Portugal, Stuart John Butler, Tim Nunn (illustrator) (Watersports Books).

Portuguese Gardens, Helder Carita, Homem Cardoso (Antique Collector's Club).

Walking in Portugal, Bethan Davies, Ben Cole (Pili Pala Press).

The Fires of Excellence: Spanish and Portuguese Oriental Architecture, Miles Danby, Matthew Weinreb (Photographer) (Garnet Publishing).

Portuguese Needlework Rugs, Patricia Stone (EPM Publications).

Portuguese Traveller: Great Sights and Hidden Treasures, BR and S. Rogers (Mills & Sanderson).

Literature

Luis Vaz de Camões

The Lusiads (Oxford World's Classics), Luis Vaz de Camões, Landeg White (intro.) (Oxford Paperbacks). Portugal's epic poem chronicling Vasco da Gama's voyages of discovery.

José Maria Eça de Queiroz

The Maias, José Maria Eça de Queiroz, Nigel Griffin (ed.), Patricia McGowan Pinheiro (transl.), Ann Stevens (tr.) (Penguin Classics). An ironic portrayal of corruption among the clergy and in high society.

Fernando Pessoa

Always Astonished: Selected Prose, Fernando Pessoa, Edwin Honig (tr.) City Lights Books.
Selected Poems, Fernando Pessoa (Penguin Modern Classics).
The Surprise of Being, Fernando Pessoa (Angel Books).
A Centenary Pessoa, Aspects of Portugal: Poetry, Fernando Pessoa, et al (Carcanet Press).
The Book of Disquiet, Fernando Pessoa, Richard Zenith (transl.) (Penguin Modern Classics).
The Poems of Fernando Pessoa, Edwin Honig (transl.) and Susan M. Brown (ed.) (City Lights Books).

José Saramago

The Gospel According to Jesus Christ, José Saramago (Harvill Press).
The Year of the Death of Ricardo Reis, José Saramago (Harvill Press).
Baltasar and Blimunda, José Saramago (Harvill Press).
The Srone Raft, José Saramago (Harvill Press).
Blindness, José Saramago (Harvill Press).
The History of the Siege of Lisbon, José Saramago (Harvill Press).

Antonio Lobo Antunes

The Inquisitors' Manual (Grove Press).
The Return of the Caravels (Grove Press).
Act of the Damned (Grove Press).
The Natural Order of Things (Grove Press).
Fado Alexandrino (Grove Press).

Some of Portugal's Best Films

As was seen in Chapter 03, Portuguese cinema enjoys only a very limited production and can be hard to find except in art houses (*see* **Portugal Today**, 'Cinema', pp.67–8). These are some of the best Portuguese films, listed in the order they were made:

A Canção de Lisboa (*Lisbon Song*, 1933), Cotinelli Telmo. A classic comedy about a student living it up on money loaned to him by his aunts.

Pai Tirano (*The Tyrannical Father*, 1941), Antonio Lopes Ribeiro. Comedy featuring a young shop assistant torn between two suitors.

Aniki-Bobó (1942), Manoel de Oliveira. A tale of poor children in Oporto, considered a classic.

Verdes Anos (Green Years, 1963), Paulo Rocha. Early Portuguese New Wave movie about a man who goes to Lisbon to make a living as a cobbler.

Trás os Montes (1976), Antonio Reis and Margarida Cordeiro. A masterpiece that captures the feel of life in the eponymous region.

Recordações da Casa Amarela (Memories of the Madhouse, 1989), João César Monteiro. A tale of madness and transgression in a popular Lisbon neighbourhood.

Viagem até o Princípio do Mundo (Journey to the Beginning of the World, 1997), Manoel de Oliveira. An autobiographical movie. Marcello Mastroianni portrays Manoel de Oliveira himself going back to his northern roots.

Ossos (Bones, 1997), Pedro Costa. Using non-professional actors, this movie takes a look at Lisbon's dark underbelly.

Tentação (Temptation, 1997), Joaquim Leitão. The story of a priest who is tempted by both the needle and the flesh. Portuguese cinema's greatest ever box office hit.

Os Capitães de Abril (Captains of April, 2000), Maria de Medreiros. Portrayal of the Carnation Revolution.

Also by Manoel de Oliveira

Douro, Faina Fluvial (1931). A silent documentary about life in the Douro region.

O Passado e o Presente (The Past and the Present, 1972). A 'theatrical' œuvre, marking de Oliveira's return to film-making after decades of inactivity.

Amor de Perdição (Love of Perdition, 1978).

The Portuguese Language

Pronunciation

Although structurally similar to Castilian Spanish, and readable if you are familiar with that language, Portuguese is more difficult when it comes to pronunciation and comprehension. Many people think that spoken Portuguese sounds like an eastern European language because of the proliferation of shushing consonants that are sometimes slurred together, and the closed and nasal vowels, some of which are ignored at the end of words.

Consonants

The capitals represent the stressed syllable, or should we say 'The CApitals represENT the STRESSed SYLLable'.

C   is hard (as in 'k') before all letters except 'e' and 'i'. Before these letters it has the sound of a liquid 's'. Thus *conceder* (to concede or grant) is pronounced 'kon-say-DARE'.

Ç   (cedilla) is a soft 'c' that comes before other vowels and is pronounced like an 's' sound as in *açucar* (sugar). Pronounce it 'a-SSOO-kar'.

Ch   is a bit softer than in English, coming out more like a 'sh', so *chá* (tea) is more like 'sha'.

J is like the 's' sound in 'treasure' or 'measure'.

Lh together make a 'lyuh' sound, a bit like the 'lli' in 'million'. *Filho/filha* (son/daughter) are thus 'FEEL-yo' and 'FEEL-ya'.

M on the end of words like *sim* is nasal and either hardly heard or more like a half-pronounced 'n'. So *sim* is more like the Spanish 'sí'.

Nh together make a 'nyuh' sound (similar to the 'ñ' in Castilian) so *vinho* is rendered 'VEEN-yo'.

Q is always hard like 'k', as in *quente* (hot), rendered 'KEN-tay'

S before a consonant or at the end of the word is more of a 'sh' sound, try *Cascais*, rendered 'kashKAISH'. Otherwise it is a liquid 's' as in English. Sagres, a town in the Algarve and a popular make of beer, is 'SAHgresh'.

X is also a 'sh', as in *baixo* (low), which is pronounced 'BY-show'.

Vowels

Vowel sounds can be flat and truncated or sometimes long and open but can easily be missed when listening to a Portuguese person speaking quickly.

Certain **accents** make Portuguese vowels longer, more nasal, easier to hear and more familiar to the English ear. These are the **tilde** (squiggle) '˜', the **circumflex** '^' and the **acute** '´'.

Thus in *alemã* (German woman, or something German and feminine) the 'ã' at the end is more like the French '-an' ending and is rendered 'a-lay-MAH' or even 'a-lay-MAIN' (if you know your French pronunciation!). In *português* (Portuguese, the language or something masculine and Portuguese) is the last syllable is a little more elongated and nasal and is rendered 'por-too-GAISH'. *Café*, (coffee or café) is easy – say it 'ka-FAY'.

Very common at the end of many words is the '-ão' sound as in *galão* (a large milky coffee). The '-ão' is like a little yelp – 'Ow!' – but cut off before it is finished so you would ask for ' um ga-LAOW'. Words ending in '-ão' in the plural become '-ões' so two large milky coffees would be *dois galões*, pronounced 'doysh ga-LOYSH'.

Vowels when they come together are usually pronounced separately as in *adeus* (goodbye), pronounced 'a-DAY-oos'. Some vowels together, though, make a sound of their own. This is the case with 'ei', as in *leite* (milk), which is like a long 'a' and pronounced 'LAY-tay' or 'ou', as in *doutor* (doctor), which sounds like 'dow-TOUR'.

Vowels with no accent over them at the end of words are sometimes not pronounced at all. Thus *carne* (meat) sounds like 'karn'.

An 'a' with an acute accent, 'à' is usually an abbreviation of 'a + a' meaning 'at the' (something feminine) so *à uma da tarde* is 'at one o'clock in the afternoon' (literally 'at the one of the afternoon'). *See* 'Asking and Telling the Time', pp.233–4.

Survival Vocabulary

Numbers

1	*um/uma**
2	*dois/duas**
3	*três*
4	*quatro*
5	*cinco*

6	seis
7	sete
8	oito
9	nove
10	dez
11	onze
12	doze
13	treze
14	catorze
15	quinze
16	dezasseis
17	dezassete
18	dezoito
19	dezanove
20	vinte
21	vinte e um/uma*
22	vinte e dois/duas*
30	trinta
40	quarenta
50	cinquenta
60	sessenta
70	setenta
80	oitenta
90	noventa
100	cem
101	cento e um/uma*
200	duzentos-as
300	trezentos-as
400	quatrocentos-as
500	quinhentos-as
600	seiscentos-as
700	setecentos-as
800	oitocentos-as
900	novecentos-as
1,000	mil
1,001	mil e um/um*
1,100	mil e cem
2,000	dois/duas mil
100,000	cem mil
1,000,000	um milhão
2,000,000	dois milhões

* one and two may be masculine or feminine in Portuguese, depending on what they refer to. Thus 'um homem, dois homens' is 'one man, two men', 'uma mulher, duas mulheres' is 'one woman, two women'. The same applies when speaking of 21 or 22, 31 or 32 (and so on) things or people, thus hundreds and thousands of masculine or feminine things are rendered differently; 200 men would be 'duzentos homens' but 200 women would 'duzentas mulheres'.

Days and Months

Sunday	*domingo*
Monday	*segunda-feira*
Tuesday	*terça-feira*
Wednesday	*quarta-feira*
Thursday	*quinta-feira*
Friday	*sexta-feira*
Saturday	*sábado*
January	*janeiro*
February	*fevereiro*
March	*março*
April	*abril*
May	*maio*
June	*junho*
July	*julho*
August	*agosto*
September	*setembro*
October	*outubro*
November	*novembro*
December	*dezembro*

Seasons

winter	*o inverno*
spring	*a primaveira*
summer	*o verão*
autumn	*o outono*

Asking and Telling the Time

'Time', the concept, is *tempo* (which also means 'weather') but when talking of the time of day Portuguese uses *hora* (s) (hours), so '3 o'clock' is *as três* ('the three') and so on.

What's the time?	*Que horas são?*
It's one o'clock/four o'clock	*é/são a uma/as duas/quatro* (literally 'it is the one', 'they are the two/four')
twenty to three	*vinte para as três*
quarter to seven	*um quarto para as sete*
five to four	*cinco para as quatro*
quarter past two	*as duas e quarto*
twenty past five	*as cinco e vinte*
half past seven	*as sete e meia*
twenty-five past three	*as três e vinte e cinco*
At what time...?	*A que horas...?*
At one o'clock, at four o'clock...	*À uma, às quatro* (literally 'at the one', 'at the four')

(at) midday, noon	*(ao) meio-dia*
(at) midnight	*(à) meia-noite*
(at) one o'clock in the morning	*(à) uma da manhã/madrugada*
(at) two o'clock in the afternoon	*(às) duas da tarde*

Note the difference between '*a uma da tarde*' (one o'clock in the afternoon) and '*à uma da tarde*' (**at** one o'clock in the afternoon) or between '*as sete da manhã/tarde*' and '*às sete da manhã/tarde*', which are 'seven o'clock in the morning/afternoon' and '**at** seven o'clock in the morning/afternoon' respectively.

Times/Periods of the Day

early hours (before sunrise)	*a madrugada*
morning	*a manhã*
afternoon	*a tarde*
night	*a noite*
today	*hoje*
tomorrow	*amanhã*
yesterday	*ontém*
one day	*um/o dia*
one week	*uma/a semana*
one month	*um/o mês*
one year	*um/o ano*

First Contacts

Yes	*Sim*
No	*Não*
Please	*Por favor*
Thank you	*Obrigado/a* (if it is a man/woman speaking)
You're welcome	*De nada*
No, thank you	*Não, obrigado/a*
Excuse me	*Queira desculpar*
What is your name?	*Como se chama?*
Which country do you come from?	*De que país é que vem?*
Do you speak English/French?	*Fala inglês/francês?*

Greetings

Hello	*Olá*
Good morning	*Bom dia*
Good afternoon	*Boa tarde*
Good night	*Boa noite*
Goodbye	*Adeus/ciao* (formal/informal)
How are you?	*Como está?*
Fine, thank you	*Bem, obrigado/a*
See you tomorrow	*Até amanhã*
Have a good journey	*Boa viagem*
Have fun	*Divirta-se*

| Good luck | *Boa sorte* |
| Feeling good? | *Bem disposto/a?* |

Signs, Notices and Public Information

attention	*atenção*
bank	*banco*
closed	*fechado*
fire Brigade	*bombeiros*
free entry	*entrada livre*
full up	*esgotado*
guide	*guia*
information	*informações*
lift	*elevador*
no entry	*entrada proibida*
open	*aberto*
open from... to...	*aberto da... às...*
please do not...	*é favor não...*
post	*correio*
push	*empurre*
in the road	*achei isto na rua*

Shops, Services and Communications

bakery	*padaria*
bar	*bar*
beer hall	*cervejaria*
butcher	*talho*
café	*café*
cake shop	*pastelaria*
cobbler	*sapateiro*
florist	*florista*
grocer's	*mercearia*
hairdresser	*cabeleireiro*
hypermarket	*hipermercado*
laundry	*lavandaria*
market	*mercado/praça*
optician	*oculista*
restaurant	*restaurante*
shoe-shop	*sapataria*
shop	*loja*
stationer's	*papelaria*
supermarket	*supermercado*
tobacconist	*tabacaria*
e-mail	*correio electrónico*
envelope	*envelope*
express mail	*correio expresso*
letter	*carta*

mail	*correio*
mobile telephone	*telemóvel*
post box	*marco do correio*
post office	*correios/estação dos correios*
postal order	*vale postal*
stamp	*selo*
telegram	*telegrama*
telephone	*telefone*
telephone box	*cabina telefónica*
telephone call	*chamada telefónica*
telephone number-	*número de telefone*

Some Phrases

Can you repair...?	*Pode consertar...?*
Is there a ... near here?	*Há um/um ... por aquí?*
Where can I buy...?	*Onde é que posso comprar...?*
Have you got any...?	*Tem...?*
When are the shops open?	*Quando é que as lojas estão abertas?*
Could you show me...?	*Podia-me mostrar...?*
Do you have this in another colour/size?	*Tem algum noutra cor/noutro tamanho?*
How much is this?	*Quanto custa isto?*
Do you have anything cheaper?	*Tem algo mais barato?*
I will take this	*Levo comigo*
It does not fit me	*Não me serve*
It is dirty/ripped/broken	*Está sujo/rasgado/partido*
I want a...	*Quero um/uma...*
I would like to buy a...	*Queria comprar um/uma...*
I need a...	*Preciso de um/uma...*
I would like to make a call to...	*Queria fazer uma marcação para...*
I would like to make a telephone call	*Queria fazer uma chamada*

Food and Restaurants

afternoon tea	*lanche*
appetite	*apetite*
ashtray	*cinzeiro*
bill/check	*conta*
bottle	*arrafa*
breakfast	*pequeno-almoço*
cigarettes	*cigarros*
dessert	*sobremesa*
dinner	*jantar*
discount	*desconto*
drink	*bebida*
eggs	*ovos*
fish	*peixe*
flowers	*flores*
food	*comida*

fork	*garfo*
fruit	*fruta*
garlic	*alho*
glass	*copo*
ham	*fiambre*
jug	*jarro*
juice	*sumo*
knife	*faca*
lunch	*almoço*
matches	*fósforos*
meal	*refeição*
meat	*carne*
menu	*ementa*
mustard	*mostarda*
napkin	*guardanapo*
olive oil	*azeite*
pepper	*pimenta*
plate/dish	*prato*
price	*preço*
salt	*sal*
sauce	*molho*
saucer	*pires*
small bottle	*frasco*
soup	*sopa*
spoon	*colher*
sugar	*açúcar*
sweet	*doce*
table	*mesa*
tablecloth	*toalha de mesa*
tea	*chá*
tea cup	*chávena*
tip	*gorjeta*
toothpick	*palito*

The Menu

bread	*pão*
butter	*manteiga*
cheese	*queijo*
tomato	*tomate*
onion	*cebola*
pasta	*massa*
rice	*arroz*
salad	*salada*
cream	*natas*
vegetables	*vegetais*
vinegar	*vinagre*
steak	*bife*
smoked ham	*presunto*

potato	*batata*
coffee	*café*
beer	*cerveja*
water (room temperature/cold)	*água natural/fresca*
water (still/sparkling)	*água sem/com gás*
wine	*vinho*
I want to reserve a table	*Queria reservar uma mesa*
Do you have table for two/four/six?	*Tem uma mesa para duas pessoas/quatro/seis?*
Do you serve dinner?	*Servem jantares?*
Can I see the menu?	*Posso ver a ementa?*
I would like a glass of water/ beer/wine please	*Queria um copo de água/cerveja/vinho por favor*
Que recomenda?	*What do you recommend?*
Como é servido este prato?	*How is this plate served?*
Is it hot or cold?	*É quente ou frio?*
This is not what I asked for	*Não foi isto que pedi*
More bread, please	*Mais pão, se faz favor*
This plate is cold	*Este prato está frio*
Bring the bill please	*A conta se faz favor*
What is this amount for?	*Esta importância refere-se a quê?*
I did not eat soup	*Não comi sopa*
Give us separate bills, please	*Faça-nos contas separadas, se faz favor*
Can you bring me an ashtray?	*Podia-me trazer um cinzeiro?*

Travel

aeroplane	*avião*
airport	*aeroporto*
arrivals	*chegadas*
boat	*barco*
bus	*autocarro*
car/automobile	*automóvel*
connections	*ligações*
departures	*partidas*
diesel	*gasóleo*
distance	*distância*
driver	*condutor*
garage	*garagem*
gas	*gás*
information	*informações*
kilometres	*quilómetros*
lost and found	*objectos perdidos*
passengers	*Passageiros*
petrol	*gasolina*
reservations	*reservas*
road	*estrada*
station	*estação*

taxi	*táxi*
ticket	*bilhete*
ticket office	*bilheteira*
train	*comboio*
tram	*eléctrico*
underground	*metro*
van	*camioneta*

Some Phrases

How do I get to Lisbon/Coimbra...?	*Para ir a Lisboa/Coimbra...?*
Which is the road to Lisbon/Coimbra?	*Qual é a estrada para Lisboa/Coimbra?*
Is this the bus/train for...?	*É este o camboio/autocarro para...?*
Where is...?	*Onde é...?*
the train/coach station?	*a estação de comboios/autocarros?*
the bus/tram stop for...?	*a paragem de autocarro/eléctrico para...?*
What time does it leave/arrive?	*A que horas parte/chega?*
Where are you going?	*Para onde vai?*
I'm going to...	*Vou a/para...*
A single/return ticket to...	*Um bilhete de ida/de ida e volta para...*
Two tickets to...	*Dois bilhetes para...*
Can you tell me where to get off?	*Pode-me dizer onde é que desço?*

Internet Vocabulary

arroba	@
barra	/ (forward slash)
barra barra	//
base de dados	database
buscar	to browse
decifrar	decode
dois pontos	: (colon)
eliminar	delete
(endereço de) email/correio electróncio	e-mail (address)
encerrar	shut down
online	online
ponto	. (dot)
rede ('*net*' for internet – both are feminine)	network
reiniciar	re-start
seleccionar	to select
traço	- (hyphen)
traço em baixo/sublinhado	_ (underline)
utente	user
www	'double u', (as in English)

Portuguese Holidays

1 January	New Year's Day (*Ano Novo*). Fireworks in some places but generally a quiet day.
4 March	Carnival (*Carnaval*). Portugal's Brazilian community add a lot of punch to the carnival proceedings.
18 April	Good Friday. Solemn processions.
25 April	Freedom Day (*Dia da Liberdade*). Commemorates the 1974 revolution; nowadays mainly the preserve of nostalgic lefties.
1 May	Labour Day (*Dia do Trabalho*). Celebrated by trade union marches throughout the country.
10 June	Portugal Day (*Dia de Portugal*).The national holiday.
a Thurs in June	*Corpus Christi*. Processions and other festivities, taken seriously.
15 August	Assumption (*Assunção da Nossa Senhora*). Feast of the Assumption.
5 October	Republic Day (*Dia da República*). Celebrates the proclamation of Portugal's first republic in 1910.
1 November	All Saints' Day (*Dia de Todos os Santos*). Also known as the Day of the Dead, florists do a roaring trade in chrysanthemums, which people lay on the graves of their dead relatives.
1 December	Independence Day (*Dia da Restauração da Independência*). Commemorates Portugal's liberation from the Spanish in 1640.
8 December	Immaculate Conception (Conceição Imaculada). Celebrates the Immaculate Conception.
25 December	Christmas Day (*Natal*).The big celebration is the night before, with families enjoying a dinner of cod (*bacalhau*), opening presents and going to midnight mass.

Dialling Codes and Postcodes

Telephone Numbers

All Portuguese telephone numbers begin with 2 followed by eight more digits so there are no real 'codes' as such; the second and third digits are the ones that give away the town to which the number corresponds. Lisbon numbers all start with 21... Oporto numbers with 22... Algarve and some southern Alentejo numbers with 28... etc.

Here is a complete list:

241	Abrantes	**262**	Caldas da Rainha
295	Angra do Heroísmo	**272**	Castelo Branco
235	Arganil	**286**	Castro Verde
234	Aveiro	**276**	Chaves
284	Beja	**239**	Coimbra
253	Braga	**292**	Corvo
273	Bragança	**275**	Covilhã

268 Estremoz		**282** Portimão	
266 Évora		**22** Porto	
289 Faro		**291** Porto Santo	
233 Figueira da Foz		**274** Proença-a-Nova	
292 Flores		**256** São João de Madeira	
291 Funchal		**295** São Jorge	
295 Graciosa		**296** Santa Maria	
271 Guarda		**243** Santarém	
292 Horta		**269** Santiago do Cacém	
277 Idanha-a-Nova		**238** Seia	
244 Leiria		**265** Setúbal	
21 Lisboa		**281** Tavira	
231 Mealhada		**279** Torre de Moncorvo	
278 Mirandela		**249** Torres Novas	
285 Moura		**261** Torres Vedras	
283 Odemira		**251** Valença	
255 Penefiel		**258** Viana do Castelo	
254 Peso da Régua		**263** Vila Franca de Xira	
236 Pombal		**252** Vila Nova da Famalicão	
296 Ponte Delgado		**259** Vila Real	
242 Ponte de Sôr		**232** Viseu	
245 Portalegre			

To call Portugal from abroad, dial **oo +351 + number**.

Postcodes

Portuguese postcodes, until recently, consisted of just four digits. The first of these was, and still is, indicative of the *distrito* (province, not 'district' in the English sense) in which the address fell. Lisbon, the city itself, known as the *'concelho de Lisboa'*, was awarded the four-digit numbers beginning with 1 and the surrounding area, Greater Lisbon, had codes beginning with 2. Thus, the headquarters of the Banco Espírito Santo, on Avenida da Liberdade 195, was in the postal district (in the English sense of the word) 1250.

The authorities have recently added a further three digits to these codes to allow for addresses to be more easily identifiable letters so that same office should now be addressed to Lisbon 1250-142. The first four digits still correspond to the same areas so if you do not know the full seven-digit code it does not matter that much, your letter will still arrive. This is good, as many Portuguese companies and even government agencies do not use the full code in their correspondence or on their websites! Eventually everyone will use the new system.

The Portuguese postcodes cover the following areas, starting from:

1000 Concelho de Lisboa, Lisbon, the area controlled by the city council.

2000 Suburban Lisbon, most of Leiria province, the Setúbal peninsula and the *distrito* of Santarém.

3000 The *distritos* of Viseu, Coimbra and Aveiro, and the far north of the *distrito* of Leiria.

4000   The *distritos* of Viana do Castelo, Braga and Oporto.
5000   The *distritos* of Vila Real and Bragança.
6000   The *distritos* of Castelo Branco and Guarda, and the *concelhos* of Nisa and Gavião (in the *distrito* of Portalegre).
7000   The *distritos* of Beja, Évora and Portalegre (except Nisa and Gavião, *see* above) and the *concelhos* of Alcácer do Sal, Grândola, Santiago do Cacém and Sines (belonging to the *distrito* of Setúbal).
8000   The Algarve.
9000   *Ilhas*, Madeira and the Azores.

Regional Climate Charts

The table below shows the average monthly temperatures (daily maximum and minimum) in degrees Centigrade and rainfall (in millimetres per month) in a representative sample of areas. Bragança is in the far northeastern corner of the country, Faro is in the far south, Funchal is the capital of the island of Madeira, Lisbon is at the southern end of central Portugal and Oporto is to the north of the country.

	Jan	Feb	Mar	April	May	June	July	Aug	Sept	Oct	Nov	Dec
Bragança												
Max	8	11	13	16	19	24	28	28	24	18	12	8
Min	0	1	3	5	7	11	13	13	10	7	3	1
Rainfall	149	104	133	73	69	42	15	16	39	79	110	144
Faro												
Max	15	16	18	20	22	25	28	28	26	22	19	16
Min	9	10	11	13	14	18	20	20	19	16	13	10
Rainfall	70	52	72	31	21	5	1	1	17	51	65	67
Funchal												
Max	19	18	19	19	21	22	24	24	24	23	22	19
Min	13	13	13	14	16	17	19	19	19	18	16	14
Rainfall	64	74	79	33	18	5	0	0	25	76	89	84
Lisbon												
Max	14	15	17	20	21	25	27	28	26	22	17	15
Min	8	8	10	12	13	15	17	17	17	14	11	9
Rainfall	111	76	109	54	44	16	3	4	33	62	89	103
Oporto												
Max	13	14	16	18	20	23	25	25	24	21	17	14
Min	5	5	8	9	11	13	15	15	14	11	8	5
Rainfall	159	112	147	86	87	41	20	26	51	105	148	168

Source: www.bbc.co.uk/weather

Churches

Most churches in Portugal are Catholic, but there are some churches for other denominations, especially in the larger cities and where there are expat communities.

Algarve

- **St Vincent's Anglican Church** in the Algarve, t 289 366 720 (Reverend Eric Britt), **www.geocities.com/stvincents2002**:

- Western congregation: **Praia da Luz** village church (Nossa Senhora da Luz). Praia da Luz is 7km west of Lagos. Services on Sundays at 11.30am.

- Central congregation: **Nossa Senhora de Fatima** church, near Almancil. Services on Sundays at 9.30am.

- Eastern congregation: **St Luke's Anglican Church**, Monte Palhagueira. Retirement village south of the road between Loulé and Sao Bras. Services on Sundays at 11.30am.

Lisbon

- Anglican: **St George's Church**, Rua São Jorge, 1200 Lisbon, t 213 906 248 (English cemetery).

- Church of Scotland: **St Andrew's**, Rua Arriaga, 13 Lisboa, t 213 957 677.

- Jewish: **Shaaré-Tikvá Synagogue**, Rua Alexandre Herculano, 59, 1250-010 Lisboa, t 213 858 604.

- Muslim: **Mesquita Central de Lisboa**, Avenida José Malhôa, 1070 Lisbon, t 213 874 142.

Porto

- Anglican: **St James**, Largo da Maternidade Júlio Dinis, 4050 Porto.

Index

Titles available in the *Working and Living* series

Working and Living: France
Working and Living: Spain
Working and Living: Italy
Working and Living: Portugal

Forthcoming

Working and Living: Australia
Working and Living: New Zealand
Working and Living: Canada
Working and Living: USA

Related titles

Starting a Business: France
Starting a Business: Spain

Titles available in the *Buying a Property* series

Buying a Property: France
Buying a Property: Spain
Buying a Property: Italy
Buying a Property: Portugal
Buying a Property: Ireland
Buying a Property: Greece
Buying a Property: Turkey
Buying a Property: Abroad
Buying a Property: Retiring Abroad

Forthcoming

Buying a Property: Cyprus
Buying a Property: Emerging European Countries